STRUCTURAL
KNOWLEDGE:
Techniques for Representing, Conveying, and Acquiring Structural Knowledge

STRUCTURAL KNOWLEDGE:
Techniques for Representing, Conveying, and Acquiring Structural Knowledge

David H. Jonassen
University of Colorado

Katherine Beissner
Ithaca College

Michael Yacci
Rochester Institute of Technology

LAWRENCE ERLBAUM ASSOCIATES, PUBLISHERS

1993   Hillsdale, New Jersey   Hove and London

Lawrence Erlbaum Associates, Inc., Publishers
365 Broadway
Hillsdale, New Jersey 07642

Library of Congress Cataloging-in-Publication Data

Jonassen, David H., 1947-
   Structural knowledge : techniques for representing, conveying, and acquiring structural knowledge / David H. Jonassen, Katherine Beissner, Michael Yacci.
      p.   cm.
   Includes bibliographical references and index.
   ISBN 0-8058-1009-9 - ISBN 0-8058-1360-8 (pbk.)
   1. Conceptual structures (Information theory) 2. Knowledge representation (Information theory) 3. Artificial Intelligence.
   I. Beissner, Katherine. II. Yacci, Michael. III. Title.
   Q387.2.J66   1993
   003'.54--dc20   92-43332
                                                 CIP

Books published by Lawrence Erlbaum Associates are printed on acid-free paper, and their bindings are chosen for strength and durability.

Printed in the United States of America

10   9   8   7   6   5   4   3   2   1

Contents

Preface   viii

**PART I: INTRODUCTION TO STRUCTURAL
KNOWLEDGE**   1

1. Structural Knowledge: Description, Rationale, and
    Assumptions   3

**PART II: REPRESENTING/ASSESSING STRUCTURAL
KNOWLEDGE**   21

Eliciting Knowledge Through

2. Word Association Proximities   25
3. Similarity Ratings   37
4. Card Sorts   45

Representing Structural Knowledge Through

5. Tree Construction Task   53
6. Dimensional Representations (Cognitive Maps)   61
7. Link Weighted Network Representations:
    Pathfinder Nets   73
8. Tree Representations: Ordered Tree Technique   83
9. Verbal Tests   89

PART III: CONVEYING STRUCTURAL KNOWLEDGE   97

Implicit Methods for Conveying Structural Knowledge Through

10.	Content Structures	101
11.	Elaboration Theory	115
12	Frames & Slots	125

Explicit Methods for Conveying Structural Knowledge Through

13.	Semantic Maps	135
14.	Causal Interaction Maps	145
15.	Concept Maps	155
16.	Graphic Organizers/Structured Overviews	165
17.	Cross Classification Tables	173
18.	Semantic Features Analysis	179
19.	Advance Organizers	189

PART IV: STRUCTURAL KNOWLEDGE LEARNING STRATEGIES: 201

20.	Pattern Notes	205
21.	Spider Maps	213
22.	Frame Games	221
23.	Networks	231
24.	Node Acquisition and Integration Technique	243
	Author Index	255
	Subject Index	259

Dedications

David Jonassen

To my brother, Stephen, for whom the pursuit of all types of knowledge has been so important.

Katherine Beissner

For Harry

Michael Yacci

To my family and friends

Acknowledgments

Many thanks to Peggy Cole for the Author Index, Chapter 22, and all of her conceptual and editorial advice.

Preface

This volume has two related purposes. First, it is intended to introduce the concept of a hypothetical type of knowledge construction that we and others have referred to as structural knowledge. As described in Chapter 1, structural knowledge goes beyond traditional forms of information recall to provide the basis for knowledge application. Assuming that you accept the validity of the concept, then the book's primary goal is to function as a handbook for supporting the assessment and use of structural knowledge in learning and instructional settings. As a handbook, its descriptions are direct and short and its structure is consistent. Every chapter except the first describes a technique for representing or assessing structural knowledge acquisition, conveying knowledge structures through direct instruction, or providing learners with strategies that they may use to acquire structural knowledge. Nearly every chapter that describes a technique includes the following hierarchical sections in the same sequence:

Description of the technique
    Rationale (theoretical or conceptual) for the technique
Examples of the technique
Applications of the technique for
    Representing and assessing structural knowledge acquisition
    Conveying structural knowledge instructionally
    Strategies for acquiring structural knowledge
Procedure for developing and using the technique
Effectiveness of technique
    Learner interactions and differences using the technique
    Interactions of the techniques with different content or task types
    Advantages of the technique
        Disadvantages of the technique
References to the literature about the technique

This consistent chapter structure is designed to facilitate access to information as well as comparisons and contrasts among the techniques.

The characteristics described above indicate that this volume is not a research handbook so much as it is a utilization handbook. Therefore, lengthy descriptions of the research are not provided. We do summarize (hopefully) all existing research as support for our recommendations but do not critique or analyze this research. If you are a researcher and want to replicate some of the research mentioned in the book or generate your own research topics, you are referred to the originally cited works to consider the methodological issues. The purpose of this book is to support the consideration of these techniques and their utilization in a variety of learning settings. Clearly, more experience and research are needed on all of the techniques described in this volume in order to assure their potential success.

The volume is divided into four parts, the first part introducing the concept of structural knowledge and the rationale for studying it and the latter three parts corresponding to the three types of applications of structural knowledge. Part II describes techniques for representing and assessing the quality of an individual's knowledge structure. Part III describes techniques that were originally intended to convey or describe content or knowledge structures to learners. Part IV focuses on learning strategies that may be used by learners to acquire structural knowledge. As described in the three subsections under applications in each chapter, these techniques may be effectively used to support activities other than those originally intended. In many of these cases, their use in other activities has not been researched, although they seem reasonable and logical.

As a handbook, this volume is meant to be used rather than simply read. We hope that its use will lead to more interesting research and deeper learning for the students who are engaged by these activities.

David H. Jonassen

Part I

Introduction to Structural Knowledge

Chapter 1 Structural Knowledge: Description, Rationale, and Assumptions

1

Structural Knowledge:
Description, Rationale, and Assumptions

DEFINITIONS OF STRUCTURAL KNOWLEDGE

Structural knowledge has several convergent definitions, all of which describe a form a knowledge representation.

Declarative, Structural, and Procedural Knowledge

Discussions of the psychology of knowing have often distinguished between declarative or procedural forms of knowledge. Declarative knowledge represents cognizance or awareness of some object, event, or idea. Ryle (1949) describes this type of knowledge as *knowing that*. When a person *knows that*, she or he is able to define or describe the objects of that knowing but are not necessarily able to use that knowledge, as declarative knowledge does not imply understanding. Declarative knowledge of ideas is often characterized as schemas (Rumelhart & Ortony, 1977). Schemas are ideational constructs that are defined by attributes that they inherit from other schemas. Declarative knowledge enables learners to come to know, or define, which forms the basis for thinking about and using those schemas.

Procedural knowledge, on the other hand, describes how learners use or apply their declarative knowledge. Ryle describes this type of knowledge as *knowing how*. Procedural knowledge entails the interrelating of schemas into patterns that represent mental performance which are in turn represented mentally as performance schemata. Solving problems, forming plans, and making arguments are examples of activities that entail procedural knowledge. In performing these activities, learners must access and interrelate relevant schemata and extract the relevant attributes to apply to the situation. Through practice, procedural knowledge schemata evolve where the mental activities are represented in more complex, performance-oriented schemata, otherwise known as scripts (Schank & Abelson, 1977). Declarative knowledge provides the conceptual basis for procedural knowledge. Most psychologists believe that without awareness of the objects of performance, performance would be impossible. Yet, certain performances or skills may be based on tacit knowledge (Polanyi, 1966), especially by experts, so articulating the declarative knowledge base would be difficult for the performer. Other performances may become so automatized that the performer is not declaratively aware of the skill.

In this volume, we propose an intermediate type of knowledge, *structural knowledge*, that mediates the translation of declarative into procedural knowledge and facilitates the application of procedural knowledge. Structural knowledge is the knowledge of how concepts within a domain are interrelated (Diekhoff, 1983). If schemas are defined by their interrelationships to other schemas, then explicit awareness of those interrelationships and the ability to explicate those relationships is essential for higher order, procedural knowledge. It is not enough to *know that*. In order to *know how*, you must *know why*. Structural knowledge provides the conceptual bases for *why*; it describes how the declarative knowledge is interconnected. Procedural knowledge is dependent on complex interconnections between ideas. For example, the dictum "warm air rises" entails connections between air and its modifier, warm as opposed to cold. That warm air rises is predicated on a causal relationship between warm and rising, the basis of the principle of convection. Structural knowledge, the understanding of these relationships, enables learners to form the connections that they need to use scripts or complex schemas.

Some researchers conceive of structural knowledge as a part of declarative knowledge, which has two dimensions — content and structure (Mitchell & Chi, 1984). Structure refers to how information within a knowledge domain is organized, which we have defined as structural knowledge. Whether structural knowledge exists as a separate type of knowledge or it is a part of declarative knowledge is a semantic distinction that does not affect it recognition as an entity or as a distinct type of knowledge.

Structural Knowledge as Cognitive Structure

Structural knowledge is also known as cognitive structure, the pattern of relationships among concepts in memory (Preece, 1976) or more specifically, "...a hypothetical construct referring to the organization of the relationships of concepts in long-term memory" (Shavelson, 1972, pp. 226-227). Structural knowledge is the awareness and understanding of one's cognitive structure.

Cognitive structure, like most psychological constructs, has numerous interpretations (Nagy, 1984). As described shortly, cognitive structure evolves from memory theory, particularly semantic memory.

Some researchers conceive of cognitive structure as an integral component of an individual's personality (Scott, Osgood, & Peterson, 1979). Individual differences in behavior are attributable in part to differences in an individual's cognitive contents. Cognitive structure evolves individually from the ascription of attributes (any objective or subjective feature) to objects in the world, which enables the definition of structural relations among concepts. Attributes may be related to one another in at least two ways — relations of association (e.g., friendliness) or relations of implication in which information is used in forming judgments in different circumstances. This object-attribute model of cognitive structure is based on Kelly's (1955) personal construct theory which focuses on the development of attribute-based personal constructs, which are used to interpret reality. Rather than being a reactive organism, Kelly believed that individuals take an active role in representing and organizing their environment, which drives their behavior rather than merely responding to environmental stimuli. Individuals revise or replace their constructs as is necessary in order to interpret their environment. The way that individuals organize and represent constructs, that is, their cognitive structure, determines how they interact with the environment.

Other Conceptualizations of Structural Knowledge

Structural knowledge has been also referred to as internal connectedness, integrative understanding, or as conceptual knowledge. Conceptual knowledge is the "integrated storage of meaningful dimensions .... in a given domain of knowledge" (Tennyson & Cocchiarella, 1986). It is more than the storage of declarative knowledge; it is the "understanding of a concept's operational structure within itself and between associated concepts." Conceptual knowledge is used to develop procedural knowledge for solving domain problems. Structural (conceptual) knowledge involves the integration of declarative knowledge into useful knowledge structures. The underlying assumption of each of these conceptions is that meaning for any concept or construct is implicit in the pattern of relationships to other concept or constructs.

Structural knowledge may also refer to an individual's knowledge structure. Knowledge structure is the information-processing term for organized networks of information stored in semantic or long-term memory (Champagne, Klopfer, Desena, & Squires, 1981, p. 97). It is a generic term, like structural knowledge, that refers to the integration and organization of constructs in an individual's memory.

Structural knowledge, like cognitive structure or knowledge structure, is a hypothetical construct. Such constructs can be reified using techniques described throughout this volume. These techniques, because they represent such important constructs, have utility as instructional and learning tools. To reiterate, a fundamental hypothesis of this volume is that analysis of structural knowledge mediates the acquisition of procedural knowledge. Before considering research support for this hypothesis, we describe some of the theoretical foundations of structural knowledge.

THEORETICAL BASES FOR STRUCTURAL KNOWLEDGE

The following theories provide the conceptual foundation for the construct, structural knowledge.

Schema Theory

Schema theory (Rumelhart, 1980; Rumelhart & Ortony, 1977) contends that knowledge is stored in information packets, or schema, that comprise our mental constructs for ideas. A schema for an object, event, or idea is comprised of a set of attributes or slots that describe and therefore help us to recognize that object or event. These slots contain relationships to other schemas. It is the interrelationships between schemas that give them meaning. For instance, most of us have a well-developed schema for *airplane* that includes attributes or slots such as wings, fuselage, seats, jet engines, flight attendants, cardboard snacks, and so on. The schema for airplane is a member of larger classes of schemata, such as transportation, business travel, holidays, or recreation. Likewise, our airplane schema has specific slots that are filled with more specific airplanes, such as a *Boeing 747* or *the plane that I flew to London*. Each individual possesses a unique schema for objects or events depending upon their experiences. Each schema that we construct represents a miniframework in which we interrelate elements or attributes of information about that topic or experience into a single conceptual unit (Norman, Gentner, & Stevens, 1976).

Individual schemas vary in complexity. They can resemble concrete or abstract concepts, such as airplane, *ice cream cone, anger* or *trust*, or they can be complex combinations of events or objects, such as *dining in a restaurant* or *my trip to London*. These more complex, *event schemas* involve episodic information as well as interrelated conceptual information encoded into the schema's slots. For instance, a schema for "hitting a homerun" may contain specific home runs that you have hit as well as rules about the application of vector forces, trajectory, and a host of other physical factors or schemas. We must understand the conceptual relationships between placement of the bat on the ball within a limited location in order to hit a homerun (procedural knowledge). We may also encode specific, event-related information, such as *the homerun in the Tiger's game*. The interrelationships between schemata and the formation of more complex schemas requires the construction of structural knowledge. We develop schemata for events or stories as well. A *story schema* is a mental structure that describes the way in which particular stories proceed, which is a reflection of the story grammar, the structures of the stories (Mandler, 1983; Mandler & Goodman, 1982). It is likely that most story schemas for primary children all begin, "Once upon a time...." Schemas are mental abstractions that we use to comprehend discourse, find our way, or solve problems. We must fill the schema's slots with the correct information through schema selection or inheritance of attributes from other schemas in order to acquire structural and procedural knowledge. Structural knowledge is built with schemas and interrelated schemas (schemata).

How do we acquire or change our schemata, that is, how do we learn? We fill slots by encoding our experiences as attributes of schema (for example, *my last trip to London*) in a process known as *accretion* (Rumelhart, 1980). Accretion can also result in the addition of new schemas that use existing schemas as their model. Schemas are *tuned* or finely adjusted to meet specific task demands or adapted to particular knowledge domains or contexts. Tuning might entail the refining of a procedure, filling-in of inferences, or adapting the schemas to new situations. When new experiences occur that cannot be described by existing schemas, they are restructured. The learner begins to *restructure* his or her knowledge by adding schemas or developing new conceptualizations for existing ones. While restructuring of knowledge is the least common learning activity, it is the most important one.

Semantic Networks

A basic premise of schema theory is that human memory is organized semantically. Schemas are arranged in networks (schemata) of interrelated concepts. These networks are known as our semantic network. Perhaps the best known conceptualization of a semantic network is active structural networks (Quillian, 1968), structures that are composed of nodes (the equivalent of schemas) and ordered, typed (e.g. subordinate, disjunctive) relationships or links connecting them (Norman et al., 1976). The nodes are token instances of concepts or propositions and the links described the propositional relationship between them.

If memory is organized as a semantic network, then learning can be conceived as a reorganization of the networks in semantic memory. These networks describe what a learner knows, which provides the foundations for learning new ideas, that is, altering and expanding the learner's semantic network through accretion, tuning and restructuring. The premise of this volume is that these semantic networks are representations of structural knowledge.

Spreading Activation Theory

Quillian's model of semantic memory, active structural networks, connects concepts together into a network. In order to search that network during comprehension, the mind starts at the nodes identified by the input words and spreads through all of the links connected to those nodes to other nodes, and through all of the links to other nodes. As nodes are activated, they are tagged so that the processor can retrace the path to the starting node. Rather than this spread of activation constantly expanding, Collins and Loftus (1975) claimed that the original signal is attenuated by traveling through more intervening nodes. Activation of nodes in the network decreases proportionate to the strength of the links, which introduced the idea of semantic similarity into the networks. Semantic similarity is a function of the number of properties that the concepts have in common. The more common properties that two concepts have, the more they are linked together through those properties, so the more closely they are related. These amendments to Quillian's model of semantic memory were necessary to accommodate the results of a number of subsequent experiments. Regarding structural knowledge, this concept of semantic similarity between concepts is an important assumption of many of the techniques for representing structural knowledge that are described here.

RATIONALES FOR STUDYING STRUCTURAL KNOWLEDGE

Semantic networks describe structural knowledge. They provide a psychological foundation for the epistemological assumptions made about structural knowledge and the inference that researchers have drawn regarding structure. These inferences that have been examined empirically provide a strong rationale for studying structural knowledge. The following descriptions briefly describe the rationales for considering structural knowledge.

Structure is Inherent in All Knowledge

"Meaning does not exist until some structure, or organization, is achieved" (Mandler, 1983, p. 4). Without structure, mental constructs could not be formed because nothing could be described. Each object may have an identity, but it could have no relation to anything else. Without structure, abstract knowledge would be impossible. This is why Mandler claims that the deeper a domain is understood the more abstract the structure must be. Abstract ideas have a greater reliance on structure.

Structural Knowledge is Essential to Recall and Comprehension

We naturally and necessarily organize our mental representations of phenomena in order to be able to access them. An extensive amount of memory research over the past century (too great to review in this volume) has clearly demonstrated that ideas with any sort of structure are better recalled than unstructured lists of ideas. The more semantically meaningful the relationships between the ideas are, the better recalled they are. Clearly, structural knowledge facilitates recall.

Knowledge of the structural interrelatedness of ideas is also essential to comprehension of those ideas. In his *Transcendental Analytic*, Kant (Zweig, 1970) argued that in acquiring knowledge from empirical events, that we develop representations called *transcendental schema*, and that these "schema of the concepts of the understanding allow the phenomena to be comprehended" (Zweig, 1970, p. 153). Schema theory, as described earlier, explains how meaning is constructed by individuals based on the structural interrelationships between the schemas that are possessed. The use of structural knowledge in comprehension is applied in everyday activities. Reading a story requires that schemas be accessed and filled in the slots of the story schema. However, if those schemas are unavailable while reading a story, then reader must fill in gaps in their memory with preestablished structural knowledge of stories (Mandler, 1983, p. 11).

Learners Assimilate Structural Knowledge

As described earlier, learning consists of building new knowledge structures by constructing new nodes and interrelating them with existing nodes and with each other (Norman, 1976). If links are formed between existing knowledge and new knowledge, the new knowledge will be integrated and comprehended better. In the lexicon of schema theory, learning is a reorganization of the learner's cognitive structure. Research has shown that during the process of learning, the learners' cognitive structures change to correspond more closely with the content structure or the teacher's knowledge structure. That is, the structural knowledge of the learners was more similar to the structural knowledge of the teacher at the end of instruction than at the beginning (Shavelson, 1972). Thro (1978) also found that learners' cognitive structures more closely resembled the instructor's cognitive structure at the end of instruction. Learning, it appears, consists of the acquisition of structural knowledge as well as declarative knowledge and the development of procedural knowledge. Restated, subject matter knowledge consists of the acquisition of structural as well as declarative and procedural knowledge.

Memory Structures Reflect the World

Just as story schemas reflect story grammars (Mandler, 1983; Mandler & Goodman, 1982), "human memory mirrors with a remarkable degree of fidelity the structure (of knowledge) that exists in the environment" (Anderson & Schooler, 1990, p.18). They used a rational analysis process to establish a causal link between the structure of memory and the structure of the environment in three disparate knowledge domains. They concluded that the usefulness or "desirability" of certain memory structures is demand-driven. That memory structures can be ascertained from a rational analysis of environmental knowledge structures make the structural knowledge as a construct that much more accessible.

Structural Knowledge is Essential to Problem Solving

A number of research studies have shown indirectly that knowledge structures are important in problem solving (Chi & Glaser, 1985). A few studies recently have directly assessed the effects of cognitive structure on problem solving skills. Robertson (1990) used think aloud protocols to assess cognitive structure. He found that the extent to which those protocols contained relevant structural knowledge was a strong predictor of how well learners would solve transfer problems in physics on a written exam. In fact, structural knowledge was a much stronger predictor than either aptitude (as measured by standardized test scores) or performance on a set of similar problems, which was a measure of procedural knowledge. He concluded that cognitive structures that connect the formula and important concepts in the knowledge base are important to understanding physics principles, more important it seems than aptitude. Gordon and Gill (1989) used question probes successfully to elicit knowledge structures in the form of graphs in two subject domains. These graphs were then used to determine the role of knowledge structures in domain-specific problem solving. The similarity of the learners' graphs (reflective of underlying cognitive structure) with the expert's (instructional graph) was found to be highly predictive of total problem solving scores (accounting for over 80% of the variance) as well as specific problem solving activities. Structural knowledge has been shown by this research to support our fundamental hypothesis -- that structural knowledge is a mediator of procedural knowledge acquisition. Domain-specific problem solving relies on adequate structural knowledge of the ideas in the domain being explored.

Expert's Structural Knowledge Differs From Novices

As would be expected, the knowledge structures of expert problem solvers differ from those of novices. Experts represent problems in different ways than novices. For instance, experts initially abstract and apply physics principles while novices focus on literal aspects of the problem (Chi, Feltovich, & Glaser, 1985). A growing body of research is linking the acquisition of structural knowledge to problem solving performance. One of the major differences between expert and novice problem solvers is that expert's knowledge includes rich sets of pattern-indexed schemata that guides problem interpretation and solution (Larkin, McDermott, Simon, & Simon, 1980). These schemata are the expert's structural knowledge about his or her field. Experts develop more elaborate schemata. They chunk schemas together. Experts represent problems in terms of abstract principles, where novices represent problems in terms of its literal characteristics.

ASSUMPTIONS AND LIMITATIONS OF STRUCTURAL KNOWLEDGE

Recently, two competing models of cognition have been identified: the symbolic processing model with the computer as its metaphor and the connectionist or parallel processing model of cognition with neural networks as its metaphor. The symbolic processing model is represented as sets of discrete facts and rules which are processed by the learner. Connectionists counter that neural nets are a better model of memory because they can learn from trials, they can function when incomplete information is available in the net, and they better resemble human processing in terms of brain functioning. An assumption of many connectionists is that cognition is situated, and therefore the connections that describe ideas are indexed by the experiences that result in those memories.

The reason for describing this dialectic is that semantic network theory, according to critics, is an example of a symbolic processing model of cognition. The tools that are described in this volume entail traditional conceptions of memory. Clancy (1992) probably best summarizes the limitations of the symbolic processing model of cognition which underlie many or most of the tools in this volume. Clancy claims that the traditional views of learning assume that human memory consists of stored facts and procedures. He challenges the "identity hypothesis" of these symbolic representation models, claiming that semantic network theorists see nets as isomorphic representations of what is stored in memory. That is, memory structures (and by inference, structural knowledge) literally exist as representations in the mind — that they represent not only behavior but also internal representational structures and mental processes. Clancy cites Lakoff (1987) who claims that these objective representations are collections of symbols that reflect an external reality, which is an objectivist interpretation of the mind as a manipulator of these symbols. Clancy goes on to attack semantic memory conceptions of knowledge that consist of mental networks that are literally searched just as a computer searches its memory stores. This implies that the semantic store of information in humans can be cognitively mapped, perhaps using the tools described in this volume.

Connectionist models believe, on the other hand, that memory is distributed in different memory locations. They see structural knowledge as neural networks that multiply encode memories — that memory is not static as symbolic representations assume. Memory changes according to the context in which the events occurred or the context in which ideas are being recalled.

We do not pretend that we can resolve these competing views of cognition. We do believe that the tools described in this volume are techniques for representing the current state of the learner's knowledge. But those states are dynamic. They change with the context in which they are produced, and they change as a function of different contexts imposed on their creation. Rather than objectivist conceptions of knowledge, we believe that as tools for reflecting on current knowledge structures, they are inherently constructivistic. What these tools generate are representations of semantic networks. We make no assumptions about where these representations reside or how they are stored in memory, though many of the authors that we cite certainly have made very clear their assumptions. In fact, we would argue that these nets are not encoded in memory at all. Rather, the tools described in this volume are representational formalisms for describing a learner's structural knowledge that may be used to represent in different ways and in different contexts the organization of ideas that are stored in memory. The ideas are stored in memory. It is not clear that the organization is stored however. The nets that we describe in this volume are not, so far as we know, isomorphisms for memory stores. Rather, we believe that structural knowledge, like declarative and procedural knowledge, can best be explained by a hybrid model of symbolic and connectionist models (Anderson, 1990; Minsky, 1991).

From our experience, it is clear that these tools and their resulting nets are contextually driven. Most of the tools described in this volume will result in different products each time they are used and certainly depending upon the social context in which they are used and most especially by the assumptions that associated with constraining contexts. That is, in many of the techniques, you try to constrain the responses by asking the learners to "think like a physicist" when you make these responses.

SUMMARY

Structural knowledge, like cognitive structures or schemata, is a hypothetical (theoretical) construct that is important to human information processing. There is no material referent for structural knowledge in the brain or anywhere else. However, structural knowledge, like schemata, is a useful construct or metaphor for describing the ways that humans construct and store knowledge. Because structural knowledge has been tied to memory processes and problem solving, it seems useful to prescribe instructional and learning strategies for fostering the acquisition of structural knowledge. Because structural knowledge has been tied to learning and knowledge acquisition, it also seems useful to assess structural knowledge growth in learners.

The graphic organizer for this volume, shown in Fig. 1.1, illustrates the assumptions and sections of this volume. The remainder of this volume is divided into three major parts; representing or assessing structural knowledge (shown on the right side of Fig. 1.1), conveying structural knowledge (shown on the left side of Fig. 1.1), and finally learning strategies that facilitate the acquisition of structural knowledge (shown on the upper left side of the figure). We now briefly describe some of the assumptions and contents of these three sections.

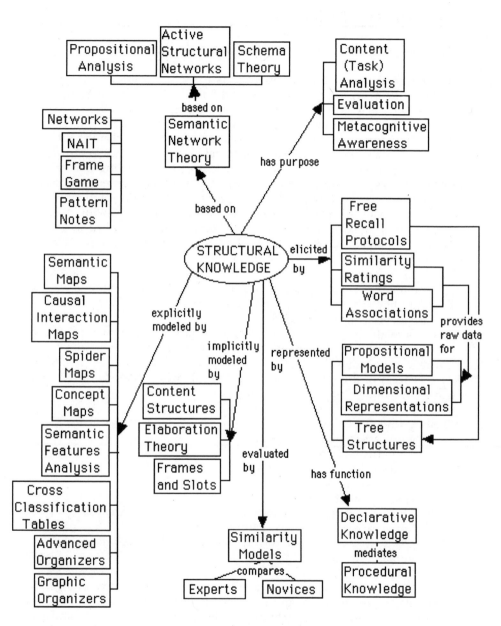

Fig. 1.1. Concept map of structural knowledge.

OVERVIEW OF THIS VOLUME

Representing/Assessing Structural Knowledge

We believe that structural knowledge is a useful construct. Therefore, methods for assessing or representing the learner's structural knowledge are needed. It is possible to measure, in realistic settings, the structural knowledge of both students and instructors and by comparing them, the student's understanding of the topic area can be evaluated (Fenker, 1975).

There are various approaches to representing cognitive structure: cognitive mapping, process tracing, and regression modeling (Shavelson, 1985). Of these the most common is cognitive mapping. Based on associative network theory, it is most appropriate for representing student representations of subject matter structure and is most consistent with our conceptualization of structural knowledge. From research described in greater detail in Chapters 2 - 8, we know that expert's maps correspond more closely to subject-matter structure than students' maps; students' cognitive structure resembles subject matter structure with instruction; alternative measurement methods produce similar structural representations; and similarity between students' cognitive structures and subject matter structure predicts achievement (Shavelson, 1974, 1985). Essential to the hypotheses of this volume is the finding that measures of structural knowledge have validity, that is, we can effectively represent the structure of learners' knowledge.

Part II of this volume describes the following methods for eliciting and representing structural knowledge:

Eliciting Knowledge
    Word association proximities
    Similarity ratings
    Card sort
Representing Knowledge Structures
    Tree construction task
    Dimensional representations: Scaling and Cluster Analysis
    Network representations: Pathfinder nets
    Tree Representations: Ordered and additive tree techniques
    Verbal tests

Most of these techniques (word associations, similarity ratings, dimensional representations, and network representations) assume a spatial metaphor for describing structural knowledge and are based on similarity data, that is, semantic proximities between concepts in memory (Nagy, 1984). These methods require the identification of a set of related concepts that define a subject domain. The process of representing structural knowledge normally occurs in two stages — eliciting the structural knowledge of the individual and then representing the underlying structures in the knowledge elicited. Knowledge of interrelationships is most frequently and effectively elicited using word association or similarity rating tasks. The interrelatedness of the elicited knowledge is then evaluated using advanced statistical techniques, like principal components or cluster analysis or multidimensional scaling to discover the structural framework underlying the set of concepts. These statistical methods transform the concept-interrelational data into interpoint distances in a space of minimal dimensionality (Fenker, 1975). Although these stages are normally combined in most descriptions, they are separated in this volume to highlight their distinctness as operations and because they may be combined in different ways.

The assumption that all of these techniques make is that semantic distance can be represented in terms of geometric space. However, the solutions generated by these procedures are often multidimensional, with each dimension representing different arrangements of the concepts. Semantic memory is complex and multidimensional, with each dimension representing a particular perspective or orientation. How concepts lie in relation to each other depends upon the context and the specific sets of concepts being interrelated. Most researchers agree though that the procedures described in Part II make it possible to operationally define cognitive structure (structural knowledge) (Fenker, 1975; Jonassen, 1987; Preece, 1976; Shavelson, 1972, 1985; Wainer & Kaye, 1974).

Conveying Structural Knowledge

If structural knowledge is integral to learning and performing higher order mental operations like problem solving, then performance should be improved by conveying the structure of information. That is the implicit assumption of each of the structural knowledge representation techniques in Part III:

Implicit Methods
>   Content structures
>   Elaboration theory
>   Frames and slots
Explicit Methods
>   Semantic maps
>   Causal interaction maps
>   Concept maps
>   Spider maps
>   Semantic features analysis
>   Cross classification tables
>   Advance organizers
>   Graphic organizers/Structured overviews

The first section of Part III describes techniques for implicitly conveying structural knowledge, that is, by mapping an organization of ideas onto materials. For instance, Meyer (1985) has conducted extensive research that shows that verbal signals in text can be used by the writer to communicate propositional knowledge at different levels of detail. Armbruster and Anderson (1985) believe that content-independent structures can be mapped onto text in the form of frames and slots. These structures provide a conceptual scaffold for assimilating the text, whether the content is in the sciences, social or behavioral science, or the humanities. Structures such as problem-solution can organize ides from any subject domain. Another elaborate set of prescriptions for mapping structures onto instructional sequences comes from elaboration theory (Reigeluth & Stein, 1983). Elaboration theory maps procedural, conceptual or theoretical structures onto content and provides elaborate prescriptions for sequencing content in lessons. These techniques all assume that structured content is more comprehensible and memorable.

The second section of Part III describes a number of techniques for explicitly mapping or illustrating the structure of content in instructional materials. Advanced organizers (Ausubel, 1968) verbally describe contexts for assimilating information, while structured overviews (Barron, 1969), spider maps (Hanf, 1971), concept maps (Novak & Gowin, 1984), and cognitive maps (Diekhoff & Diekhoff, 1982) graphically depict the organization of content during instruction. These methods are based on the use of concept maps for representing knowledge. They assume that by explicitly showing subject matter structure or the expert's cognitive structure, learners will assimilate an appropriate organizational scheme as well as the information to be learned. The maps function as scaffolding for assimilating and better comprehending the ideas in a content domain.

Structural Knowledge Learning Strategies (Acquiring Structural Knowledge)

Learning is a generative process (Wittrock, 1974). That is, learners must relate information to prior knowledge in order to convey meaning to that information. Learning is a constructive process, in which learners to some degree construct their own reality from sensory perceptions (Jonassen, 1991). A constructivist approach assumes that humans construct knowledge by organizing complex entities, they are autonomous and purposive in their intellectual behavior, and they are knowing beings (Magoon, 1977). To the extent that we ascribe to these hypotheses, we need to provide learners with skills or techniques for acquiring knowledge, in this case structural knowledge. The techniques for representing cognitive structure (structural knowledge) that are described in this volume support a constructivist approach by enabling learners to model their knowledge representations, which in turn enables educators to better understand how learners go about developing their theories for representing reality and solving instructional problems (Erickson, 1984)

The skills that are needed by learners to include cognitive learning strategies, which are generalizable, learning-to-learn "mental operations or procedures that a student may use to acquire, retain, and retrieve different kinds of knowledge and performance (Rigney, 1978, p.165). Learning strategies are intended to increase the number of links between presented information and prior knowledge, which makes them generative. There are different classes of learning strategies designed to facilitate different types of learning (Jonassen, 1985; Tessmer & Jonassen, 1988) and meta-learning (Brezin, 1980). This section briefly describes some of the learning strategies that facilitate the acquisition of structural knowledge.

Part IV describes a number of learning strategies for acquiring structural knowledge.

> Pattern noting
> Frame game
> Networking
> Node acquisition and integration technique

These methods, like those for conveying structural knowledge, are based on the semantic network assumptions that support the representational techniques described in Parts II and III, although not all of them assume a spatial metaphor. As pointed out earlier, these techniques engage students in higher-order thinking such as exemplifying, categorizing, integrating, elaborating, and analyzing. Mapping techniques such as pattern notes and concept maps requires students to graphically analyze subject matter in order to illustrate its structures. There are also some well verified study strategy systems such as networking (Dansereau, Collins, McDonald, Holley, Garland, Diekhoff, & Evans, 1979), analysis of key ideas and the node acquisition and integration technique (Diekhoff, Brown, & Dansereau, 1982) that require students to analyze and describe subject matter structure by defining the interrelationships between ideas. These strategies are more sophisticated and require a number of hours to learn.

REFERENCES

Anderson, J.A. (1990). Hybrid computation in cognitive science: Neural networks and symbols. *Applied Cognitive Psychology, 4*, 337-347.

Anderson, J.R.. & Schooler, L.J. (1990). *Reflections of the environment in memory.* Pittsburgh, PA: Carnegie Mellon University, Department of Psychology.

Armbruster, B.B., & Anderson, T.H. (1985). Frames: Structures for informative texts. In D.H. Jonassen (Ed.), *The technology of text*, Vol. 2 Englewood Cliffs, NJ: Educational Technology Publications.

Ausubel, D.P. (1968). *Educational psychology: A cognitive view.* New York: Holt, Rinehart & Winston.

Barron, R.F. (1969). The use of vocabulary as an advance organizer. In H.L. Herber & P.L. Sanders (Eds.), *Research on reading in the content area*. Syracuse, NY: Syracuse University Press.

Brezin, M.J. (1980). Cognitive monitoring: From learning theory to instructional applications. *Educational Communications and Technology Journal, 28*, 227-242.

Champagne, A.B., Klopfer, L.E., Desena, A.T., & Squires, D.A. (1981). Structural representations of students' knowledge before and after science instruction. *Journal of Research in Science Teaching, 18*, 97-111.

Chi, M.T., Feltovich, P.J., & Glaser, R. (1985). Categorization and representation of physics problems by experts and novices. *Cognitive Science, 5*, 121-152.

Chi, M.T., & Glaser, R. (1985). *Problem solving ability*. In R.S. Sternberg (Ed.), Human abilities: An information processing approach. New York; W.H. Freeman.

Clancy, W. (1992). Representations of knowing: In defense of cognitive apprenticeship: A response to Sanberg & Wielinga. *Journal of Artificial Intelligence in Education, 3* (2), 139-168.

Collins, A.M., & Loftus, E.F. (1975). A spreading-activation theory of semantic processing. *Psychological Review, 82*, 407-428.

Dansereau, D. F., Collins, K. W., McDonald, B. A., Holley, C. D., Garland, J. C., Diekhoff, G. M., & Evans, S. H. (1979). Development and evaluation of a learning strategy training program. *Journal of Educational Psychology, 71*, 64-73.

Diekhoff, G.M. (1983). Relationship judgments in the evaluation of structural understanding. *Journal of Educational Psychology, 75*, 227-233.

Diekhoff, G.M., Brown, P., & Dansereau, D.F. (1983). A prose learning strategy based on network and depth of processing models. *Journal of Experimental Education, 50*(4), 180-184.

Diekhoff, G.M., & Diekhoff, K.B. (1982). Cognitive maps as a tool in communicating structural knowledge. *Educational Technology, 22* (4), 28-30.

Erickson, G. (1984). Theoretical and empirical issues in the study of students' conceptual frameworks. In P. Nagy (Ed.), *The representation of cognitive structures* (pp. 13-30). Toronto, Canada: Ontario Institute for Studies in Education.

Fenker, R.M. (1975). The organization of conceptual materials: A methodology for measuring ideal and actual cognitive structures. *Instructional Science, 4*, 33-57.

Gordon, S.E., & Gill, R.T. (1989). *The formation and use of knowledge structures in problem solving domains*. Tech. Report AFOSR-88-0063. Washington, DC: Bolling AFB.

Hanf, M. B. (1971). Mapping: A technique for translating reading into thinking. *Journal of Reading, 14*, 225-230; 270.

Jonassen, D.H. (1985). Learning strategies: A new educational technology. *Programmed Learning and Educational Technology, 22* (1), 26-34.

Jonassen, D.H. (1987). Assessing cognitive structure: Verifying a method using pattern notes. *Journal of Research and Development in Education, 20* (3), 1-14.

Jonassen, D.H. (1991). Objectivism vs. constructivism: Do we need a new philosophical paradigm? *Educational Technology, 31* (3), 3-12.

Kelly, G.A.(1955.).*The Psychology of Personal Constructs*. New York: W.W. Norton.

Lakoff, G. (1987). *Women, fire, and dangerous things: What categories reveal about the mind*. Chicago: University of Chicago Press.

Larkin, J.H., McDermott, J., Simon, D.P., & Simon, H.A. (1980). Expert and novice performance in solving physics problems. *Science, 208*, 1335-1342.

Magoon, A.J. (1977). Constructivist approaches in educational research. *Review of Educational Research, 47*, 651-693.

Mandler, J. (1983). *Stories: The function of structure*. Paper presented at the annual convention of the American Psychological Association, Anaheim, CA, August 26-30, 1983 (ED 238 247).

Mandler, J., & Goodman, M.S.(1982). On the psychological validity of story structure. *Journal of Verbal Learning and Verbal Behavior, 21*, 507-523.

Meyer, B.J.F. (1985). Signaling the structure of text. In D.H. Jonassen (Ed.), *The technology of text*, Vol.2. Englewood Cliffs, NJ: Educational Technology Publications.

Minsky, M. (1991). Logical versus analogical or symbolic versus connectionist or neat versus scruffy. *AI Magazine*, 35-51.

Mitchell, A.A., & Chi, M.T. (1984). Measuring knowledge within a domain. In P. Nagy (Ed.), *The representation of cognitive structure* (p. 85-109).Toronto, Canada: Ontario Institute for Studies in Education.

Nagy, P. (1984). Cognitive structure and the spatial metaphor. In P. Nagy (Ed.), *The representation of cognitive structure* (p. 1-11).Toronto, Canada: Ontario Institute for Studies in Education.

Norman, D. A. (1976). *Studies in learning and self-contained education systems*, 1973-1976. Tech Report No. 7601. Washington, D.C.: Office of Naval Research, Advanced Research Projects Agency. (ED 121 786)

Norman, D.A., Gentner, S. & Stevens, A.L. (1976). Comments on learning schemata and memory representation. In D.Klahr (Ed.), *Cognition and instruction*. Hillsdale, NJ: Lawrence Erlbaum Associates.

Novak, J.D., & Gowin, D.B. (1984). *Learning how to learn*. Cambridge: Cambridge University Press.

Polanyi, M. (1966). *The tacit dimension*. New York: Doubleday.

Preece, P.F.W. (1976). Mapping cognitive structure: A comparison of methods. *Journal of Educational Psychology, 68*, 1-8.

Quillian, M.R. (1968). Semantic memory. In M. Minsky (Ed.), *Semantic information processing*. Cambridge, MA: MIT Press.

Reigeluth, C.M., & Stein, F. (1983). The elaboration theory of instruction. In C.M. Reigeluth (Ed.), *Instructional design theories and models: An overview of their current status*. Hillsdale, NJ: Lawrence Erlbaum Associates.

Rigney, J. (1978). Learning strategies: A theoretical perspective. In H.F. ONeil (Ed.), *Learning strategies*. New York: Academic.

Robertson, W.C. (1990). Detection of cognitive structure with protocol data: Predicting performance on physics transfer problems. *Cognitive Science, 14*, 253-280.

Rumelhart, D.E. (1980). Schemata: The building blocks of cognition. In R.J. Spiro, B.C. Bruce & W.F. Brewer (Eds.), *Theoretical issues in reading comprehension: Perspectives from cognitive psychology, linguistics, artificial intelligence, and education*. Hillsdale, NJ: Lawrence Erlbaum.

Rumelhart, D.E., & Ortony, A. (1977).The representation of knowledge in memory. In R.C. Anderson, R.J. Spiro, & W.E. Montague (Eds.), *Schooling and the acquisition of knowledge*. Hillsdale, NJ: Lawrence Erlbaum.

Ryle, G. (1949). *Collected papers, Vol II. Critical essays*. London: Hutchinson.

Scott, W.A., Osgood, D.W., & Peterson, C. (1979). *Cognitive structure: Theory and measurement of individual differences*. New York: V.H. Winston.

Schank, R. & Abelson, R. (1977). *Scripts, plans, goals, and understanding*. Hillsdale, NJ: Lawrence Erlbaum Associates.

Shavelson, R.J. (1972). Some aspects of the correspondence between content structure and cognitive structure in physics instruction. *Journal of Educational Psychology, 63*, 225-234.

Shavelson, R. (1974). Methods for examining representations of subject matter structure in students' memory. *Journal of Research in Science Teaching, 11*, 231-249.

Shavelson, R.J. (1985). *The measurement of cognitive structure*. Paper presented at the annual convention of the American Educational Research Association, Chicago, April 3, 1985.

Tessmer, M., & Jonassen, D.H. (1988). Learning strategies. In N.D.C. Harris (Ed.), *The world yearbook of education*. London: Kogan Page.

Tennyson, R.D., & Cocciarella, M.J. (1986) An empirically based instructional design theory for teaching concepts. *Review of Educational Research, 56*, 40-71.

Thro, M.P. (1978). *Individual differences among college students in cognitive structure and physics performance.* Paper presented at the annual meeting of the American Educational Research Association, Toronto, Canada.

Wainer, H., & Kaye, K. (1974). Multidimensional scaling of concept learning in an introductory course. *Journal of Educational Psychology, 66,* 591-598.

Wittrock, M.C. (1974). Learning as a generative activity. *Educational Psychologist, 11,* 87-95.

Zweig, A. (1970). *The essential Kant.* New York: New American Library.

Part II

Representing/Assessing Structural Knowledge

Eliciting Knowledge Through

Chapter 2 Word Association Proximities
Chapter 3 Similarity Ratings
Chapter 4 Card Sorts

Representing Structural Knowledge Through

Chapter 5 Tree Construction Task
Chapter 6 Dimensional Representations (Cognitive Maps)
Chapter 7 Link Weighted Network Representations: Pathfinder Nets
Chapter 8 Tree Representations: Ordered Tree Technique
Chapter 9 Verbal Tests

INTRODUCTION

Representing and assessing structural knowledge is a three stage process. First, it is necessary to elicit the knowledge from the respondents (learners, students, test takers, etc.). A variety of techniques support this activity, as indicated in Fig. II.1. The techniques that are most established and effective for eliciting structural knowledge, word associations and similarity ratings, are described in this volume.

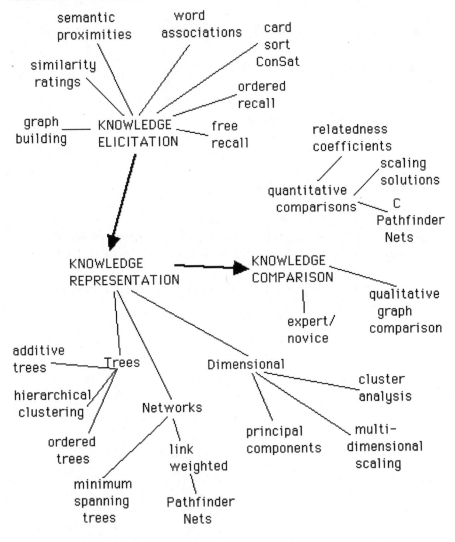

Fig. II.1. Processes for representing and assessing structural knowledge.

Once knowledge has been elicited from the respondents, its structural aspects must be evoked. Again, the most effective techniques, tree constructions, dimensional representations, Pathfinder nets, and verbal test are described here.

Finally, in order to assess structural knowledge acquisition, learners' knowledge representations are typically compared with the teacher's, an expert's, or some content representation. Methods for making these comparisons are discussed within the context of the knowledge representation chapters in this volume.

2

Eliciting Knowledge Through Word Association Proximities

DESCRIPTION OF WORD ASSOCIATION PROXIMITIES

One of the primary means for eliciting a learner's structural knowledge is by having learners generate controlled or free word association lists. For each concept in a knowledge domain, say Newtonian mechanics, students generate a list of associated words that immediately come to mind when presented with each concept in a domain as a stimulus. For instance, when asked to free associate to the term *speed*, they might respond with a list that includes *velocity, acceleration, distance*, etc. In order to elicit structural knowledge of a domain, learners are also asked to free associate each of the concepts in a domain. So, when asked to associate the term *acceleration*, the student might say *velocity, car*, etc.

The lists of words in the knowledge domain are compared in order to assess the relatedness between each of the concepts. If concepts show up on the other associates lists, they are related. So, in the previous example, we can conclude that *speed, velocity*, and *acceleration*, because they appeared on each list of associates, are related. The strength of the association is a function of their order of appearance on the lists of associates. The higher up on the associates list that terms appear, the more strongly the concepts are related. The more overlap between the two word lists, that is, the more words that each pair of lists has in common, the more strongly related are the two words.

Relatedness coefficients that quantify the degree of relatedness between two concepts may be calculated from different types of lists: from a *free word association* list or from a *controlled word association* list. A free association task gives a student an initial stimulus word and asks the student to generate as many related words as the student can think of within a specified time period. A controlled association task asks a student to both generate the words and rank order the words as they are generated. A controlled association task may limit the domain by asking the students to draw words from a specific subject matter domain (e.g., relate and rank only specific *physics* concepts to the stimulus word). The controlled association test has an additional property that allows for a more precise assessment of the overlap between lists by expressing the degree of relatedness in a correlation coefficient that represents the degree of relatedness between the two concepts.

Rationale

Generating associated word lists is based on the theory of long term memory that claims that ideas that are related in long-term memory have a semantic proximity. Semantic proximity assumes that ideas are closer together, that is, more easily paired, when they are more strongly related. For example, in tests of color relatedness, semantic proximity has been shown to be supportive of the way that colors are organized, lending validity to the construct.

Semantic relatedness from word association lists assumes that words that are related or more strongly connected in long-term memory are retrievable from memory as related pairs. The word association tasks require a student to make these connections explicit.

EXAMPLES OF WORD ASSOCIATION PROXIMITIES

As mentioned previously, there are two types of word association graphing procedures, a *free association* task and a *controlled word association* task. A free association task in the domain of psychology might look like the following example. The free association task requires learners to write down as many words as they can that are associated with the selected term, in this example, the term behaviorism, within a specified time limit (usually one minute).

BEHAVIORISM

BEHAVIORISM	*psychology*
BEHAVIORISM	*stimulus*
BEHAVIORISM	*response*
BEHAVIORISM	*reinforcement*
BEHAVIORISM	*rewards*
BEHAVIORISM	*punishment*
BEHAVIORISM	*rats*
BEHAVIORISM	*pigeons*
BEHAVIORISM	*Skinner*

The student fills in the blanks with as many terms as possible that are associated with the selected term, with such terms as *stimulus, response, Skinner,* etc.

An alternative form of the word association task is done using a controlled word association procedure, in which the learner ranks the words as he or she associates them. Students are instructed to fill in the blanks in their order of importance, that is, in the order of the strength of its relationship to the target word. Clearly, such a task is subject to error though it does provide more information than the free word association task. For example:

BEHAVIORISM

1. *stimulus*

2. *response*

3. *reinforcement*

4. *behavior*

5. *psychology*

The controlled word association task is scored in a manner similar to the free association task. Using the assumption that the more strongly related ideas are the first to be generated, the controlled association test weights each generated word by keeping track of the order in which the words are retrieved. The controlled word association procedure factors in the various retrieval order rankings of each learner. For the free word association lists, relatedness coefficients (RC) are calculated for each pair of words as a quantitative measure (of the degree of relatedness between them.

The various RC values between pairs of concepts are then organized into a matrix which displays each student's set of relationships between pairs of given concepts. The matrix presents each of the coefficient relationships between each pair of concepts. The structure implied by these coefficients is typically represented through the use of multidimensional scaling (MDS), a statistical technique that produces a dimensional representation of the relationships depicted in the coefficient matrix (see Chapter 6).

APPLICATIONS OF WORD ASSOCIATION PROXIMITIES

Representing/Assessing Structural Knowledge

The primary purpose of generating word associates lists is to elicit structural knowledge, that is to elicit through recall information about the structural interrelatedness of ideas in a learners' memory. The word association task is a form of the knowledge elicitation part of the structural knowledge representation task. The information collected during this task is analyzed using techniques described in Chapter 6.

Conveying Structural Knowledge

The primary application of this process is to represent the knowledge structures. However, as part of the knowledge representation process, it is frequently used to generate cognitive maps (see Chapter 6) of the expert or teacher to used by a teacher to convey the underlying structure of a knowledge domain. These maps provide learners with a structural overview of the content domain being studied (see Graphic Organizers, Chapter 21).

Acquiring Structural Knowledge

Word association graphing is not generally used to help the learner acquire structural knowledge, but rather is normally applied to the assessing structural knowledge that a learner has already acquired. It might be possible to use word association graphs in actual instruction, however the analysis procedure is difficult and tedious, making it an impractical strategy.

PROCEDURE FOR DEVELOPING WORD ASSOCIATION TASKS

The following description steps through the entire procedure of creating and using a word association task. First, a *free association* procedure is detailed, followed by a *controlled word association* procedure.

Free Association Procedure

1. First, determine the major concepts in the course or content domain. These can be determined by achieving consensus from a panel of experts or simply by a teacher's determination of what concepts are most important. For research purposes, these concepts should be the primary organizing concepts of the subject matter, although the relationships between *any* concepts can be assessed by this procedure. This type of test

has utility at varying levels. That might mean, for example, that the word association assessment procedure could be used for a unit level test, or even a module-level test. The threats to the validity at these lower levels are discussed later. In this example (a course in sports), the teacher is interested in the relationships between FOOTBALL and BASKETBALL, among others.

2. After selecting the stimulus words, center each word at the top of a page. Each page should have one stimulus word/concept.

3. Repeat the word several times (at least 10 times) down the left border, leaving space next to each word for the learner to write related terms. The completed page for football would look like this:

FOOTBALL

FOOTBALL   _____

FOOTBALL   _____

FOOTBALL   _____

FOOTBALL   _____

FOOTBALL   _____
etc.

4. Instruct each student to generate as many other words as she or he can that are related to this concept within a specified time period (usually 1 to 1 1/2 minutes per page).

5. If this procedure is to be used to assess structural knowledge in a specific content domain, you may want to constrain the learners responses by suggesting a particular conceptual orientation when you give directions. For instance, "When thinking about related ideas, it is important to 'think like a psychologist." The idea is to suppress random or irrelevant responses and to constrain responses to domain-related ideas.

Controlled Word Association Procedure

1. The initial step is the same for both types of test: it is necessary to first determine the concepts that are of interest.

2. Each stimulus word/concept is centered at the top of a page, the same as the free association test.

3. Students are instructed to relate other concepts from the *same subject matter domain*, labeling the most highly related "1," the second most related "2," etc. This page would look like the following:

FOOTBALL

1.
2.
3.
4.
5.

Generally, the student is given a limited amount of time (such as 1 to 1 1/2 minutes per page). Preece (1976) reports using "filler" pages in between concepts (unrelated topics, which are not scored but are inserted between each page of the test) to reduce the amount of redundancy that is based on test instrument proximity rather than semantic proximity. Although this doubles the length of the test, it should help to reduce this effect. You may also want to consider constraining the responses as described earlier.

Scoring for Both Procedures

Scoring these tests are somewhat complex, but with reasonable math skills, the initial part of the scoring (building a matrix) can be done by hand.

The general formula is borrowed from Garskoff and Houston (1963) and is considerably simplified for our purposes. The original formula contains a measure to control for the shape of the distribution, which has been eliminated. However, in most cases, the formula supplied here will produce almost the same results as the original, more complex formula (Martys, 1991, personal conversation). The simplified Garskoff and Houston formula:

$$\frac{\text{RELATED WORDS (RW)}}{\text{TOTAL NUMBER OF POSSIBLE RELATED WORDS (TN)}} \quad \text{or} \quad \frac{\text{RW}}{\text{TN}}$$

To score the tests, construct a blank matrix with all of the concepts tested crossed with themselves. An excerpt from the example matrix would look like the matrix on the next page. Take the first pair of concepts, in this case football and basketball, and look at the test sheets for the first student. You'll need to renumber the responses so that the most related has the highest number.

	Football	Basketball	Soccer	Tennis
Football				
Basketball				
Soccer				
Tennis				

For example, if this were the student's response sheet:

FOOTBALL

1. kick
2. run
3. pass
4. crowd
5. tackle

You would renumber it like this:

FOOTBALL

1. kick (5)
2. run (4)
3. pass (3)
4. crowd (2)
5. tackle (1)

You would then do the same for the second concept sheet:

BASKETBALL

1. shoot (5)
2. pass (4)
3. crowd (3)
4. run (2)
5. defense (1)

List the words that are common to both sheets. Then, write down the values that are listed on both sheets.

In this example:

	FOOTBALL		BASKETBALL	
run	(4)	x	(2)	= 8
pass	(3)	x	(4)	=12
crowd	(2)	x	(3)	= 6
				+_____
				26 = RW

The denominator (TN) will always equal 54, as long as only five values are used for each stimulus word.

$$\frac{RW}{TN} = \frac{26}{54}$$

Therefore, the RC for these two terms, football and basketball, is RW/TN or 26/54 which in a decimal form equals .481. This number goes into the matrix in the intersection between FOOTBALL and BASKETBALL. The higher the number, the more overlap there is between lists, and therefore the more related the two terms are. The RC is, in effect, a correlation coefficient between the words.

The procedure is repeated for each pair of concepts that are tested, until a final matrix is completed. This matrix can be analyzed using knowledge representation techniques described in Chapters 6 and 7. Those procedures will produce a visual map that cluster the most related concepts closer together on the map to reflect the semantic proximities that are described numerically in the matrix. However, even without mapping proximities, one can examine the matrix to see which concepts are most related for each student. The correlation coefficients may be compared between individuals to assess the degree of similarity in their structural knowledge of the domain.

EFFECTIVENESS OF WORD ASSOCIATION LISTS

The free association test has a higher face validity than controlled word associations or tree construction (see Chapter 5) tasks and has a reliability of .87 (Preece, 1976). It would appear that this type of test may accurately elicit the underlying relations of a learner's structural knowledge. However, due to its unconstrained nature, there may be many relationships that go beyond the subject matter domain. Also, if instructions do not constrain responses, the free association test gives students a chance to wander far from the relationships of interest.

Visually analyzing a matrix can assist the teacher in diagnosing student misconceptions and the instructional designer in conducting formative evaluation. For example, if a student has a high RC between two ideas that are not generally highly related, it might signal the instructor to do some additional probing, as it may suggest misunderstandings in the subject matter that have not been perceived, or it may signal to an instructional designer that there is an inadequacy in the instructional materials.

Content/Task Interactions

Word association graphing has used in a variety of subject matter domains.

- Word associations have been shown to be effective (Geeslin & Shavelson, 1975) in assessing mathematics structure. There appear to be no interactions with tasks or domains. It is a technique that can be used in any knowledge domain.

- Goldsmith, Johnson, and Acton (1991) found that raw relatedness coefficients were less accurate in predicting examination scores than Pathfinder nets (see Chapter 8).

Learner Interactions

Though no research is available, individual differences in the ability to generate word association lists likely exist. Individual differences, such as ideational fluency (Guilford, 1967), the ability to generate alternative divergent, verbal responses, may very likely constrain the size of the word list that is generated.

- Preece's (1976) found that this procedure was correlated with a tree construction task at a group level. This might suggest the use of this procedure as a formative evaluation tool, rather than as an alternative to achievement testing. There is little research investigating learner style interactions with results of word association tasks.

Advantages of Word Association Tasks

- Both word association tasks have high face validity, in that they require the learner to actually produce the terms that are related, not simply select them from a list or rate the similarity between them (as in Chapter

3). In this sense, they may be the most accurate measure of a learner's actual cognitive structure, as Preece (1976) suggested.

• The tests take little time to produce for an instructor. Other than identifying the key terms of interest, preparation of the materials is reasonably easy.

Disadvantages of Word Association Tasks

• Nagy (1984) suggests that this type of assessment data be used in *conjunction* with achievement testing. By itself, the results may be overgeneralized. He claims that assessing structural knowledge is still in its infancy, and this type of data should not be used alone, but should be used in conjunction with other data to assess students.

• A word of caution about over-interpreting this type of assessment procedure is given by Stewart (cited in Nagy, 1984), who suggests that terms can be recalled without any real meaning of the underlying concepts, simply because the terms are learned in contiguity with other terms. This could be supported by the levels of processing model of memory, suggesting that information can be processed at a shallow level without ever attending to the semantic meaning of a term. This might suggest situations in which a learner can generate terms that are related without necessarily comprehending the exact relationships between terms, simply because the learner remembered hearing them mentioned at the same time during instruction.

• This procedure does not judge the accuracy of the two lists of terms. For example, both the football and basketball list used in the previous example could have generated identical, yet unrelated lists, such as: *telephone, eyebrow, dictionary,* and *pizza.* If the two lists were identical, the relationship between terms would be high, yet would show no underlying knowledge of the subject matter whatsoever. This would show that the learner makes similar relationships between the terms, but the relationships would not be the types that are usually of interest in instruction.

• These methods do not provide any information about the dynamic properties of the structure.

• Most studies have used a relatively small amount of information, such as that from a chapter or two from a textbook.

Naveh-Benjamin, McKeachie, Lin, and Tucker (1986) also provided some criticism of this type of research.

- Nearly all of the techniques represented in this chapter transform the data into distance matrices to describe the semantic distances between the concepts in the domain. The problem is that such an analysis removes the data several steps from their original data and can miss some regularities because it averages the data . For instance, cases with extreme ratings would be averaged with middle judgments, obtaining a scaled value that would ignore the extreme ratings.

- Different aspects of the cognitive structure of the students are not specified. Most of the research has used general distance from a standard structures as the measure for structure development. Comparing cognitive structure needs to consider the number of dimensions and other factors.

REFERENCES

Garskoff, B.E., & Houston, J.P. (1963). Measurement of verbal relatedness: an idiographic approach. *Psychological Review, 70*, 277-288.

Geeslin, W.E., & Shavelson, R.J. (1975). Comparison of content structure and cognitive structure in high school students' learning of probability. *Journal of Research in Mathematics Education, 12*, 109-120.

Goldsmith, T.E., Johnson, P.J., & Acton, W.H. (1991). Assessing structural knowledge. *Journal of Educational Psychology, 83*, 88-96.

Guilford, J.P. (1967). *The nature of human intelligence.* New York: McGraw-Hill.

Nagy, P. (1984). *The representation of cognitive structures.* Toronto, Canada: Ontario Institute for Studies in Education.

Naveh-Benjamin, M., McKeachie, W.J., Lin, Y.G., & Tucker, D.G. (1986) Inferring students' cognitive structures and their development using the "ordered tree technique". *Journal of Educational Psychology, 78*, 130-140.

Preece, P.F. W. (1976). Mapping cognitive structure: A comparison of methods. *Journal of Educational Psychology, 68*, 1-8.

3

Eliciting Knowledge Through Similarity Ratings

DESCRIPTION OF SIMILARITY RATINGS

Similarity ratings are the most direct method for rating the similarity between concepts in an individual's cognitive structure. Similarity ratings essentially ask individuals to rate in terms of a constant scale the degree of similarity between pairs of concepts or ideas. This method identifies a group of related concepts, asking the respondent to rate the degree of similarity or dissimilarity between each of the pairs of concepts. These ratings are summarized in a distance matrix which depicts the degree of similarity or dissimilarity for all pairs of concepts. This method may be contrasted with the indirect method for determining similarity ratings through word association tasks (see Chapter 2). However, Johnson, Cox, and Curran (1970) found that the similarity ratings that resulted from these two methods were highly correlated.

Rationale

The rationale for rating or comparing the similarity between concepts assumes a spatial metaphor for depicting cognitive structure. As indicated in Chapter 1, structural knowledge or cognitive structure describes the pattern of relationships among concepts in memory (Preece, 1976) Although it is a hypothetical construct, it can best be reified spatially. Constructs in an individual's cognitive structure are differentially related, that is, some are closely related while others are more distantly related. This semantic distance is most often conceived in terms of geometric distance. More closely related concepts appear closer in geometric space while more semantically dissimilar concepts are further apart. The representations that are developed from proximity rating using MDS (Chapter 6) and Pathfinder nets (Chapter 8) both assume that the geometric distances between concepts in n-dimensional space reflect the psychological proximity of the concepts in the individual's cognitive structure. The similarity ratings method is the simplest and most direct method for identifying those distances.

EXAMPLE OF SIMILARITY RATINGS

The ratings from a pairwise similarity rating exercise are typically represented as a half-matrix of correlation coefficients as in Fig. 3.1, where each intersection in the matrix depicts the individual's rating of the similarity between those two concepts. The example provided is a similarity matrix produced by a beginning physics student who generated his own list of concepts related to lasers.

```
1 Lasers          .8
2 Power           .9 .1
3 Wavelength      .7 .5 .8
4 Photons         .9 .6 .8 .9
5 Light           .8 .8 .9 .9 .5
6 Energy          .8 .2 .7 .5 .9 .5
7 Mirrors         .8 .9 .8 .7 .8 .6 .9
8 Amplify Medium  .8 .9 .1 .6 .8 .2 .8 .9
9 Gain            .6 .6 .6 .4 .6 .8 .2 .6 .2
10 Heat           .8 .9 .6 .6 .2 .9 .1 .7 .8 .8
11 Energy Source  .6 .9 .3 .7 .5 .2 .1 .3 .2 .1 .2
12 Focus          .9 .9 .1 .0 .0 .3 .3 .3 .1 .6 .8 .5
13 Physical Size  .7 .6 .1 .0 .4 .9 .3 .5 .3 .4 .8 .6 .6
14 Cost           .4 .9 .1 .4 .1 .7 .5 .9 .9 .8 .5 .0 .3 .4
15 Efficiency     .9 .1 .9 .6 .8 .8 .8 .9 .1 .1 .7 .0 .0 .0 .0
16 Frequency      .9 .9 .9 .5 .9 .9 .6 .8 .2 .5 .7 .8 .9 .8 .8 .9
17 Applications   .9 .9 .7 .1 .6 .9 .3 .5 .2 .7 .8 .2 .6 .6 .1 .7 .9
18 Safety         .6 .3 .0 .3 .0 .5 .5 .6 .1 .7 .5 .0 .7 .1 .2 .0 .8 .6
19 Reliability    .8 .1 .1 .6 .4 .8 .4 .7 .1 .3 .8 .0 .0 .1 .5 .1 .9 .0 .1
20 Pulse Length   .7 .1 .6 .2 .8 .1 .3 .6 .1 .1 .2 .8 .1 .2 .5 .6 .8 .3 .2 .1
21 Beam Dispersion .8 .3 .1 .8 .7 .0 .8 .9 .1 .1 .5 .1 .0 .6 .3 .8 .9 .0 .0 .3

                   20 19 18 17 16 15 14 13 12 11 10 9 8 7 6 5 4 3 2 1
```

Fig. 3.1. Similarity matrix of laser concepts.

APPLICATIONS OF SIMILARITY RATINGS

Representing/Assessing Structural Knowledge

Similarity ratings have been used exclusively as a knowledge elicitation task for identifying the strength of relationships in order to ascertain the underlying structure of a group of related ideas. The primary application of the similarity rating technique is to generate similarity matrices for structural knowledge representation. The structure of the similarity matrices may be accessed by using a variety of statistical algorithms to identify the underlying clusters or dimensions, including principal components (Diekhoff & Diekhoff, 1982), cluster analysis, multidimensional scaling (see Chapter 6), or Pathfinder networks (see Chapter 7). The most common method for analyzing similarity ratings in order to represent a learner's cognitive structure is multidimensional scaling (Fenker, 1975)

Conveying Structural Knowledge

Diekhoff and Diekhoff (1982) used the similarity rating procedure to generate cognitive maps for teacher use as a tool in communicating structural knowledge to students. Essentially, they were using similarity ratings as an assessment method to capture the teacher's knowledge representation, which would in turn be used as an overview or conceptual organizer in teaching class.

Acquiring Structural Knowledge

The applications of semantic rating are meant only for assessing or representing structural knowledge. The process, if repeated, may have some strategic benefits to learners if the learners compared the relative changes in their knowledge structures, though that hypothesis has never been tested.

PROCEDURE FOR DEVELOPING SIMILARITY RATINGS

Although the actual process of similarity rating appears to be fairly straightforward, there are several important decisions which, if made haphazardly, will produce a score that has little meaning. These considerations are (a) who or what produces a set of ratings, experts or novices; (b) which content is selected; (c) and producing a mental set in the learners that will enable the students to generate appropriate ratings.

Expert Ratings. Expert ratings can be created in several ways. One method would be to select a panel of experts that are highly familiar with the subject matter. They can each produce a set of relationship judgments, and these can then be averaged (median ratings are often used) to produce the expert judgments. An alternative method is to pool the relationship judgments of students who have been previously successful in the class. A third method is to use the relationship judgments of the course instructor.

Content Selection. Obviously, the content selected for the concept pairs should pertain to the subject matter of the course or the content being studied. However, when devising this type of test, one should choose pairs that are roughly of equal importance, as this type of assessment technique does not allow for any "weighting" of the relative importance of the concept pairs. Put another way, a trivial pair of concepts will affect the score as much as a vital pair of concepts. Therefore, it is suggested that the test construction be limited to only the most important concepts.

Learner's Mental Set. Careful instructions must be created that give the student an idea of the general range of relationship judgments. An example of how to score the pairs should also be given to the student in the test's instructions. So, if you are interested in assessing learners' knowledge of physics, instruct them to "think like physicists when completing the rating task."

1. Select a group of concepts that are representative of a content area. Most often, single concepts are chosen. However, similarities between more elaborate concept statements may also be rated. For instance, Stanners and Brown (1982) had students compare such statements as:

   Behavior is unconsciously motivated.
   Personality is a product of learning.

2. Construct a matrix in which all possible pairs of concepts are represented. Each pair should be presented to the student in a random order.

3. Consider embedding this type of assessment technique within or in addition to other testing techniques. For example, in a traditional midterm exam, the test might be constructed in several sections. There might be traditional test techniques (such as multiple choice questions or fill-in questions) along with a relationship judgment section of the test.

4. Create a simple example of the procedure. Remember that many students will not be familiar with this type of assessment technique. Use obvious examples in the test instructions, such as

   ROBIN------PIGEON rated as a 8 or 9
   ROBIN------PENCIL SHARPENER rated as a 1

5. Present each pair of concepts together and ask the student to rate the strength of the relationship between each pair on a scale of 1-9 (some researchers use 1-7, 1-15, or other scales), where 1 indicates little or no relationship between the concepts and 9 indicates a very strong or equivalence relationship between the concepts.

   1 |--| 9
        Unrelated   Related

On a scale of 1-9, rate the degree of similarity between the following concepts:

   momentum — acceleration

6. Convert these ratings to decimals (i.e. 1=.1, 9=.9) and summarize in a half matrix such as in Fig. 3.1.

7. Consult Chapters 6 or 8 for the methods that may be used to determining the underlying structural representation of the ratings in the matrix.

EFFECTIVENESS OF SIMILARITY RATINGS

Learner Interactions

Most of the research using similarity ratings has been done with college students. No studies have compared the validity or reliability of similarity ratings with different populations of learners. Similarity ratings are intended to capture individual differences in knowledge structures, so individual differences in knowledge, especially prior knowledge, will naturally affect the ratings of each individual.

Content/Task Interactions

Similarity ratings have been used to elicit structural knowledge in different content areas, including physics (Johnson et al., 1970) and psychology (Brown & Stanners, 1983; Diekhoff & Diekhoff, 1982; Wainer & Kaye, 1974). No studies have compared the validity or reliability of similarity ratings between content domains. Most researchers believe it to be an evaluation method that is independent of the content domain.

Advantages of Similarity Ratings

- It is a simpler method than word association method described in Chapter 2.

- Although similarity ratings appear to be quite subjective, research shows good reliability in their judgments over time, and judgments from different experts show a high degree of similarity (Diekhoff & Wigginton, 1982).

Disadvantages of Similarity Ratings

- On the other hand, distances derived from direct similarity ratings have been found to be limited in reliability (Reitman & Rueter, 1980). They change with the directions or context in which they were collected, or they may change from day to day.

- Analyses of distance matrices require that distances are symmetric, yet psychological processes often produce distances that are asymmetric (Reitman & Rueter, 1980).

- This is a tedious process that is useful for a limited set of concepts. The number of pairwise comparisons is (n*n-1)/2 the number of concepts in the list. So, for example, a list of 15 concepts results in 105 comparisons, but a list of 25 concepts results in 300 comparisons. Such a list would require well more than 1 hour for even the most dedicated performer to complete. Fatigue will become a problem.

- One of the weaknesses with this type of test is the vague definitions of relatedness. The scope of relationships are not clearly defined by previous researchers, and although Diekhoff (1983) reports that an example was sufficient to convey "relatedness" to the test-taker, this appears to be a construct that needs more clarification. For example, how similar are a ROBIN and an EAGLE. Compared to a ROBIN and PIGEON used earlier, these terms have limited similarity. However, compared to a ROBIN and a PENCIL SHARPENER, these same two items are likely to receive a higher rating.

- In like manner, the overall scope of the test may produce distorted relationships. For example a test limited strictly to relationships between pairs of birds will produce a lower relationship between ROBIN and EAGLE than would a test that covers relationships between several animal classes. It would perhaps be best not to mix and match a broadly divergent range of related pairs, but rather to limit the use of this type of assessment to limited domains, such as within a particular lesson or module.

- It would appear that sequencing of the pairs in a test is likely to produce distorted relationships. Therefore, a random sequencing of the pairs is essential.

- Since all possible pairs of concepts being considered must be rated to develop the cognitive map, the reliability of relatedness ratings can vary considerably. Diekhoff (1983) notes that under such conditions even experts would have difficulty reliably judging the degree of relatedness between concept pairs.

REFERENCES

Brown, L.T., & Stanners, R.F. (1983). The assessment and modification of concept interrelationships. *Journal of Experimental Education, 52,* 11-21.
Diekhoff, G.M. (1983). Testing through relationship judgments. *Journal of Educational Psychology, 75,* 227-233.

Diekhoff, G.M., & Diekhoff, K.B. (1982). Cognitive maps as a tool in communicating structural knowledge. *Educational Technology, 22*(4), 28-30.

Diekhoff, G.M., & Wigginton, P. (1982, April). *Using multi-dimensional scaling-produced cognitive maps to facilitate the communication of structural knowledge.* Paper presented at the annual meeting of the Southwestern Psychological Association, Dallas, TX. (ERIC Document Reproduction Service No. ED 218 245)

Fenker, R.M. (1975). The organization of conceptual materials: A methodology for measuring ideal and actual cognitive structures. *Instructional Science, 4*, 33-57.

Johnson, P.E., Cox, D.L., & Curran, T.E. (1970). Psychological reality of physical concepts. *Psychonomic Science, 19*(4), 245-246.

Preece, P.F.W. (1976). Mapping cognitive structure: A comparison of methods. *Journal of Educational Psychology, 68*, 1-8.

Reitman, J.S., & Rueter, H.H. (1980). Organization revealed by recall orders and confirmed by pauses. *Cognitive Psychology, 12*, 554-581.

Stanners, R.F., & Brown, L.T. (1982). Conceptual interrelationships based upon learning in introductory psychology. *Teaching of Psychology, 9*(2), 74-77.

Wainer, H., & Kaye, K. (1974). multidimensional scaling of concept learning in an introductory course. *Journal of Educational Psychology, 66*, 591-598.

4

Eliciting Knowledge Through Card Sorts

DESCRIPTION OF CARD SORTS

The card sort exercise is similar to a learning exercise used in many preschools and kindergartens, in which the child is shown a group of pictures and asked "which of these belong together?" Such questions are followed by explanations of how some of the pictures represent similar ideas or functions, while the other picture or pictures do not fall in the same category. In this basic sorting task the basis for categorization of concepts is usually obvious for adults. However, when dealing with categories of more complex and abstract concepts, the basis for groupings are often less clear. The card sort technique is an advanced level sorting task that can be used to identify how concepts in a content area are organized in a learner's knowledge structures.

A typical card sort exercise involves presenting subjects with a series of cards on which concept words are written and sometimes briefly defined. The subject is then instructed to sort concepts according to similarity of meaning (Miller, 1969). In a modification of this card sort exercise subjects can be instructed to sort the cards into groups in some meaningful manner, and to label the groups and any subgroups (Hirschman & Wallendorf, 1982; Stein, Baxter & Leinhardt, 1990). Analysis of the resulting organization of concepts provides insight into the manner in which the subject views the content area.

Rationale

The Russian psycholinguist, Lev Vygotsky, and his associates investigated the meaning of words assigned by individuals using sorting tasks somewhat similar to the card sort technique described here. These researchers took drawings of common items and asked their subjects to indicate which ones were alike. In one incident described by this group, a peasant was shown drawings of a hammer, a saw, a log, and a hatchet. This peasant indicated that all of the objects belonged together. The researchers explained that others had grouped three of the items together, the hammer, the saw, and the hatchet because they were all tools. The peasant replied

that anyone who would make such a grouping probably had enough fire-
wood (Luria, 1979).

Miller (1969) describes the card sorting technique as a method for
examining meanings of words. Sorting concepts according to similarity of
meaning, or according to some other meaningful criteria results in a
grouping of concepts, assumed to be organized in a hierarchical manner.
When investigating cognitive structure, the group in which one selects to
place a particular concept provides insight into the individual meaning
that one assigns to concepts. Some may tend to group items in a way that
is functional for themselves, as did the peasant from Vygotsky's study,
while others may choose other grouping criteria.

EXAMPLES OF CARD SORTS

Whereas card sorts can be used for meaningful sorting of any number of
complex concepts, the results of a simple card sort exercise are depicted
here. Herbaceous flowering plants can be organized according to several
different factors, including hardiness, color of bloom, season of bloom, and
whether the plants are annuals or perennials. The figures here show how
cards with name of flowering plants were organized by subjects with dif-
fering levels of knowledge about the plants. The most highly differentiated sorting (Fig. 4.1) shows the plants grouped as annuals vs.

PERENNIALS		ANNUALS	
Shade tolerant	**Full Sun**	**Shade Tolerant**	**Full Sun**
Spring bloom:	Spring bloom:	Impatiens	Marigold
Bleeding heart	Crocus	Browallia	Zinnias
Woodland Phlox	Candytuft		
	Snapdragons		
Globe flower	Tulips		
	Sunflowers		
Jacob's ladder			Petunias
Summer bloom:	Summer bloom:		
Hostas	Black-eyed Susans		
Gooseneck	Purple Coneflower		
Loosestrife	Shasta Daisy		
Fall bloom:	Fall bloom:		
Japenese anemone	Hardy Aster		
Azure Monkshood	Autumn Joy		

Fig. 4.1. Card sort resulting in a three-level hierarchical organization of
     plants.

perennials, as requiring full sun vs. shade tolerant, and by season of bloom. Other, less differentiated sortings are also possible. If a learner was unaware of the sun requirements for plants the same cards could be sorted into two tiered hierarchies (Fig. 4.2). A grouping made by a subject with even less knowledge of the difference between plants is depicted in Fig. 4.3, who grouped plants as annuals or perennials only.

PERENNIALS   **ANNUALS**

Spring bloom: Marigold
Bleeding heart   Browallia
Woodland Phlox   Sunflowers
Candytuft   Zinnias
Globe flower   Impatiens
Crocus   Snapdragons
Jacob's ladder   Petunias
Tulips
Summer bloom:
Hostas
Black-eyed Susans
Gooseneck Loosestrife
Purple Coneflower
Shasta Daisy

Fall bloom:
Japenese anemone
Hardy Aster
Azure Monkshood
Autumn Joy

Fig. 4.2. Card sort resulting in a two-tiered hierarchy of plants.

APPLICATIONS OF CARD SORTS

Card sorts can be used as classroom activities prior to review sessions or to stimulate discussions in a content area. Students can be asked to sort a series of concepts into meaningful groups and to assign each group a title. The various organizational schemes developed by students can then be discussed in large or small group sessions.

Learners can be given the results of a card sort (i.e., unlabeled clusters of words) and instructed to determine how the concepts in each grouping are related. This exercise can be completed individually and then shared in group discussions, or it may be used as the basis for a small group activity.

PERENNIALS   **ANNUALS**

Bleeding heart   Browallia
Azure Monkshood   Petunias
Candytuft   Zinnias
Autumn Joy   Impatiens
Crocus   Sunflowers
Jacob's ladder   Marigold
Hostas   Snapdragon
Black-eyed Susans
TulipsGooseneck Loosestrife
Purple Coneflower
Globe flower
Japenese anemone
Hardy Aster
Woodland Phlox
Shasta Daisy

Fig. 4.3. Card sort resulting in a one-tiered hierarchy of plants.

Representing/Assessing Structural Knowledge

The card sort technique was developed as a technique to identify how a learner or group of learners organize information in memory. When instructed to sort concepts according to similarity of meaning the relative semantic proximity of concepts can be determined. Miller (1969) described a series of computations that allow analysis of card sort data to identify the relative semantic "distance" between all terms included in the card sort.

When instructed to sort cards in some meaningful manner, without further instructions as to the type of meaning or organizational scheme to impose upon the concepts, learners gain additional insight into how these selected concepts are clustered in memory. In some cases the organization structure imposed by a subject will provide indications of knowledge deficits that may prevent that subject from applying knowledge to solve problems. Another possibility is that a learner may organize concepts according to superficial, surface characteristics such as similarity in appearance, sound, or rhyme. This attention to surface characteristics rather than attending to the meaning of concepts may interfere with ability to use those concepts (see, for example, Stein et al., 1990).

Conveying Structural Knowledge

Groupings identified through card sort exercises indicate that a series of concepts are related in some manner. The basis for the relationship between concepts can be conveyed through the use of labels or titles for the groups of categories. Card sorts completed by experts tend to reflect more differentiated organizational structures than those completed by novices (Stein et al., 1990). The organizational structures imposed by experts on a series of concepts can be helpful in conveying these important relationships to learners. An instructor can present his or her organization of concepts in a content area as a summary of key concepts covered in a unit of study. Alternatively, this grouping may be presented prior to instruction as an organizer of information to follow. When a card sort exercise is completed by groups of experts the compiled results of the sort conveys the primary organizational structure used by experts to view a content area.

Acquiring Structural Knowledge

The process of sorting concepts requires consideration of how concepts are related and what features they share. This task itself requires learners to consider structural relationships and may help learners identify new relationships between concepts. One method of completing a card sort requires the sorter to arrange the cards in one manner, and then do a second sort using different grouping criteria (Stein et al., 1990). When learners are forced (or at least urged) to sort cards a second time they gain an increased understanding that there are different ways to organize knowledge. In addition, in the process of completing the second sorting task new structural relations may become apparent.

PROCEDURE FOR DEVELOPING AND USING CARD SORTS

1. Select the concepts of interest for sorting. Concepts included in the exercise should differ along a number of dimensions (e.g., function vs. appearance). Write the word(s) for each concept on a separate card.

2. Arrange the cards in random order and present them to the learner.

3. Instruct the learner to sort the cards into groups and to label each group.

4. After the first sorting is complete, if desired, ask the learner to sort the cards a second way. Learners who are able to complete a second meaningful sorting of the concepts demonstrate that they are not rigid in their definitions of the concepts, and that they understand that concepts can be grouped in different ways.

5. Analyze the groupings identified by the learner. Did the learner identify subgroups within major groups? This reflects a greater degree of differentiation among concepts.

6. Continue to analyze the groupings. Are concepts sorted according to meaningful criteria, or do the criteria for sorting appear random, or su-

perficial? What is the semantic relationship between the concepts in each group? Develop a definition and/or conceptual title for each group. You may want to ask the learners the criteria by which they formed groups.

7. Compare the groupings identified by learners to the groupings obtained by experts in the field to identify how the learners' perception of the concepts differs from those of the experts.

8. If possible, interview learners' whose groupings differ from other learners' or experts' to identify the basis for differences in groupings.

EFFECTIVENESS OF CARD SORTS

Research to date has used card sorting techniques as a tool for gathering data on relatedness of concepts. However, little research into the accuracy of this tool in conveying or assessing cognitive structure has been conducted.

- Hirschman and Wallendorf (1982) found that only 50% of subjects in their study used the same type of organizing scheme in two successive card sort tasks, indicating questionable reliability of the technique. However, the two tasks used different groups of concepts which might logically be organized differently in memory. In addition, fatique may have impacted upon subjects' performance in the second sorting task. Thus, no firm conclusions can be made about the technique's reliability.

- Stein et al. (1990) used the card sort technique to investigate a mathematics instructor's structural knowledge in the area of mathematical functions. Through the card sort and an interview they found that that the teacher's knowledge was limited in several areas, and that his knowledge was organized in a superficial manner. Analysis of his teaching in the content area showed that instruction was narrowed in accordance with his knowledge structures. This study provides evidence that the card sort technique is a useful tool for assessing structural knowledge.

- Miller (1969) found the card sort task to be a useful tool for identifying relative distances between concepts that are organized in a hierarchical structure.

Learner Interactions

Little research has been conducted on the card sort technique. However, it is clear that the some individuals are able to sort concepts into more highly differentiated groups than others, based on their organization of knowledge in the content area (Stein et al., 1990). Hirschman and Wallendorf (1982) identified five different types of sorting patterns, ranging from highly organized/well-differentiated groups to idiosyncratic grouping patterns in which the criteria for grouping is not clear. The primary learner interaction identified in studies to date is the organization of knowledge in the content area.

Content/Task Interactions

Card sorts can be used in any content area. Studies to date include the use of card sorts to investigate knowledge structures related to mathematical functions and graphing (Stein et al., 1990), and to identify organization of concepts for consumer research (Hirschman & Wallendorf, 1982). Card sort techniques are also used in vocational counseling to identify learner's interests in various occupations (Jones, 1979; Williams, 1978).

Advantages of Card Sort

- The sorting task is a well-structured task that can be comprehended by most learners.

- Card sorts can be used to identify organization of knowledge in a content area and to identify areas of knowledge deficiency.

Disadvantages of Card Sort

- Card sorting tasks are restrictive, allowing a concept to be included in only one group, rather than several groups simultaneously.

- The card sorting task limits subjects to consideration of the similarities and differences of only those concepts presented on the cards. Thus, a limited "picture" of each subject's cognitive structure can be assessed with this technique. This is contrasted with other techniques such as free word association tasks, or some graphical techniques in which learners may include any concepts from memory in the analysis.

REFERENCES

Hirshman, E. C. ,& Wallendorf, M. R. (1982). Free-response and card-sort techniques for assessing cognitive content: Two studies concerning their stability, validity and utility. *Perceptual and Motor Skills, 54,* 1095-1110.

Jones, L. K. (1979). Occu-Sort: Development and evaluation of an occupational card sort system. *Vocational Guidance Quarterly, 28,* 56-62.

Luria, A. R. (1979). *The making of mind: A personal account of Soviet psychology.* Cambridge, MA: Harvard University Press.

Miller, G. A. (1969). A psychological method to investigate verbal concepts. *Journal of Mathemential Psychology, 6,* 169-191.

Stein, M. K., Baxter, J. A., & Leinhardt, G. (1990). Subject matter knowledge and elementary instruction: A case from functions and graphing. *American Educational Research Journal, 27,* 639-663.

Williams, S. K. (1978). The vocational card sort: A tool for vocational exploration. *Vocational Guidance Quarterly, 26,* 237-243.

5

Representing Structural Knowledge Through Tree Construction Tests

DESCRIPTION OF TREE CONSTRUCTION TESTS

Tree construction tests are an alternative method of representing structural knowledge. Like the other techniques (Chapters 6 - 8), this technique is based on the assumption of semantic proximity, which states that ideas that are more closely related can be conceived as being "closer" in cognitive space. Tree construction tests consist of sets of concepts that are sequentially linked by the learner. The links are not labeled and the exact nature of the relationships is defined as "similarity" or "most related to." In addition to the linkages between concepts, the relative strength of each linkage is given through the ordinal numbering of each connection. That is, one can determine which links are the strongest by retracing the order in which the learner connected the concepts.

Tree construction tests are a "rapid method of obtaining proximity measures" (Preece, 1976) and their value may be in the ease with which they can be administered and scored. Preece reported that free and controlled word association tests took 35-40 minutes to administer while a tree construction test took less than 10 minutes for most subjects.

The tree construction test requires students to build a connected structure (alternatively called a directed graph), using terms that are pre-supplied by the tester. The tree construction test is similar to a pattern note (see Chapter 22) in that both assessment measures require the students to connect words that represent concepts. In both techniques, it is the variety of *connections* that the student makes that are of interest to the instructor. However, the tree construction test differs from a pattern note in that the concepts that are to be linked are supplied in advance by the instructor. Therefore, the tree construction test might be conceived as a pattern note with pre-supplied concepts. Unlike a pattern note, it has the advantage of constraining the range of responses that a student may supply. Consequently, it is easier to interpret, because it is limited to terms that may be of interest academically. The pattern note, in contrast, may be more accurate an assessment of a student's structural knowledge simply because it is so unconstrained, i.e., it may include *any* relationships that are of interest to a student.

EXAMPLES OF TREE CONSTRUCTIONS

Figure 5.1 shows an example of a tree construction that was built by a student on the topic of computer assisted instruction.

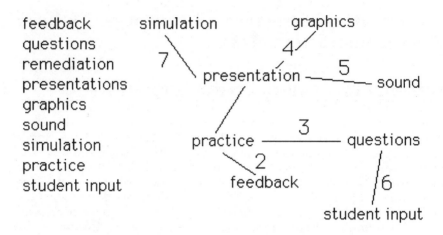

Fig. 5.1. Tree construction on computer assisted instruction.

The tree construction test supplies the learner with a list of terms, and instructs the learner to begin linking the terms together. For example, a course in computer assisted instruction might supply the following terms (along with many others):

> feedback
> question content
> response mode
> branching
> presentation

The learner is told to select two terms that are more closely related (or alternatively more *similar*) than any other pair, and to cross them from the list. Then, the two terms are written on a sheet of paper and connected with a line. The line is labeled "1."

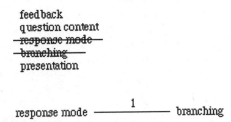

Then, from the remaining words, a word is selected that is most closely connected to either of the two words already selected. This word is in turn crossed from the list and joined to the word that it is most closely related to in the structure. The line connecting the new term is labeled "2."

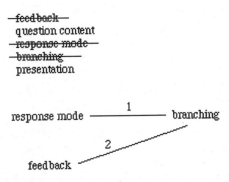

The student is then instructed to select a term which is most closely connected to any of the three words which have been selected so far. This term is crossed from the list, added to the structure with a line, which is labeled "3."

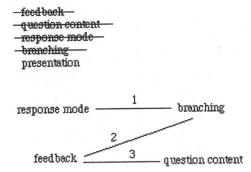

This process continues until all terms are removed from the list and integrated into the structure. In each case, the to-be-added term can be connected to any term in the structure, and the line is labeled consecutively. Preece (1976) used 15 terms in a tree construction test, but there is no particular reason why more or fewer terms could not be used. For example, Waern (1972) reports a variety of semantic proximity tasks that use 8-22 terms.

APPLICATIONS OF TREE CONSTRUCTION TESTS

Tree construction tests are primarily used as a means of assessing structural knowledge. They are used without further data reduction as a pictorial means of capturing structural knowledge of a learner. The data can also be further reduced using a procedure detailed in the following section.

Representing/Assessing Structural Knowledge

The tree construction test produces a graphic representation of the connections within a student's structural knowledge, and therefore, in many cases, no further reduction of the data is necessary. That is, the result of the test produces a "picture" of a learner's structural knowledge and also provides clues regarding the order in which linkages occurred.

However, in testing the validity of the tree construction task, Preece developed a rather complex method of scoring that increases the validity of the tree construction test. According to Preece's method, the test is scored by counting the number of links that connect any two terms, and then taking the square root of that number. In the earlier example, *response mode* and *feedback* are connected by one link, and hence receive a value of "1." The square root of that number is also "1." This number is then entered into a half matrix which relates all pairs of terms. In a like manner, the terms *response mode* and *question content* are connected by two links, and therefore receive a value of "2." The square root of 2 is "1.4." These values are entered into a half matrix. A procedure described by Waern (1972) suggests that a "cutoff" value be established. A cutoff value in essence decides (somewhat arbitrarily) that items in the matrix below (or in this case *above*) a certain value are eliminated from the tree. Items above the cutoff value are then treated as "connections" and graphed on the tree, producing a graphic representation of structural knowledge that has eliminated several of the lesser connected terms. It would appear that this method is not entirely useful for many applications, and that an unscored graph may have more utility since it continues to represent all of the original data. However, it may be useful in trying to average the structural knowledge of many students or experts, and it may have value as a data reduction tool.

Note that the ordinal values of the links (the sequential numbering of the links from 1 to 15) are *not* used in the scoring procedure. As yet, there are no procedures for integrating this information into the scoring of the tree construction test. However, this is an area that may still be qualitatively explored by an instructor by noting the varied strengths and sequence of the construction process.

Conveying Structural Knowledge

The tree construction test conveys the structural knowledge of a learner, not within a text or within the subject matter. As such, it reflects the general linkages between concepts within a given learner's cognitive structure and so are not useful for conveying structural knowledge.

Acquiring Structural Knowledge

The tree construction test is not used as a means for students to acquire structural knowledge. Rather, it is used to assess structural knowledge already acquired by a learner. Although the selection of terms from within a domain requires some prior knowledge of that domain, the selection of terms for inclusion in the test is done by a teacher, not a learner. Therefore, the tree construction test does not directly relate to a student's acquiring structural knowledge, unless one considers formalizing the links between concepts to be a learning experience.

PROCEDURE FOR DEVELOPING TREE CONSTRUCTION TESTS

1. Choose terms that are of basically the same level of detail and importance from a content domain or subject area. For example, in selecting mechanics concepts, the terms *area, volume, density, velocity, acceleration, force, pressure, work,* and *power* were selected (Preece, 1976). Note that in this example all can be expressed in terms of each other (e.g., volume = area x distance). These are all appropriately at the same level and type of abstraction. An inappropriate term might be *Newton*, because he is not of the same class of terms. That is, he is not a mechanical concept, but rather a theorist. However, if the instructor were interested in the student's view of each concept's relative relatedness to Newton, then, of course, this mixture of terms would be acceptable.

2. Produce a list of terms for the student. This is done by simply supplying the students a list of approximately 10-15 terms from which to choose.

3. Ask the student to begin by choosing the two terms that are most closely related and to connect the two terms with a line. As stated previously,

the numbering of the links sequentially (starting with 1 to 15) is optional because this data is not currently used in scoring the test. However, if
the instructor is qualitatively interested in such data, the student should
be instructed to number the links.

4. The student should be told to cross each term from the list after the term
   is added to the structure. In that way, no term gets used twice.

5. In order to score the tree constructions, you must count the links and
   compare them with the links created by an expert. This score may compare the total number of links in the learner's and expert's trees, or it
   may compare the ordinal position of each of the links in each set. The
   closer the sequences match, the more accurate the learner's tree is.

Optional Method

By requiring that all new terms be added to the existing structure,
we may influence the ordinal sequence of labels. For example, if in a list
of terms the two most strongly related terms are *evil* and *dangerous* then
those might be the first linked pair. The second most strongly connected
pair might be *dog* and *carnivore*, but these would not show up as the next
terms to be added to the structure. In fact, only a term that is strongly associated with either *evil* or *dangerous* may be added next. Thus, using the
ordinal sequence numbers may be very misleading in some cases.

Rapoport (1967) determined that an optional method of tree construction tests will produce essentially the same data, while eliminating
the necessity for always connecting a new term to the existing structure. In
the optional method, students are told to link the most closely associated
pair (e.g., evil and dangerous). However the next term chosen does not
have to be added to the existing structure yet. So, a student could then
link *dog* and *carnivore* or create yet another linked pair that is not
connected to the original structure. The only requirement in using this
optional method is that when the test is concluded, all substructures must
be linked together. That is, the structure must all be connected.

When the tree structure is constructed using the optional method,
Rapoport (1967) has determined that the two resulting structures are structurally equivalent, and can be scored by counting the links as detailed before. However, the ordinal numbers of the links may be quite different,
and may give an instructor different data regarding the strengths of the
connections in the structure.

EFFECTIVENESS OF TREE CONSTRUCTION TESTS

The tree construction test may be used to assess a learner's cognitive space
or structural knowledge. Like many of these structural knowledge assess-

ment measures, it is not recommended that the tree construction test be used as the sole assessment measure for any course. However, interesting information can be discovered about how a student has perceived the subject matter that has been taught. Also, gross misconceptions of material may be uncovered through using this procedure.

• Preece (1976) determined that the tree construction test is not highly correlated (.35) with free word association test or the controlled word association test when using individual data. This implies that the tree construction test may not be a highly valid measure of individual structural knowledge.

• Rapoport (1967) showed that the optional method of scoring produced structures that were structurally equivalent to the regular method of building the structures, i.e., whether or not a student adds to the existing structure or is allowed to build "sub-structures" and link them later produces graphs that are essentially the same.

• Waern (1972) suggests a method of scoring the test that allows for reduction of the data in a systematic way. This may be useful in averaging the graphs of several student or several subject matter experts.

Learner Interactions

Although some research (Rapoport & Fillenbaum, 1972) used males and female subjects, there was little difference related to gender. It is possible that this type of test might be more appealing to some learning styles, and might be enjoyed more by learners who have a higher tolerance for ambiguity. Although there is no research to support this contention, it is possible that the ill-defined nature of "similarity" and "most closely related" will confuse students who require more structure in their learning, such as field dependent learners.

Content/Task Interactions

Researchers have studied several content areas including colors (Rapoport & Fillenbaum, 1972), the family of "have" verbs (Rapoport & Fillenbaum, 1972), and emotions (Dietze, 1963). At present, there is no research that suggests that the subject matter interacts with the functioning of the tree construction test.

Advantages of Tree Construction Tests

• Tree construction tests are relatively quick for a teacher to design, requiring only a list of terms from within a domain of interest.

• Tree construction tests can be completed quickly by a learner.

• Without further data reduction, these tests provide a quick visual "snap-shot" of a learner's structural knowledge.

Disadvantages of Tree Construction Tests

• The nature of the relationships between concepts is limited to "is similar to" or "is more strongly related to." That is, the semantic nature of the links is not defined.

• The methodology for further reduction of these data is rather lengthy.

REFERENCES

Dietze, A.G (1963). Types of emotions or dimensions of emotions? A comparison of typal analysis with factor analysis. *Journal of Psychology, 56*, 143-159.

Preece, P.F.W. (1976). Mapping cognitive structure: A comparison of methods. *Journal of Educational Psychology, 68*, 1-8.

Rapoport, A. (1967). A comparison of two tree-construction methods for obtaining proximity measures among words. *Journal of Verbal Learning and Verbal Behavior, 6*, 884-890.

Rapoport, A., & Fillenbaum, S. (1972). An experimental study of semantic structures. in A.K.Romney, R.N.Shepard, & S.B.Nerlove (Eds.), *Multidimensional scaling: Theory and application in the behavioral sciences*, Vol. II. New York: Seminar Press.

Waern, Y. (1972). Structure in similarity matrices: A graphic approach. *Scandinavian Journal of Psychology, 13*, 5-16.

6

Representing Structural Knowledge Through Dimensional Representations (Cognitive Maps)

DESCRIPTION OF COGNITIVE MAPS

Dimensional representations of knowledge structures begin with a set of semantic similarities that have been elicited from the learner (see Chapters 2 and 3) in which the degree of semantic similarity between ideas is represented as a value, usually between 0 and 1.0. Concepts that are more closely related (cow...horse) are closer to 1.0, and concepts that are less closely related (automobile...bird) have a relatedness rating closer to 0. These relatedness values are collected in a half matrix where each concept in a knowledge domain is collected and related to all other concepts (see Chapter 3 for example). The procedures described in this chapter attempt to use that matrix of values to spatially represent each concept as a point in coordinate space so that the distances between each concept reflects the observed semantic proximities between them. That is, the semantic distance between the concepts are spatially related in terms of geometric distance between the objects. The resulting spatial models are often referred to as cognitive maps, which are spatial representations of cognitive structure (Geeslin & Shavelson, 1975a; Shavelson, 1974).

Cognitive maps derived in this way provide dimensional representations of knowledge structures, as compared with link-weighted network representations (Chapter 7) and tree representations (Chapter 8). These methods are alternative means for representing the underlying structure of knowledge by analyzing proximity data. Dimensional representations are derived by analyzing proximity data using multidimensional scaling (MDS), cluster analysis, or principal components analysis, although MDS is the most commonly used procedure.

Multidimensional scaling (Kruskal, 1964; Shepard, 1962) is a powerful technique for extracting the latent structure from similarity judgments or relatedness coefficients. Its purpose is to transform relational data (estimates of the degree of relatedness between objects) into points representing the distances between those objects in a minimum number of dimensions. MDS represents each concept to be mapped as a point in coordinate space. It arranges the concepts in n-dimensional space where the metric distance represents the semantic, perceptual, or conceptual distance between the objects being related. MDS provides three valuable types of information: spatial, dimensional, and metric (Schvanenveldt, Durso, Goldsmith, Breen, Cooke, Tucker, & DeMaio, 1985). The data is presented in a spatial map which illustrates the relative distances between concepts. It considers the relationships of each concept to all others in the domain and positions these concepts along different dimensions of space in a way that reflects these relations. This global information is important in interpreting relationships. Finally, MDS supplies metric data that relates the distances between concepts in multidimensional space, which assists in comparing maps or relating them to other quantitative measures.

Rationale

Cognitive mapping is based on the assumption that the relationships between ideas or concepts can be made overt based on semantic proximity; that is, more semantically related ideas will appear "closer" in geometric representations of cognitive space. Fenker (1975) states three assumptions or properties of cognitive maps:

1. Information about a topic area is organized and interpreted on the basis of a set of dimensions which represent organizational features of the topic area.
2. These dimensions can be represented in n-dimension geometric space.
3. There are many relationships that can exist among concepts. Similarity, degree of association, and the extent to which one concept implies another are examples of these types of relationships. That is, the nature of the semantic relationship is implicit in the relationship but has to be interpreted.

Dimensional representations are based on schema theory and active structural networks (see Chapter 1). We can gain some understanding of an individual's cognitive structure by examining how that individual rates the relationships between concepts in memory. Dimensional representations graphically depict the proximity of all identifiable links to any schema in an individual's cognitive structure.

EXAMPLES OF COGNITIVE MAPS

Figure 6.1 illustrates a dimensional representation (cognitive map) of the relationships between concepts in photography as rated by an amateur photographer. Concepts related to correct exposure are clustered on the left hand side of the map, while concepts dealing with the content of the photograph are clustered on the right. Figure 6.2 is a cognitive map of types of physical treatments used by physical therapists. Note that three clusters of concepts are depicted on the map. The first cluster of "NMES" and "TENS" represents two types electrical stimulation treatments used by therapists. A second cluster of cold packs, ice massage, and cold immersion represent cooling treatments, while a third cluster includes various types of heat treatments.

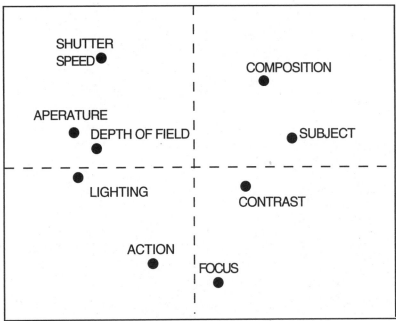

Fig. 6.1. Cognitive map of photography concepts.

APPLICATIONS OF COGNITIVE MAPS

Cognitive maps can be used for a number of instructional purposes, both for conveying and assessing cognitive structures.

Representing/Assessing Structural Knowledge

Cognitive maps are primarily used as assessment tools to determine the degree to which learners have achieved an integrated knowledge structure. Learners may be asked to rank pairs of concepts according to their similarity, and the resulting maps may be compared to a map constructed by an expert. This type of comparison may be used to identify areas in which further instruction is indicated, or to identify those areas in which the learner's cognitive structure is sufficiently similar to experts as to indicate no need for further instruction.

- Rips, Shoben, and Smith (1973) showed that distances in subjects' spatial representations would predict categorization times. Semantic distance between concepts predicted quite highly the reaction times required to verify statements such as "A robin is a bird."

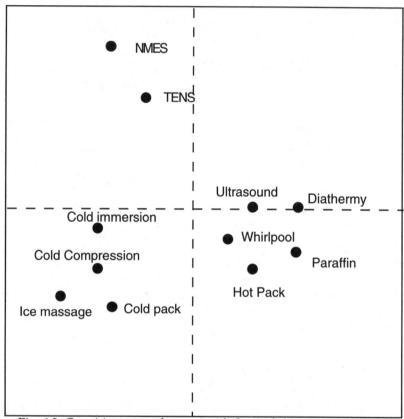

Fig. 6.2. Cognitive map of a group of physical therapy treatments.

- Stanners and Brown (1982) confirmed the use of scaling of concepts for memory representation using eleven sentence concepts. They found that graduate students' structures showed more grouping while under-graduates' were more diffuse and less structured.

However, cognitive mapping is a procedure primarily intended to assess a learner's structural knowledge through the ranking of pairs of re-lationships. The procedure is intended to ultimately construct a "picture" that accurately represents the relationships that exist in the learner's cog-nitive structure. Therefore, cognitive mapping is a reasonably easy in-strument or technique that can assess structural knowledge. The assessment procedure is based upon asking a learner to make relationship judgments. Relationship judgments entail rating the relatedness between pairs of words representing subject matter (see Chapter 3).

Completed cognitive maps depict the individual's perception of the relative relatedness of key concepts in a topic area. The completed maps do not indicate how the concepts are related but do help to distinguish between groups of concepts. Careful analysis of cognitive maps can reveal the manner in which the concepts are related. Cognitive maps derived from experts' assessments of concept relatedness can be used to assist in conveying the structural relationships between concepts.

Students' numerical judgments regarding the relatedness of concept pairs can be useful in identifying the student's organization of knowledge. Many researchers (described later) have evaluated the use of cognitive maps as a measure of structural knowledge, and found a significant relationship between the degree of similarity between students' and experts' maps and students' final course grades. The cognitive maps of learners may also be compared visually or statistically with an expert's set of judgments or using correlation analysis of the coordinates produced by the scaling procedure.

- Shavelson (1972) found that over a learning period, the correspondence of the students' cognitive structures corresponded more closely with the instructor's as their achievement increased.

- Wainer and Kaye (1974) used individual differences scaling procedures with developmental psychology students to show movement of student structures toward the instructors in the three-dimensional solutions. They reported a correlation of r=.15 between student's grades and similarity to the instructor's structural map. This suggests that there are a variety of bases for assigning grades, and that cognitive mapping might avoid certain weaknesses in general student evaluation measures.

- Fenker (1975) found a significant relationship between students' course grades and a score that indicated the similarity between their cognitive maps and experts' cognitive maps. This gives some indication that students with cognitive maps similar to those of experts perform better in a course than those students whose cognitive maps are less similar to experts' maps.

- Geeslin and Shavelson (1975b) found convergence between learners' cognitive structures and content structure after programmed instruction in probability. They also found a moderate correlation between the correspondence and problem-solving achievement.

- Thro (1978) found greater correlations between students' associative structures and the instructor's associative structure after exposure to course content. The correspondence of associative structures along with prior achievement significantly predicted final achievement scores in physics.

- Expert programmers recalled more lines of randomly presented code than novices (Adelson, 1981) using free recall. Scaled averages of the distance matrices of intersubject recall similarity showed greater clustering and similarity among experts, with novices clustering around syntax concerns and experts clustering around conceptual, routine-oriented.

- Diekhoff (1983) demonstrated that relationship judgment tests are significantly correlated with essay tests and with multiple-choice tests. Although the correlations are significant, they are moderate, and this implies that relationship judgment tests should perhaps be used in conjunction with other testing methods rather than replacing them.

- Stanners, Brown, Price and Holmes (1983) found strong relationships of the ratings with essay performance and that the commonality in student representations accounted for substantial variance in essay scores.

Conveying Structural Knowledge

Conveying cognitive structures an expert's map can be used to show similarities between ideas. These maps can then be used to generate discussion regarding the manner in which concepts are related or unrelated. Similarly, maps generated by a learner can be compared to maps generated by experts to identify differences in perceptions in the content area.

A composite cognitive map can be generated by averaging the rating scores assigned by members of some group and using those average scores as the basis for the map. When the ratings are assigned by experts, this type of composite cognitive map has been used to depict and/or identify an "ideal" cognitive map (Fenker, 1975). These maps can be compared to learner's maps to identify areas of similarity and dissimilarity.

Likewise, discussions centered on comparing student's and instructor's maps could also help to identify areas in which students need to address more effort in studying.

- Following use of cognitive maps to guide discussions in review sessions, learners performed better on essay tests than students who attended a review session in which only definitions of concepts were reviewed (Diekhoff & Diekhoff, 1982). In addition, after review sessions in which instructor's cognitive maps were reviewed and discussed learners' own relationship judgments were found to be more similar to the instructor's.

Acquiring Structural Knowledge

Cognitive maps can assist a learner in acquiring structural knowledge in at least two ways. First, the process of rating each pair of concepts in terms of their degree of similarity is, in itself, an exercise in developing structural knowledge. When rating each pair of concepts one must consider how those concepts are related on any number of dimensions. More dimensions imply more complex knowledge structures, which engage learners in deeper level interpretations. For example, Berg and Wainer (1973, cited in Wainer & Kaye, 1974) had students rate French poems in terms of their similarity. Those students who read the poems in an English translation perceived only one dimension of similarity between poems, that of the main ideas and imagery. In contrast, students who read the poems in the original language perceived a second, rhetorical dimension along which the poems varied.

A second way that cognitive maps can assist the learner in acquiring structural knowledge is from analysis of the map itself. After similarity ratings have been converted into the cognitive map, the map must be examined to identify the dimensions along which concepts differ. Analysis of the cognitive maps drawn by experts can assist learners in identifying the similarities between concepts in a field.

* Diekhoff and Diekhoff (1982) report that using this cognitive mapping procedure as a means of reviewing units enhanced students essay test scores, increased the reliability of each student's cognitive map, and increased the correlations between student and expert cognitive maps.

PROCEDURE FOR DEVELOPING COGNITIVE MAPS

This part of the process is less procedural than the knowledge elicitation process described in Chapters 2 and 3. The matrix of relatedness coefficients or similarity ratings are analyzed most often using MDS. MDS provides spatial representations of similarity data. Given proximities or distances between each of a set of entities, MDS finds the solution that spatially represents those proximities between each other.

1. Collect relatedness coefficients or semantic similarity judgments in a half matrix where each concept is related to all other concepts in the knowledge domain (see Chapters 2 and 3).

2. Enter the matrix in a nonmetric, multidimensional scaling procedure. Alternatively, use cluster analysis, or principal components analysis. This process will require the use of a computer and fairly sophisticated statistics software. Statistical help with these procedures is typically hard to locate.

3. Analyze the clusters and dimensions. Using minimum stress as a criterion, determine how many dimensions provide the best goodness of fit for the matrix. The maximal solution may be two, three, four, or multidimensional. Too many dimensions are difficult to analyze. Most MDS procedures present the concept clusters in two-dimensional representations, so a 3-dimensional solution would generate 3 2-dimensional maps (AB, AC, and BC). Identify the semantic similarities of each of the clusters in each two-dimensional representation. Compare the clusters at each end of each dimension. For instance, the cluster on the left side of Fig. 6.2 represents cold therapies while the cluster on the right side represent warm therapies. So, the left-right dimension (the abscissa of the graph) represents a warm-cold dimension. That is, an important distinction among physical therapies is the warm-cold distinction. Continue to describe the clusters and dimensions for each dimension. These clusters and dimensions represent the underlying structure of the knowledge domain. Most knowledge domains have multidimensional structures. This is an important, albeit difficult, concept for learners to grasp.

EFFECTIVENESS OF COGNITIVE MAPS

Most often, cognitive maps derived from scaling techniques have been used to describe a construct derived from memory structures, cognitive structure, as well as changes in cognitive structure. They provide a reliable measurement tool for assessing cognitive structure (Geeslin & Shavelson 1975a; Shavelson, 1972). Additionally:

• Johnson, Cox, and Curran (1970) found a high convergence between a geometric model and the distances in scaling solutions of both similarity data and word associations.

• The reliability of cognitive maps is somewhat questionable in the early stages of a course. Fenker (1975) noted that the cognitive maps generated by learners prior to instruction on given concepts were not reliable; nor were they accurate, when compared to maps of the same concepts generated by experts.

• Brown and Stanners (1983) found that explicitly teaching students relationships in order to bring their coordinate systems closer to the author's did not work. However, using a more interactive teaching strategy where learners compared their systems with the teacher's produced a substantial shift toward the instructor's coordinates. There was a moderate relationship between common space in the solutions and quiz performance.

Learner Interactions

McDonald (1989a, 1989b) found that learners who have reached the stage of formal operational thought were able to produce cognitive maps on geometric concepts that were more similar to experts' maps than learners who were in the concrete operational stage of cognitive development. Likewise, learners who were formal operational at the time that they learned geometric concepts showed more stability in their cognitive maps than learners who were concrete operational at the time they learned the concepts. In fact, formal operational learners produced cognitive maps that were more similar to an expert map one year after completing the geometry course than they did immediately after completing the course (McDonald, 1989b).

To date there has been no research conducted into other learner attributes that may be conducive to learning from cognitive maps. Neither has there been further research into those learner characteristics that may be conducive to the development of maps. However, since the development of cognitive maps requires rating of relationships on a numerical scale rather than depicting the relationships spatially, it seems likely that visual/spatial aptitudes are not requisite for constructing this type of map. Instead, the ability to translate concept similarities into numerical ratings is required.

Content/Task Interactions

Cognitive maps have been generated in a wide variety of fields. Multidimensional scaling has been used to generate cognitive maps in literature (Berg & Wainer, 1973; Wainer & Berg, 1972), psychology (Diekhoff, 1982; Diekhoff & Diekhoff, 1982; Wainer & Kaye, 1974) , physics (Johnson et al., 1970), mathematics (McDonald, 1989a, 1989b), and communications (Pettey, 1984). There is no evidence that cognitive mapping is more effective or applicable to a particular content area, though the most consistent results appear to have occurred using content areas with very well-defined and consistent content structures, such as Newtonian physics. However, any content area in which pairs of concepts can be rated as related or unrelated can serve as the basis for a cognitive map.

Advantages of Cognitive Maps

The relationship judgment tasks have the advantage of a limited domain. That is, only items that are of practical interest to a course need be rated by the learner. This might be analogous to asking multiple-choice questions rather than open-ended essay questions in a traditional test: The number and types of responses are predetermined by the test designer.

• Cognitive mapping using dimensional representations is a practical answer to assessing a student's mastery of higher level knowledge beyond recall.

• It may be used as an alternative to essay tests, which are subject to many biases and are also time consuming to score. The objectivity of essay tests are also questioned, although they can be improved upon by using scoring protocols.

• Diekhoff (1983) suggests that relationship judgments may be a useful measure of a group's structural knowledge. This may have utility as a means of formative evaluation of instructional materials. For example, if a designer is unsure of whether or not the materials are working for a given target population, a quick relationship judgment test could be administered and compared with either course objectives or a subject matter expert's map.

• Cognitive maps convey relationships between concepts in a graphical manner.

• Constructing a relationship judgment-type of test is easier than constructing a multiple choice test.

• Cognitive maps provide a relatively objective measure of an individual's cognitive structure in a given content area (Jonassen, 1987).

Disadvantages of Cognitive Maps

• Construction of the cognitive map using dimensional representations requires the use of advanced statistical routines, such as multidimensional scaling, principal components, or cluster analysis. These routines are available in only selected computer-based statistical packages which tend to be more expensive and more difficult to use. The maps would be extremely difficult to construct without a computer.

REFERENCES

Adelson, B. (1981). Problem solving and the development of abstract programming languages. *Memory and Cognition, 9*, 422-433.

Berg, W., & Wainer, H. (1973). What's lost in translation? An application of multidimensional scaling. Chicago: University of Chicago, Department of Psychology. (Mimeographed)

Brown, L.T., & Stanners, R.F. (1983). The assessment and modification of concept interrelationships. *Journal of Experimental Education, 52*, 11-21.

Diekhoff, G.M. (1982). Cognitive maps as a way of presenting the dimensions of comparison within the history of psychology. *Teaching of Psychology 9*(2), 115-116.

Diekhoff, G.M. (1983). Testing through relationship judgments. *Journal of Educational Psychology, 75,* 227-233.

Diekhoff, G.M., & Diekhoff, K.B. (1982). Cognitive maps as a tool in communicating structural knowledge. *Educational Technology, 22*(4), 28-30.

Fenker, R.M. (1975). The organization of conceptual materials: A methodology for measuring ideal and actual cognitive structures. *Instructional Science, 4,* 33-57.

Geeslin, W.E., & Shavelson, R.J. (1975a). An exploratory analysis of the representation of a mathematic structure in students' cognitive structure. *American Educational Research Journal, 12,* 21-39.

Geeslin, W.E., & Shavelson, R.J. (1975b). Comparison of content structure and cognitive structure in high school student's learning of probability. *Journal of Research in Mathematics Education, 6,* 109-120.

Johnson, P.E., Cox, D.L., & Curran, T.E. (1970). Psychological reality of physical concepts. *Psychonomic Science, 19,* 245-247.

Jonassen, D.H. (1987). Verifying a method for assessing cognitive structure using pattern notes. *Journal of Research and Development in Education, 20*(3), 1-14.

Kruskal, J.B. (1964). Multidimensional scaling by optimizing goodness of fit to a non-metric hypothesis. *Psychometrika, 29,* 1-27.

McDonald, J.L. (1989a). Cognitive development and the structuring of geometric content. *Journal for Research in Mathematics Education, 20*(1), 1-21.

McDonald, J.L. (1989b) Accuracy and stability of cognitive structures and retention of geometric content. *Educational Studies in Mathematics, 20,* 425-448.

Pettey, G.R. (1984). *A first step toward a search for meaning in the reliance--political interest typology.* Paper presented at the Annual Meeting of the Association for Education in Journalism and Mass Communication, Gainesville, Florida (ERIC Document Reproduction Service No. ED 247 577).

Rips, L.J., Shoben, E.J., & Smith, E.E. (1973). Semantic distance ad the verification of semantic relations. *Journal of Verbal Learning and Verbal Behavior, 12,* 1-20.

Schvanenveldt, R.W., Durso, F.T., Goldsmith, T.E., Breen, T.J., Cooke, N.M., Tucker, R.G., & DeMaio, J.C. (1985). Measuring the structure of expertise. *International Journal of Man-Machine Studies, 23,* 699-728.

Shavelson, R.J. (1972). Some aspects of the correspondence between content structure and cognitive structure in physics instruction. *Journal of Educational Psychology, 63,* 225-234.

Shavelson, R.J. (1974). Methods for examining representations of a subject-matter structure in a student's memory. *Journal of Research in Science Teaching, 11,* 231-249.

Shepard, R.N. (1962). The analysis of proximities: Multidimensional scaling with an unknown distance function. *Psychometrika, 27,* 125-140, 219-246.

Stanners, R.F., & Brown, L.T. (1982). Conceptual interrelationship on learning in introductory psychology. *Teaching of Psychology, 9*(2),74-77.

Stanners, R.F., Brown, L.T., Price, J.M., & Holmes, M. (1983). Concept comparisons, essay examinations, and conceptual knowledge. *Journal of Educational Psychology, 75,* 857-864.

Thro, M.P. (1978). relationships between associative and content structure of physics concepts. *Journal of Educational Psychology, 70,* 971-978.

Wainer, H., & Berg, W. (1972). The dimensions of de Maupassant: A multidimensional analysis of students' perception of literature. *American Educatonal Research Journal, 9,* 485-492.

Wainer, H., & Kaye, K. (1974). Multidimensional scaling of concept learning in an introductory course. *Journal of Educational Psychology, 66,* 591-598.

7

Representing Structural Knowledge Through Link Weighted Network Representations: Pathfinder Nets

DESCRIPTION OF PATHFINDER NETS

Pathfinder networks (PFNets) are configurations in which concepts (objects, events, actions, or entities) are represented as nodes and relationships as links connecting the nodes (Schvaneveldt, Durso, Goldsmith, Breen, Cooke, Tucker, & DeMaio, 1985). Links may be symmetric (undirected) or asymmetric (directed), unlike dimensional representations which assumes symmetric relationships between concepts. The links are assigned a value or weight that reflects the strength of the relationship between the nodes in terms of the distance between one node and another. These weights determine the length of the path. So, different ways of calculating weights will produce different graphs. Not every node in a PFNet is necessarily linked to every other node. In fact, links are limited in the network by the distance estimates (semantic distances between each pair of concepts) that are calculated by the Pathfinder program (Schvaneveldt, Durso, & Dearholt, 1985, 1987, 1989). A link is added if the minimum distance between concepts for every possible path is greater than the distance estimate for that pair (Cooke & McDonald, 1987). The distance estimate provides a weight to each link. With a complete set of distance estimates, these are represented as a complete graph of nodes connected by links (Schvaneveldt, Durso, Goldsmith, Breen, Cooke, Tucker, & DeMaio, 1985).

Pathfinder nets are derived from an algorithm that transforms a proximity matrix (see Chapters 2 and 3) into a network structure in which each concept or object in the matrix is represented by a node and the proximities are represented by how closely the objects are linked. The algorithm searches through the nodes to find the closest indirect path between objects. The algorithm retains only the links with a minimum-length path between two concepts, so in the resulting net, not all concepts are not directly connected to all other concepts, as is implied by dimensional representations (see Chapter 6). So Pathfinder extracts the latent structure in the data rather than transforming it as multidimensional scaling (MDS) does when developing dimensional representations. Therefore, it better represents local or pairwise comparisons between concepts in a knowledge domain but does not provide the global information (dimensional) information that MDS does. Another uniqueness of Pathfinder nets is that they do not force a hierarchical solution, as do the tree representations (see Chapter 8).

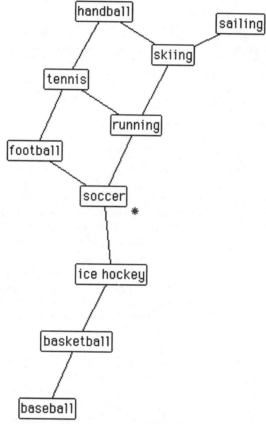

Fig. 7.1. Pathfinder net of sports concepts.

Rationale

The quantitative foundations of Pathfinder nets is in the mathematical study of graph theory which is concerned with the general properties of networks. Graph theory has been applied to the computational theory of psychological similarity in the form of Pathfinder networks (Dearholt, Schvaneveldt, & Durso, 1976; Schvaneveldt, Dearholt & Durso 1988). PFNets a) regard semantic similarity matrices as a network adjacency matrix (from graph theory), b) compute the semantic distance between nodes, and c) reduce the number of links by restricting the distance between any two nodes that are linked.

Conceptually, PFNets are rooted in semantic networks (see Chapter 1), which are a popular technique for defining knowledge representations (Aidinejad, 1988; Meyer & Schvaneveldt, 1976). Semantic nets are most commonly viewed as directed graphs (from graph theory). Unlike computational graphs, however, what distinguishes semantic nets is that they have semantic relationships implied in the links, whereas most graphs are unlabeled.

EXAMPLES OF PATHFINDER NETS

The first example (Fig. 7.1) is a simple comparison of major sports and how they are related. The longitudinal dimension obviously relates to individual or pair (top) vs. team (bottom) sports.

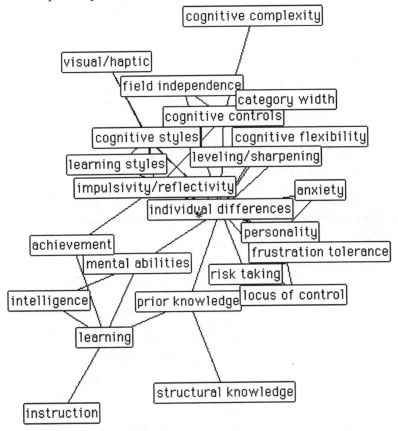

Fig. 7.2. Pathfinder Net of learner characteristics concepts.

In the second example of a PFNet (see Fig. 7.2), the domain of individual differences and learning is explored. The central node is "individual differences" which was the major topic in the course for which this net was prepared. That is, individual differences is the most central node because so many other concepts are linked to that node. The longitudinal dimension relates to generalized processing skills (top) to knowledge acquisition (bottom). The clusters are cognitive controls/styles near the top, personality variables (lower right) and ability measures (lower left).

APPLICATIONS OF PATHFINDER NETS

Representing/Assessing Structural Knowledge

The primary, intended purpose for PFNets has always been to represent knowledge structures. Determining differences in knowledge structures can help to explain differences in human performance. Several ways to apply this information have been suggested by Schvaneveldt et al. (1988):

- predicting performance for the purpose of selecting applicants, such as pilot trainees
- comparing how similarly an individual thinks to a group's understanding
- identifying a consensus understanding of a group.

Predicting school performance or learning based upon PFNets is another application. This application is predicated upon comparing the structural similarity of two graphs. In order to do so, the nets must be produced from expert (teacher) ratings and student ratings (see Chapter 3) using a common set of concepts. Graph similarity is a function of the similarity of the patterns of edges that define how two graphs are linked (Goldsmith & Davenport, 1990). Structural similarity may also be compared by identifying the subjects of hierarchically ordered objects. Goldsmith, Johnson, and Acton (1991) used the algorithm in the pathfinder program and found that the similarity between each student's net and the instructor's net (calculated using a set-theoretic algorithm included in the Pathfinder program) was highly predictive of examination scores over the course of the semester.

Schvaneveldt et al. (1988) found that PFNets were useful for comparing expert and novice pilots. In comparing naive, novice, intermediate, and expert computer programmers, Cooke and Schvaneveldt (1988) were able to clearly distinguish between the groups based upon their PFNets. They found that correlations between nets within each of the above groups was higher than for the more advanced groups. Experts, it appears, all have a more coherent cognitive structure. When asked to classify the nature of the links generated in the PFNets, advanced groups were better able to classify the nature of the relationships than naive and novice programmers. Novices and experts clearly do not think alike, and PFNets are a simple but effective means for illustrating those differences.

Rather than expert/novice distinctions, PFNets can also be used to compare how people with different perspectives or careers conceive of the same content domain. Gillan, Breedin, and Cooke (1992) compared two groups of experts, human factors specialists and software experts on their organizations of 50 human-computer interaction concepts. They found that the human factors experts produced nets with more interrelated subnetworks, while software experts' nets consisted of more central groups along dimensions related to technology, implementation and user characteristics without the subnetworks. The human factors experts organized the concepts more consistently according to user characteristics. The nets of both groups, however, were much better organized than those of novices.

Conveying Structural Knowledge

PFNets can also be used during content or task analysis to identify critical information as components of the knowledge structures that tend to be present in all or most experts (Schvaneveldt et al., 1988). Identifying expert models, for instance for building intelligent tutoring systems, could be facilitated by having experts rate concepts for PFNets.

Cooke and McDonald (1987) used PFNets to elicit knowledge for building knowledge based expert systems. They found PFNets especially useful because they provide a means for combining the knowledge of multiple experts and because they require less effort from the experts than traditional means of interviewing for knowledge elicitation. McDonald, Paap, and McDonald (1990) demonstrated a method for using PFNets for structuring a hypertext information system. Although the system has not been implemented, the principle that representing information as an expert would should produce a more comprehensible hypertext knowledge base (Jonassen, 1991).

Acquiring Structural Knowledge

PFNets can also be used to extract semantic information from text using a related Pathtrieve system (McDonald, Plate, & Schvaneveldt, 1990). This system uses a graphical interface to help readers draw out semantic information from text that they are studying.

PROCEDURE FOR DEVELOPING PATHFINDER NETS

The procedure for producing PFNets is completely automated by a series of computer programs, KNOT (Knowledge Network and Orientation Tool), which is available from Interlink, Inc. through the Computing Research Laboratory at New Mexico State University. The following steps briefly describe the process.

1. Beginning with a matrix of semantic similarity ratings (described in Chapter 3 and implemented in the KNOT computer programs, analyze the matrix using the Pathfinder algorithm. This produces a matrix of relatedness coefficients.

2. Create a spatial layout from this set of coordinates using the Layout function in KNOT.

3. In order to average nets, use the Average function that is built into the KNOT program.

4. In order to compare the similarity between two nets using the C algorithm, which is implemented in a program known as Similarity, select the Similarity function and identify the nets to be compared.

EFFECTIVENESS OF PATHFINDER NETS

The effectiveness of Pathfinder nets to describe knowledge structures or predict learning and memory performance has been evaluated most frequently by comparing Pathfinder results with spatial or dimensional representations derived from multidimensional scaling. Both PFNets and MDS solutions were found to be useful in correctly classifying experts and novices, however MDS solutions outperformed PFNets on classifying expert/novices and experts/experts (Schvaneveldt et al., 1988).

Goldsmith et al. (1991) found that the similarity between each student's net and the instructor's net was more highly predictive of examination scores over the course of the semester than using either raw relatedness data or MDS representations. Cooke, Durso, and Schvaneveldt (1985, 1986) compared PFNets and MDS solutions as predictors of free recall and serial recall tasks. In the serial recall task, lists that were organized according to PFNets resulted in faster learning than those organized by multidimensional space. In free recall tasks, PFNets were more predictive of recall order than the spatial, multidimensional representations. They concluded that PFNets better capture the organizational relationships that are important for recall than do the spatial relationships (MDS).

Learner Interactions

Perhaps the most frequent application of PFNets has been to distinguish between the knowledge structures of experts and novices. In these studies, typically, PFNets are calculated for both groups and then compared based upon their consistency, coherence, and similarity to each other. The assumption that experts will have distinctly different knowledge structures than novices has been supported (Cooke & Schvaneveldt, 1988; Gillan et al., 1992).

Content/Task Interactions

An insufficient amount of research has been conducted on Pathfinder Nets to document content interactions. Since the research group that has developed and promoted Pathfinder Nets has a computer science background, most of the research has focused on computer science concepts such as human computer interactions (Gillan et al., 1992), and computer and programming languages (Cooke & McDonald, 1987; Cooke & Schvaneveldt, 1988). Goldsmith et al. (1991) showed that similarity between the students nets and the instructors net was very predictive of their course grade in statistics. Pathfinder nets were less effective at classifying expert and novice pilots based upon their structure of concepts related to fighter pilot maneuvers. It is highly probable that Pathfinder nets will be more or less effective in reflecting knowledge structures in different knowledge domains. Like most of the other representation techniques (see Chapters 6 and 8), Pathfinder nets will likely be more reliable in tightly structured knowledge domains. We look for research in the areas of social sciences and the humanities.

Advantages of Pathfinder Nets

- Identifies meaningful links between concepts (unlike multidimensional scaling) by requiring minimal strengths of relationships between concepts.

- PFNets focus on the local relationships among concepts whereas multidimensional scaling provides more global information about the concept space (Schvaneveldt et al., 1988).

- PFNets provide information concerning the structure of knowledge that may be used to represent that knowledge in an information or instruction system (Cooke & McDonald, 1987).

- PFNets provide a means for combining the knowledge from multiple experts.

- PFNets require less introspection and cognitive effort from the learner than traditional means of interviewing for knowledge elicitation.

REFERENCES

Aidinejad, H. (1988). *Semantic networks as a unified model of knowledge representation.* (Memorandum in Computer and Cognitive Science, MCCS-88-117). Las Cruces, NM: Computing Research Laboratory, New Mexico State University.

Cooke, N.M., Durso, F.T., & Schvaneveldt, R.W. (1985). *Measures of memory organization and recall* (Memorandum in Computer and Cognitive Science, MCCS-85-11). Las Cruces, NM: Computing Research Laboratory, New Mexico State University.

Cooke, N.M., Durso, F.T., & Schvaneveldt, R.W. (1986). Recall and measures of memory organization. *Journal of Experimental Psychology: Learning, Memory and Cognition, 12,* 538-549.

Cooke, N.M., & McDonald, J.E. (1987). The application of psychological scaling techniques to knowledge elicitation for knowledge based systems. *International Journal of Man-Machine Studies, 26,* 533-550.

Cooke, N.M., & Schvaneveldt, R.W. (1988). Effects of computer programming experience on network representations of abstract programming concepts. *International Journal of Man-Machine Studies, 29,* 407-427.

Dearholt, D.W., Schvaneveldt, R.W., & Durso, F.T. (1985). *Properties of network derived from proximities* (Memorandum in Computer and Cognitive Science, MCCS-85-11). Las Cruces, NM: Computing Research Laboratory, New Mexico State University.

Gillan, D.J., Breedin, S.D., & Cooke, N.J. (1992). Network and multi-dimensional representations of the declarative knowledge of human-computer interface design experts. *International Journal of Man-Machine Studies, 36,* 587-615.

Goldsmith, T.E., & Davenport, D.M. (1990). Assessing structural similarity of graphs. In R. W. Schvaneveldt (Ed.), *Pathfinder associative networks: Studies in knowledge organization* (pp. 75-87). Norwood, NJ: Ablex.

Goldsmith, T.E., Johnson, P.J., & Acton, W.H. (1991). Assessing structural knowledge. *Journal of Educational Psychology, 83,* 88-96.

Jonassen, D.H. (1991). Representing the expert's knowledge in hypertext. *Impact Assessment Bulletin, 9* (1), 1-13.

McDonald, J.E., Paap, K.R., & McDonald, D.R. (1990). Hypertext perspectives: Using Pathfinder to build hypertext systems. In R. W. Schvaneveldt (Ed.), *Pathfinder associative networks: Studies in knowledge organization* (pp. 197-211). Norwood, NJ: Ablex.

McDonald, J.E., Plate, T.A., & Schvaneveldt, R.W. (1990). Using Pathfinder to extract semantic information from text (pp.149-178). In R. W. Schvaneveldt (Ed.), *Pathfinder associative networks: Studies in knowledge organization* (pp. 75-87). Norwood, NJ: Ablex.

Meyer, D.E., & Schvaneveldt, R.W. (1976). Meaning, memory structure, and mental processes. *Science, 192,* 27-33.

Schvaneveldt, R.W., Dearholt, D.W., & Durso, F.T.(1988). Graph theoretic foundations of Pathfinder networks. *Computers and Mathematics with Applications, 15,* 337-345.

Schvaneveldt, R.W., Durso, F.T., & Dearholt, D.W.(1985). Pathfinder: Scaling with network structures (Memorandum in Computer and Cognitive Science, MCCS-85-9). Las Cruces, NM: Computing Research Laboratory, New Mexico State University.

Schvaneveldt, R.W., Durso, F.T., & Dearholt, D.W.(1987). Pathfinder: Networks from proximity data (Memorandum in Computer and Cognitive Science, MCCS-87-90). Las Cruces, NM: Computing Research Laboratory, New Mexico State University.

Schvaneveldt, R.W., Durso, F.T., & Dearholt, D.W. (1989). Network structures in proximity data. In G. Bower (Ed.), *The psychology of learning and motivation: Advances in research and theory* (Vol. 24, pp. 249-284). New York: Academic Press.

Schvaneveldt, R.W., Durso, F.T., Goldsmith, T.E., Breen, T.J., Cooke, N.M., Tucker, R.G., & DeMaio, J.C. (1985). Measuring the structure of expertise. *International Journal of Man-Machine Studies, 23*, 699-728.

8

Representing Structural Knowledge Through Tree Representations: Ordered Tree Technique

DESCRIPTION OF TREE REPRESENTATIONS

A tree is a connected graph which represents the ordered relationships between concepts hierarchically. Some trees are derived from similarity ratings (see Chapters 2 and 3), like the dimensional representations described in Chapter 8, while others are derived from the order of concepts remembered in a free recall or prompted recall activity. Trees represent concepts in a knowledge domain as external nodes on a tree. Trees are not cyclical, that is, any two nodes in the tree are connected by only a single path. Each node has only a single entry path. The distance between two concepts is measured by the length of the path connecting them.

The ordered tree technique (OTT) was developed as a technique for identifying the underlying structure of information in memory from analyzing relatedness of the items generated in a free-recall task. The assumption of the technique is that concepts are organized into chunks and that individuals recall concepts as units, recalling all of the concepts in one chunk before moving onto another (Reitman & Rueter, 1980). These chunks are mentally organized into a tree whose nodes to be recalled are terminal nodes (those on the right side of Figs. 8.1 and 8.2) and intermediate nodes that describe the organizing concepts that define the chunks. During recall, this hierarchy organizes the retrieval of the ideas and thereby determines the sequence or order of recall. These chunks may consist of concepts that can be recalled in only one specific order, the reverse order, or any order. For instance, the individual in Fig. 8.1 probably recalled the "young adulthood" concepts before going onto the "middle adulthood" concepts and so on. The OTT is considered to be a representation of a subject's knowledge structure (Naveh-Benjamin, McKeachie, Lin, & Tucker, 1986). It produces organizations that are easy to interpret.

Rationale

The fundamental assumption of OTT is that information in memory is organized hierarchically. That is, people chunk information into similar units that are subsumed under more general concepts, that are chunked under more general concepts, and so on. When asked to recall information about a topic, individuals will typically recall all items about a chunk of information before moving onto another chunk of information. For example, if asked to recall information about congress, most people would recall for example everything about the House of Representatives before moving onto the Senate. Each chunk represents a part of the individual's cognitive structure.

So, the OTT is based on a theory of mental organization that contends that sets of concepts are organized hierarchically in such a way that the bottom concepts in the hierarchy represent the single ideas and the higher level nodes represent inferred higher order grouping concepts. The chunking or grouping of ideas in memory facilitates storage and retrieval of that information. Chunking of items in memory is inferred by the OTT through the tendency of groups of words to appear together on free recall lists. That is, information is retrieved from memory in ordered ways (Reitman & Rueter, 1980).

EXAMPLES OF ORDERED TREE TECHNIQUE

The OTT produces an ordered tree of concepts from a knowledge domain. Examples of the technique follow in Figs 8.1 and 8.2.

APPLICATIONS OF THE ORDERED TREE TECHNIQUE

The only meaningful application of the OTT is assess the underlying organization in memory, that is, to assess structural knowledge.

Representing/Assessing Structural Knowledge

The primary purpose of the OTT is to infer information about individuals' cognitive structures. Therefore, it is useful only for assessing structural knowledge and not as a means for conveying structural knowledge or as a strategy for developing structural knowledge. As an assessment tool, it has been used to show that the memory structures of novices differ from those of experts, and that experts' structures were quite similar (McKeithen & Reitman, 1981).

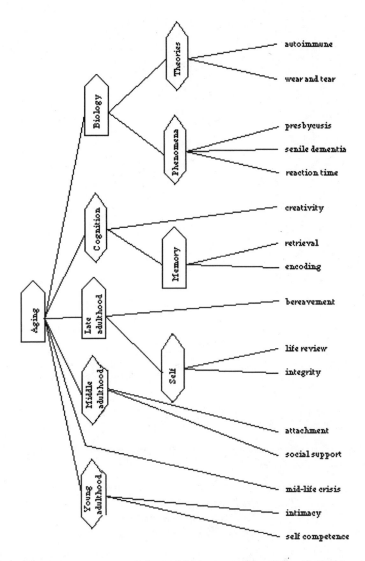

Fig. 8.1. Cognitive representation of instructor from Naveh-Benjamin, Lin, and Tucker, 1986.

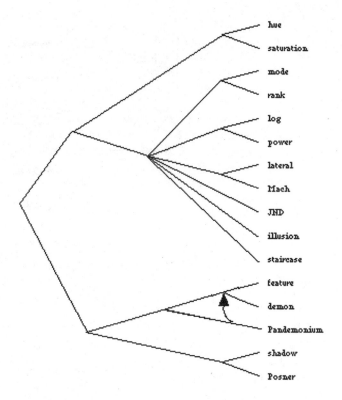

Fig. 8.2. Instructor's organization of psychology keywords (from Reitman
       & Rueter, 1980).

PROCEDURE FOR USING ORDERED TREE TECHNIQUE

The technique described here is a version of the technique used by Naveh-
Benjamin et al. (1986), which was an adaptation of the technique used by
Reitman and Rueter (1980).   This is a simpler method that does not re-
quire the effort and time required by Reitman and Rueter.

1. Identify a set of important concepts that represent a reasonable sample of
   the concepts covered in a course or content domain. This number probably should not exceed 20 or 25 concepts because of the length of the
   task.

2. Divide the words into a matrix (e.g., 4 by 5 for a 20-word list) and place
   the matrix and number of words in the matrix on the edge of each sheet
   of paper. Duplicate this sheet of paper four times, ensuring that the order of the words in the matrix on each page is different.

3. Ask the learners as part of a review session or as an exam to arrange in a vertical order in the blanks the concepts in such a way that closely related concepts in terms of their meanings would appear close to each other.

4. For the next three or four pages, ask the students to do the same except that they should begin with a particular word. Provide a distracter task between the completion of each page. Tell the students not to look back at previous pages. (Reitman and Rueter recommended as many trials as there were words, though the structure can be derived reliably with far fewer trials, according to Naveh-Benjamin et al. (1986).

5. The ordered tree is generated for each student using an algorithm developed by Reitman and Rueter (1980) to analyze each of the recall orders. The algorithm recursively examines the strings of concepts in a top-down manner looking for chunks. It identifies the largest nonoverlapping chunks (those in which the concepts are always next to each other though not necessarily in the same order). The set of chunks forms a lattice which is then converted into a tree, such as those in Figs. 8.1 and 8.2.

6. Assess the amount of organization by analyzing the depth (number of levels in the tree), the average size of the lowest level chunks, the average number of branches at each level, and the variety of recall orders.

Or

Calculate PRO (possible recall orders). This quantity is the natural logarithm of the number of differ recall orders that can be gained by traversing the tree, that is, the number of possible recall order that contain its chunks. At each node, you calculate the number of recall orders, sum the lot, and take the logarithm of that quantity. This provides a measure of the organization of a tree.

EFFECTIVEESS OF ORDERED TREE TECHNIQUE

Very little research has been conducted using the OTT. It is useful as an assessment tool only to the extent that free-recall or ordered recall methods for assessing knowledge or comprehension of a content domain are deemed appropriate.

• Reitman and Rueter (1980) found that by recalling a known set of items from different starting points (using different concept cues) can reliably reveal the underlying organization in the list of concepts.

- It is a useful technique for distinguishing between the memory structures of experts and novices (McKeithen & Reitman, 1981).

Advantages of Ordered Tree Technique

Reitman and Rueter (1980) and Naveh-Benjamin and his colleagues (1986) cite the following advantages of the OTT.

- The OTT provides more reliable representations than those generated from distance matrices, because it does not use averaging techniques to create the matrices .

- The technique provides information about the amount of organization in a given cognitive structure. This is measured by the amount of clustering of concepts separating ideas into groups.

- The OTT also shows the hierarchical depth of a individual's cognitive structure. This measure is indicated by the number of higher order general concepts subsuming lower level, more detailed concepts.

- The OTT allows researchers to compare the similarity between the cognitive structures of different individuals.

Disadvantages of Ordered Tree Technique

Naveh-Benjamin and his colleagues (1986) cite the following disadvantage of the OTT.

- Difficulties in performing free-recall tasks can hide the underlying organization in memory. They corrected the problem by providing learners with lists of ideas rather than relying on retrieval of information, thereby focusing more on the structural aspects of memory.

REFERENCES

McKeithen, K.B., & Reitman, J.S. (1981). Knowledge organization and skill differences in computer programmers. *Cognitive Psychology, 13*, 307-325.

Naveh-Benjamin, M., McKeachie, W.J., Lin, Y.G., & Tucker, D.G. (1986) Inferring students' cognitive structures and their development using the "ordered tree technique." *Journal of Educational Psychology, 78*, 130-140.

Reitman, J.S., & Rueter, H.H. (1980). Organization revealed by recall orders and confirmed by pauses. *Cognitive Psychology, 12*, 554-581.

9

Representing Structural Knowledge Through Verbal Tests

RATIONALE FOR VERBAL TESTS

Most of the methods for representing and assessing structural knowledge that were described in the previous chapters rely on sophisticated statistical analysis to display structural knowledge representations. The techniques that are described in this chapter employ simple verbal questions that are analyzed descriptively, so that they are easier to use and therefore useful by more people. However, their validity and reliability have not been supported by much research. Like the techniques described in this volume, the conceptual rationale for rating or comparing the similarity between concepts assumes that structural knowledge may be described by the pattern of relationships among concepts in memory (Preece, 1976). Some constructs in an individual's knowledge structure are closely related while others are more distantly related. This semantic distance is conceived in terms of geometric distance, so more closely related concepts rated higher than concepts that are more distantly related. In addition to quantifying the degree of relatedness between concepts in a content domain, awareness and understanding of the nature of the underlying relationships between concepts is important. Asking students to describe those relationships also focuses on the comprehension of structural relatedness among the concepts in memory. Three types of verbal tests are described briefly in this chapter: semantic relationship tests, relationship judgments (similarity ratings), and analogies.

SEMANTIC RELATIONSHIP TESTS

Description and Examples of Semantic Relationship Tests

The simplest method of assessing the learner's comprehension of the nature of the relationships between concepts in the content domain is to ask the learner to describe or classify the conceptual nature of the relationships between important concepts. Concepts within a content domain are typically presented and discussed during instruction. In order to assess the learners understanding of these relationships between concepts, merely ask the learner to classify the nature of the relationship between selected pairs of concepts. Although many possible links may be defined, most concepts are related in one of the following ways:

> has part/is part of
> has kind/is kind of
> causes/is caused by
> precedes/comes after
> describes (defines)/is description (definition) of
> assists/is assisted by
> has example/is example of
> justifies (rationalizes)/is justified (rationalize) by
> has characteristic/is characteristic of
> has opposite/ is opposite of
> models/is modeled by

Notice that these categories describe relationships in both directions. They are asymmetric. That is, the relationship in one direction between concepts is different than the relationship in the other direction. For example, "congress *has part* Senate" or "Senate *is part of* congress." The relationship between two concepts may be directional or nondirectional. That is, you may state the relationship in one direction or both. Most typically, relationship tests consist of multiple-choice questions that present two concepts and ask students to select the best relationship.

_____ software engineering ..... problem exploration tools
     a. contains
     b. is an instance of
     c. is superordinate to
     d. precedes

_____ node ..... associative link
     a. is selected by an
     b. describes the
     c. is a characteristic of
     d. is the same as

This type of question could also be presented in a short answer format.

capital   _____   assets

Applications of Semantic Relationship Tests

Little literature on the use of type of test is available. Jonassen and Wang (in press) used this type of test to assess gains in structural knowledge after reading a semantically structured hypertext.

Procedure for Developing and Using Semantic Relationship Tests

1. Identify the major concepts in the content domain that is being studied.

2. Present pairs of the concepts and ask the learner to select the option that best describes the relationship. If the nature of the relationships were explicitly described in the instructional materials, these statements should paraphrase the statements from the instructional materials. Alternatively, present the pair of concepts and ask the learners to fill in a blank with the relationship.

3. Scoring consists of identifying the number of correct classifications. Scores could also be rank judgments, indicating the closeness with which the classification matched the correct one.

RELATIONSHIP JUDGMENTS (Similarity Ratings)

Description and Examples of Relationship Judgments

Relationship judgments or similarity ratings typically require the learner to evaluate the strength of the relatedness between two concepts. They assess definitional knowledge, such as that measured by multiple-choice tests. However, they are also useful for assessing structural knowledge. Relationship judgments have the same rationale and largely use the same methods as those described in Chapter 3. That is, semantic relatedness is based on the idea of semantic distance, which is conceived in terms of geometric distance. More closely related concepts appear closer in geometric space while more semantically dissimilar concepts are further apart. The primary difference here is that rather than rating all combinations of pairs of concepts in a domain in order to develop dimensional representations of structural knowledge (Chapter 6) or Pathfinder representations (Chapter 7), verbal tests including similarity ratings use only a sample of all possible pairs of concepts and compare the learner's ratings directly with the experts without any further structural manipulations.
    Examples of this procedure include:

On a scale of 1 - 9, indicate the strength of the relationship between the following concepts (with 1 indicating no relationship and 9 indicating equivalence):

        _ _ _ _ _   active structural networks — schema theory
        _ _ _ _ _   evaluation — reflective judgments

Alternatively, relationship judgments may be presented as true-false questions (Diekhoff, 1982):

> Answer TRUE or FALSE. The concepts, <u>information processing</u> and <u>cognitive psychology</u> are closely related terms.

Applications of Relationship Judgments

The primary application of relationship judgments is to elicit structural knowledge from learners as described in Chapter 3. However, rather than using the relationship judgments as raw data for scaling, the raw scores may be compared directly to the ratings of experts in order to determine the degree of similarity between teacher or expert knowledge and learners' knowledge. Diekhoff (1983) compared relationship scores with scores on essays that asked learners to "discuss the nature of the relationships within each of three pairs of concepts." Diekhoff (1983) has also used this type of test item to assess structural knowledge of psychology students.

Procedure for Developing and Using Relationship Judgments

1. Identify the major concepts in the content domain that is being studied.

2. Present pairs of the concepts and ask the learner to judge the strength of the relationship between them. Diekhoff (1983) pointed out that many students have difficulty grasping the idea of relatedness , so he recommended providing simple examples that call on common knowledge, such as:

    CAT—DOG   Answer: 8 or 9, indicating a strong relationship
    DOG—CUP   Answer: 1 or 2, indicating little or no relationship

3. Relationship judgments may be scored in at least two ways:

Correlational Scoring

(a) Ask two or more experts in the content domain to judge the relationships (up to 10 judges). Compute the median scores of their judgments.

(b) Compute Pearson product-moment correlations between the expert judgments and the learner's judgments. This score reflects the degree of agreement of each learner with the experts. The higher the score (approaching 1.0), the more similar the learner's judgments are to the experts.

True-False Scoring

(a) Ask two or more experts in the content domain to judge the relationships (up to ten judges).

(b) Identify pairs of concepts with high relationships (8 or 9) and some with low relationships (1 or 2).

(c) Present the pairs of concepts and ask the learner to judge (TRUE or FALSE) whether the pair is highly related or barely related.

(d) Calculate the number of correct answers.

ANALOGIES

Description and Examples of Analogies

Analogies may be used to assess structural knowledge by describing two concepts and asking the learner to first identify the relationship between those concepts and then to map that relationship on two other concepts. Typically this is accomplished by requiring the learner to select from a list of concepts the one that best fulfills the implied relationship in the first pair. For example, these questions were used by Jonassen and Wang (in press) to assess structural knowledge acquisition from a hypertext that was semantically structured.

> searching : accessing information :: _____ : problem solving
> > a. instruction
> > b. idea processing
> > c. integrating
> > d. authoring

> navigating hypertext : hypermap :: integrating information: _____
> > a. synthesizing information
> > b. organizational structure
> > c. problems in browsing
> > d. dynamic control

The rationale for analogies as indicators of structural knowledge lies in schema theory (described in Chapter 1). When learners encounter new information, they seek to interpret it in terms of existing schemata. Analogical reasoning is a process of mapping existing schemata onto new information (Rumelhart & Norman, 1981), that is, mapping the relationships between existing information onto new information. The essence of analogies is the transfer of knowledge from one situation to another by a

process known as mapping, that is, finding aspects of correspondence between one set of concepts and another (Gick & Holyoak, 1983). Restated,
analogies are devices for mapping relational structures from one object or
domain of knowledge to another, a process called structural mapping
(Gentner, 1983, 1986). Relationships between objects are mapped from the
base pair to the target pair based on relationships and not the similarity of
attributes. This mapping process assesses structural knowledge at a higher,
more complex level. Rather than merely describing the degree or relatedness or the nature of the relationship between pairs of concepts, learners
must map structural similarities of one set of concepts onto another. This
complex form of structural knowledge is generally more difficult for
learners.

Applications of Analogies

Most often, analogies are used to assess "higher order learning."
Analogical reasoning is difficult, so learners tend not to score as highly as
on other types of tests. Analogies were used by Jonassen and Wang (in
press) who found that learners who browsed semantically structured hypertext were not assisted in completing analogies.

Procedure for Developing Analogies

Just as analogies are more difficult for learners to complete, they are also
more difficult to write.

1. Identify the major concepts in the content domain that is being studied.

2. Select a pair of the concepts and determine the nature of the relationship between them. Select another concept from the list that is similar
   in some way to one of the first pair of concepts. Examine the other concepts in the list to determine if any of them has the same type of relationship to the concept that you just picked as does the first pair. This is
   an iterative process of selecting, testing, and judging. Expect that this
   process will take time and mental effort.

3. Repeat this process for other questions.

EVALUATION OF VERBAL TESTS

Advantages of Verbal Tests

• Quicker and simpler method for evaluating structural knowledge, because it eliminates the process of multidimensional scaling (see Chapter
  6) (Diekhoff, 1983).

- Verbal tests are easier, because comparing relationship judgments does not require judging all possible pairs of concepts in a domain, as is required for scaling (Diekhoff, 1983).

- These tests are useful for assessing declarative and structural knowledge.

- These tests probably have high reliability though more research is needed for proof.

Disadvantages of Verbal Tests

- Verbal tests do not interrelate a domain of concepts or depict the structural relationships among domain concepts. Typically, they are limited to only a pair of concepts at a time, though they could be presented multiply in a matching format.

- Analogies test are difficult and often produce a floor effect in learners.

REFERENCES

Diekhoff, G.M (1982). Cognitive maps as a way of presenting the dimensions of comparison within the history of psychology. *Teaching of Psychology, 9,* 115-116.

Diekhoff, G.M. (1983a). Relationship judgments in the evaluation of structural understanding. *Journal of Educational Psychology, 75,* 227-233.

Gentner, D. (1983). Structure mapping: A theoretical framework for analogy. *Cognitive Science, 7,* 155-170.

Gentner, D. (1986). *Evidence for structure-mapping theory of analogy and metaphor.* Office of Naval Research Report # N00014-85-K-0559. Urbana, IL: Department of Computer Science, University of Illinois.

Gick, M.L., & Holyoak, K.J. (1983). Schema induction and analogical transfer. *Cognitive Psychology, 15,* 1-38.

Jonassen, D.H., & Wang, S. (in press). Acquiring structural knowledge from semantically structured hypertext. *Journal of Computer-Based Instruction.*

Preece, P.F.W. (1976). Mapping cognitive Structure: A comparison of methods. *Journal of Educational Psychology, 68,* 1-8.

Rumelhart, D.E., & Norman, D.A. (1981). Analogical processes in learning. In J.R. Anderson (Ed.), *Cognitive skills and their acquisition.* Hillsdale, NJ: Lawrence Erlbaum Associates.

Part III

Conveying Structural Knowledge

Implicit Methods for Conveying Structural Knowledge Through

Chapter 10   Content Structures
Chapter 11   Elaboration Theory
Chapter 12   Frames & Slots

Explicit Methods for Conveying Structural Knowledge Through

Chapter 13   Semantic Maps
Chapter 14   Causal Interaction Maps
Chapter 15   Concept Maps
Chapter 16   Graphic Organizers/Structured Overviews
Chapter 17   Cross Classification Tables
Chapter 18   Semantic Features Analysis
Chapter 19   Advance Organizers

INTRODUCTION

The first two parts of this book have attempted to convince you how important structural knowledge is to comprehension and application of information. Part I described a rationale for considering structural knowledge, and
Part II described a number of methods for assessing it. If you accept the
premises of the first two parts of this volume, that structural knowledge is integral to comprehension and should be assessed along with declarative and
procedural knowledge, then Part III shows ways that structural knowledge
may be taught or at least modeled for learners. This part makes the instructional assumption that if structural knowledge is important to learn, then it is
important to teach as well.

Part III describes a number of techniques for conveying (modeling, depicting, illustrating) the structure of domain content. In the parlance of advanced organizers (Chapter 19), this information provides an "ideational scaf-

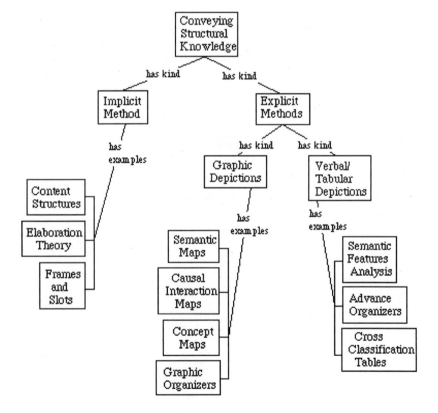

Fig. III.1. Techniques for conveying structural knowledge.

fold" or a foundation for holding ideas together. Memory research has consistently shown that better organized information is better remembered. Much of the reading research described in the Chapters 10-12 has shown that organized text also improves comprehension. So, the methods in Part III seek to depict the organization of ideas for the learners. They convey the structural knowledge to be learned.

The methods for conveying structural knowledge are illustrated in the graphic organizer above. The organizers is arranged hierarchically. There are two kinds of methods for conveying structural knowledge — implicit and explicit. Implicit methods (Chapters 10 - 12) are designed to impose a structure by organizing the material (usually verbal) according to the structure. That is, the structure is implicit in the material. These methods are not truly implicit, as the structure is often signaled for the learner. However, the organization is internal or inherent in the material. Explicit methods are those which are external to the material to be learned. That is, they are typically adjunct material which is not part of the information to be learned that are added to the instructional materials to provide an explicit foundation for the material to be learned. They are extrinsic to the material to be learned. These methods are most often in the form of maps (Chapters 13 - 16), such as the figure above. However, tables and other verbal depictions may also be used (Chapters 17 - 19). Each of these methods intends to organize learning by conveying the structure of the ideas to be learned.

10

Implicit Methods for Conveying Structural Knowledge Through Content Structures

DESCRIPTION OF CONTENT STRUCTURES

Any topic can be viewed as a network of interrelated ideas, organized in a heterarchical fashion. However, text is necessarily linear and, as such, cannot reveal all of the interrelationships between ideas simultaneously. Therefore, to convey meaning effectively a writer must impose a structure onto a topic in order to create a linear flow of text, while revealing the multiple relationships between ideas.

While advances in technology are creating new media for communication and instruction, text-based instruction is still the norm. When reading text, a number of variables can affect how well the author's message is understood by the reader. The reader's prior knowledge with the content area can play a key role in their understanding of a text passage. Other individual differences, such as cognitive style and aptitude, may also affect how well a learner is able to understand a text passage. In addition, variables within the text passage itself may affect the comprehensibility of the passage. One text variable of importance is the structure used to organize the text passage.

Content structures are writing plans that are used to determine the sequence and content of instruction to promote understanding of the author's perspective on the content area. Through an analysis of prose, Meyer has identified five types of top-level structures: description, collection, causation, problem/solution, and comparison (Meyer, 1975, 1982, 1985). Based on the content area, and what the author believes to be important about the topic, a writing plan is developed which emphasizes one of these five structures. Other content structures have been identified by researchers in this area. Some of the more common structures are simple listing, comparison/contrast, temporal sequence, cause/effect, and problem/solution (Armbruster, 1984). The similarity between these content structures and the ones identified by Meyer are evident. For the purposes of this chapter, Meyer's terminology is used when discussing content structures.

Rationale

Research has shown that when text is organized in a coherent manner readers can process the text more rapidly and remember more of what is read (Meyer, 1985). Content structures can be used to organize text in such a way as to promote an understanding of the author's perspective on the topic, and to highlight the relationships between ideas. The use of organizing structures facilitates the identification and retention of main ideas. By emphasizing main ideas the content structure creates "hooks" on which other detailed information can be anchored and stored in memory. Thus, as main ideas are recalled, the detail that supports these ideas is also recalled.

EXAMPLES OF CONTENT STRUCTURES

Descriptive writing plans present information about a topic by presenting it's attributes, or characteristics. This type of plan is the least complex organizational scheme, since descriptive content structures arrange ideas hierarchically. In this manner the main idea is presented first, followed by subordinate ideas. A descriptively organized text passage focuses on hierarchical relationships, and does not depict other, more complex interrelationships between ideas. For example, a descriptive text passage about wines might present characteristics used to judge the quality of wine, such as body, bouquet, clarity, color, acidity, and aftertaste. Alternatively, a descriptive passage might focus on a particular type of wine, such as a Chardonnay. The passage might detail some of the characteristics of Chardonnay, discuss the growing conditions most conducive to producing an exceptional wine, or describe definitive features of the winemaking process that are essential to producing Chardonnay. The content of the passage, as well as it's sequence, is decided by the author based on their reasons for writing the passage. The descriptive nature of the passage precludes any great detail about

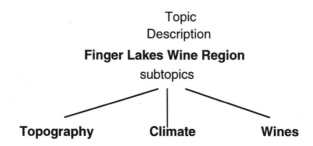

Fig. 10.1. Description content structure.

relationships between, for example, growing conditions and the character of the wine. Descriptive passages simply present the facts as the author sees them. An example of a descriptive content structure about the Finger Lakes Wine Region of New York state is shown in Fig. 10.1.

Collection plans take a group of topics related in some manner and describes their attributes. In essence, a collection plan is a group of meaningfully related descriptive passages. Meyer describes two types of collection plans. The first is collection plans that group topics by association. Again taking the example of wines, a collection passage might describe attributes of various wine regions around the country. Such a content structure is shown in Fig. 10.2. When grouping descriptive passages by association, as in this example, the order of presentation of the topics does not matter. In contrast, when meaningful relationships between the topics is possible, topics can be grouped by sequence. For example, if the passage was describing steps in the winemaking process, sequencing the descriptions in the order that the functions being described are performed provides greater organization to the passage. Figure 10.3 shows a collection of descriptions sequenced according to the steps in the process of printing black and white photographs. Collection content structures that are grouped by sequence can be seen as being more organized than collections grouped by association or description content structures.

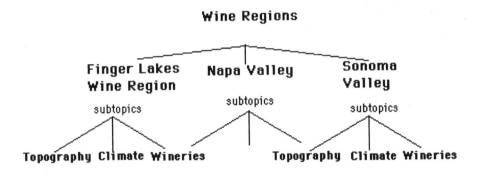

Wine Regions

Finger Lakes Wine Region   Napa Valley   Sonoma Valley

subtopics   subtopics   subtopics

Topography   Climate   Wineries   Topography   Climate   Wineries

Fig. 10.2. Content structure for a collection of descriptions grouped by association.

The next type of writing plan, causation, is also well structured. Text passages that convey cause and effect relationships are best represented in a passage that first presents the antecedent event, followed by the consequence of the event. This type of structure is familiar in "if . . . then" logic statements. A text passage on the effects of different weather conditions on wine quality or a description of the effects of oak aging on wines might assume a causation structure. In photography, the effects of various lens apertures on the final photograph might also be presented in a causation content structure.

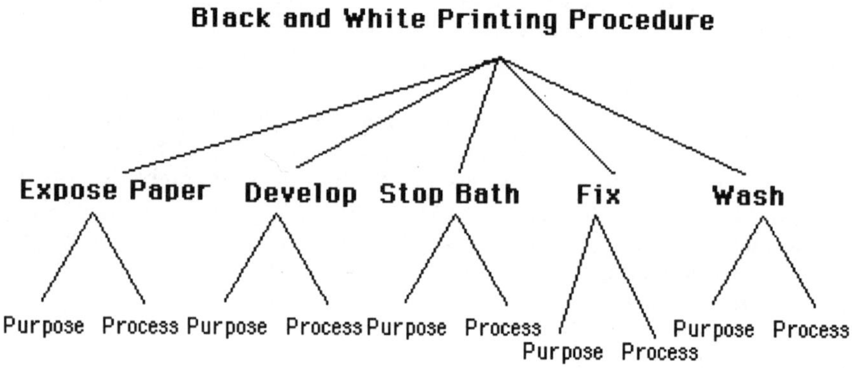

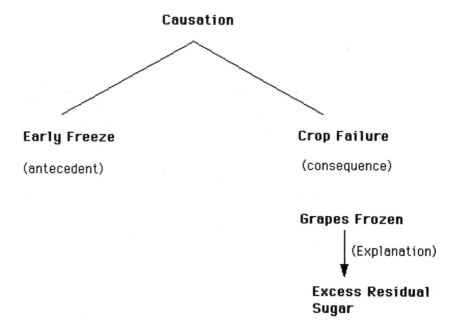

Fig. 10.3. Content structure for a collection of descriptions grouped sequentially.

Fig. 10.4. Causation content structure.

Problem/Solution structures are even more highly organized than causation structures. Elements of the causation structure must be grouped, be sequential, and be causally or quasi-causally related. Problem/solution structures have each of these characteristics, plus one additional characteristic. In the problem/solution structure, at least one element in the solution must be related to an antecedent to the problem. Taking a photography example, if the problem is that all photographs turn out too light, the solution would be to vary one of the settings that controls exposure. The writing plan for this type of content structure would first present the antecedent events (e.g., present the various settings used to produce a photograph), then present the problem, or consequence of the events (the underexposed prints). The text passage would conclude with a discussion of the possible solutions to the problem of overexposure.

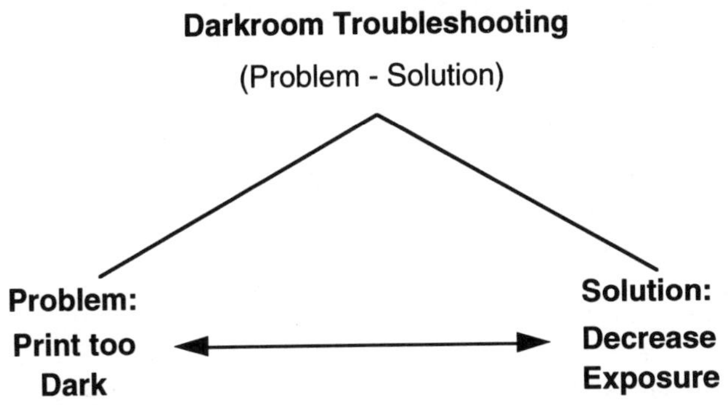

Darkroom Troubleshooting

(Problem - Solution)

Fig. 10.5. Problem-solution content structure.

A final content structure that can be used in writing is the comparison structure. This type of content structure takes two or more related topics and compares and contrasts them across a number of different categories. Comparative content structures are used to highlight the similarities and differences between topics. For example, Fig. 10.6 shows a content structure that might be used to compare and contrast IBM and Macintosh computers. Note the similarities in appearance between comparative content structures, and content structures for a collection of descriptions (e.g. Fig. 10.2). The difference between these types of structures lies in the sequencing of text. A collection of descriptions will completely describe one topic area, then move on to the next area. When writing from a comparison content structure, the characteristic of one topic is followed by a description of the same characteristic of the second topic.

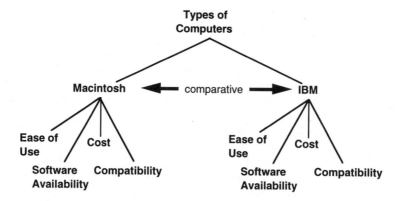

Fig. 10.6. Comparative content structure.

Often content can be structured in several different ways. Selection of a particular content structure is dependent upon the goals of the instruction, and on the level of the learner. For example, this volume is organized by a collection of description plans. Description plans provide learners with information on a topic by presenting its attributes or characteristics. Collection plans take a group of topics that are linked in some manner and describes their attributes. Although a collection plan is used here, one could easily present this same content with a different structure. For example, a problem/solution plan could be used. The problem could be presented as a need to increase learners' acquisition of the structure or organization of a content domain, thus improving retention and recall. The solution would then be presented as using one of the three methods for structuring discourse described here. Similarly, writing plans for this same content could be developed using comparison or causation structures.

APPLICATIONS OF CONTENT STRUCTURES

Content structures can be used as guidelines for designers (or authors) in preparing instructional materials, replacing the traditional outline. Content structures provide a more detailed guide for writing than traditional outlines, and more clearly identify relationships between ideas that should be emphasized in the text.

Additionally, content structures may be of use in evaluating existing instructional materials for use in the classroom. Because learners can be taught to recognize and use an author's content structure to assist in the recall information, it seems logical that we should be certain that texts (or other instructional materials) use the type of content structure that is appropriate for the learners. An example may help to clarify this point. Suppose a goal is to teach students about environmental problems and their potential solutions. Obviously, a text with a problem/solution content structure would be most appropriate for this objective. Descriptively organized texts, or texts that use a comparison structure, would not be as effective in conveying this information. It appears that texts that have a content structure that is in harmony with instructional objectives would best serve to facilitate learning.

Representing/Assessing Structural Knowledge

Although content structures are primarily intended for use by writers of textbooks, learners can be taught to use content structures when preparing essays or term papers. When used in this manner, the structure chosen for content organization reveals the learner's structural knowledge in the content area. For example, one student writing a paper on the major events and battles in the American Civil War might select a collection of descriptions format, while another might chose a cause/effect or problem/solution framework. Use of these different structures can provide insight into the depth to which the learner has integrated the essay content.

Conveying Structural Knowledge

Content structures convey structural knowledge implicitly, through the organization of text and explicitly through the signaling of those text structures (Meyer, 1985). Thus, the sequence in which content is presented to the reader conveys the structure of the content area as perceived by the writer.

In addition to using writing plans and content structures to organize text, writers can use *signals* to cue readers to the important ideas or relationships in a text passage. Signals are noncontent words that explicitly convey the relationships between ideas. "For example," is a signal that the next statement is an example of the previously stated concept. Here, "or example is an example of a signal. Other signals include words such as in contrast, interestingly, therefore, and next. Using titles is another form of signaling. Titles help readers organize the content by explicitly convey relationships by previewing information from text. Other preview statements may present the organization of a chapter or text passage by briefly outline the content to be covered. Use of signals to convey content structure appear to have the most effect on learners with lower reading comprehension (Meyer, 1985).

Acquiring Structural Knowledge

Aside from the uses of content structures for conveying and assessing structural knowledge, content structures provide minimal opportunity to increase learners structural knowledge. However, some activities may permit learners to expand their knowledge of the content structure. For example, an instructor might require learners to write an essay on a topic using a specific content structure. If a text book or other sources on which the essay is based is written in a descriptive format, learners could be required to restructure the content into a causal essay. In the process of planning and organizing the essay, then, learners will need to identify relationships between events or ideas, thus expanding their structural knowledge.

PROCEDURE FOR DEVELOPING CONTENT STRUCTURES

1. Select a the topic of the instruction. Does the purpose for writing include more than one topic, or will you be writing about a more limited subject area?

2. Select an organizational plan. Determine which manner of organizing material would best emphasize the important points to be conveyed. As indicated earlier, there is no one, correct writing plan for any given content area. The selection of a top-level structure is dependent upon the designer's own purpose for writing, his or her schema surrounding the topic area, and the information available regarding the target audience for the instruction.

3. Diagram the structure. From this top level structure, a tree diagram is developed that depicts the hierarchical arrangement of ideas to be conveyed. For example, if you will be using a problem/solution format for writing, begin with the problem solution diagram.

   List your problem on the left side of the diagram. What kinds of antecedent events lead to the problem? What are the important facts about these events that need to be conveyed? Add these main ideas, and the details that support them to your diagram. Then, continue on to the solution side of the diagram, and determine the possible solutions that should be presented. Add these to your diagram, again with supporting details.

4. Write according the content structure. The diagram serves as a guide in writing, reminding you to make the necessary links between ideas. The subsequent sequencing of content, based on the content structure diagram, is usually superordinate content prior to subordinate content. This type of sequencing helps learners remember the overall gist of the content, and fit details into their developing schema on the topic.

5. Add signals. Use noncontent words to explicitly convey the nature of relationships between ideas. Terms such as in contrast, similarly, importantly, highlight the main ideas and their relationships to other

ideas. Other signals can be used to identify the content sequence, such as adding preview statements that indicate how the passage will be organized.

6. Review your writing. Make sure that main ideas are sequenced before details, and that the signals that were used convey the correct types of relationships between content.

EFFECTIVENESS OF CONTENT STRUCTURES

Most of the research on the effect of content structures has focused on learners' ability to recall content. This has been tested through the use of recall protocols, which are obtained by having subjects write down everything they remember from the text passage. The recall protocols are then analyzed for the number of idea units contained, and the organization of the recall protocol. To the degree that the recall protocols are examined for organization, especially as related to the match between subject's recall organization and author's text organization, these studies assess the effectiveness of content structures for conveying structural knowledge.

• Subjects who received a text passage on chess pieces organized by either the names of the pieces or by a specific attribute of chess pieces (e.g., direction of movements, point values, etc.) were better able to recall content than subjects who received the same information with random organization of sentences (Frase, 1969).

• Meyer (1975) found that subjects recalled content of a target paragraph better when that paragraph was high in the content structure of a longer text passage.

Further research on the use of structures in discourse shows that learners who are able to identify and use the author's (or speaker's) plan in recalling content are able to remember more information regarding that content that readers who do not identify and/or use the author's plan.

• Frase (1969) found that subjects who were informed of the organization of a text passage did not differ significantly in the amount of content recalled than subjects who were not informed of the structure of the passage on initial testing. However, after a series of three trials informed subjects did recall significantly more content than uninformed subjects, indicating that knowledge of structure may have a cumulative effect on ability to recall content.

• After receiving training in the identification and use of four types of writing plans, ninth graders were able to recall twice as much information from text passages as a control group that received no training on text structures. These differences held true when reading and recalling text passages one day after training was conducted, and again three weeks later (Bartlett, 1979).

- Subjects who used the author's organizing structure to structure their own written statements recalling a text passage read one week earlier recalled more of the main ideas from the text passage than subjects who used a different organizing structure (Meyer, Brandt, & Bluth, 1980).

- Providing learners with the top level structure used in a passage does not appear to facilitate recall and comprehension. These findings held true for four types of content structures: claim/counterclaim, claim/support/conclusion, cause/effect, and problem/solution (Slater, Graves, & Piche, 1985).

- In a study of the differential effects of the basic types of organizing structures four groups of young adults listened to one text passage read aloud. The four groups each heard different versions of the same content, each with different organizing structures (collection, causation, problem/solution, and comparison). After listening to the passage, learners' recall of the passage was tested by having them write down everything they remembered from the passage in sentence-format. Subjects who listened to the causation and comparison passages recalled a significantly larger number of idea units than subjects who listened to the same content presented in a collection structure. Performance on the "probed" recall test (responses to direct questions about content) showed that subjects listening to the comparison passage scored higher than subjects who listened to the collection passage. Subjects who listened to the problem/solution passage were more likely to reorganize the content into a different structure than the original passage. Subjects in the groups that heard the other passages tended to organize their recalls in the same manner as it was presented (Meyer & Freedle, 1984).

Learner Interactions

Because content structures are used by writers to design text, learners do not need to acquire any new skill to benefit from writers' use of this technique. However, as noted earlier, training in the identification of content structures results in increased use of the author's structure when recalling content (Bartlett, 1979). When the author's structure is used to guide recall of content, more main ideas and details are recalled (Meyer, Brandt, & Bluth, 1980).

It also appears that learners with good reading comprehension search for the author's organizing structure without training and use this structure to assist in recall of the content (Meyer et al., 1980). Learners with lower comprehension abilities do not consistently use the author's organization to assist in recall. Such readers use what Meyer and colleagues refer to as the "default/list" strategy. When reading text using this strategy the reader has no systematic method for gathering meaning from the text passage, but instead attempts to remember ideas from text without linking the ideas in a meaningful manner. As a result, persons with low reading comprehension tend to have poor recall of main ideas, and the content that is remembered is recalled in a list-like fashion without meaningful connections between facts.

The results of these studies indicate that training students in the identification and use of content structures can help to improve their comprehension and recall of content. Additionally, it appears that learners with average and poor levels of reading comprehension would benefit most from this form of training.

However, as students mature, there is a greater tendency to recognize authors' writing plans and use these plans to organize the content they recall from the passage (Meyer, 1982). College graduates used the author's writing plan to organize their recall protocols more often than students at a competitive 4-year college, and these students in turn outperformed students from 2-year community colleges.

Content/Task Interactions

Research on the use of content structures has not focused upon differential effects for different content types. While certain types of content may be better represented by different content structures, precise designation of the most appropriate structure for a given content type has not been made.

However, research has focused on the differential effects of various content structures. Text that is organized according to comparison content structures appear to facilitate recall better than description or collection structures (Meyer & Freedle, 1984). Additionally, using different content structures appears to affect the type of content recalled. For example, two text passages were prepared with essentially the same content, but with different organizing plans. One of the passages emphasized chronological ordering of events, while the second passage emphasized comparison of ideas. Subjects who read the passage emphasizing the sequencing and timing of events remembered more specific facts than subjects who read the comparative passage, while subjects who read the comparison passage remembered more causal and comparative relationships than subjects reading the time-ordered passage (Meyer, 1982). This emphasizes the need for writers to consider the learning goal when preparing text passages.

Advantages of Content Structures

- Meyer's (1985) work on content structure and the research into the differential outcomes of alternative structures provide us with some guidelines for writing and understanding discourse. From research on content structures we know that when learners can identify and use an author's organizational scheme, they can identify and recall more content than if a text is presented in a disorganized fashion. Thus, it seems that direct instruction in identifying different content structures can assist learners in comprehending and recalling discourse.

- The five organizational plans that have been identified by Meyer can be used as guidelines for designers (or authors) in preparing instructional materials, replacing the traditional outline.

- Content structures can be used to assist learners in organizing their writing.

- Research findings have indicated that when content is presented according to more complex structures (e.g., causation or problem-solution) students are better able to recall content than when presented in a simpler (descriptive) structure.

Disadvantages of Content Structures

- Research on content structures has been limited to an analysis of written or spoken prose. There has been no linkage of this type of structuring strategy to other types of instruction, such as computer-based instruction.

- Another disadvantage of emphasizing content structures and using signals in text is the potential effect it has on learners. As noted previously, the purpose of writing text in an organized fashion and implicitly or explicitly conveying content structure is to help the learner acquire the author's perspective on the content area. Learners may have entirely different perspectives on the topic(s), which may be supplanted by the author's perspective. This, of course, is not a disadvantage of only the content structures approach to designing text but of textual material in general. Certainly classroom activities or supplemental individual exercises can be designed to explore the learner's perspectives and expand on his or her purposes for seeking instruction.

REFERENCES

Armbruster, B. B. (1984). The problem of "inconsiderate text." In G. G. Duffy, L. R. Roehler, & J. Mason (Eds.), *Comprehension instruction: Perspectives and suggestions.* New York: Longman.

Bartlett, B.J. (1979). Top-level structure as an organizational strategy for recall of classroom text. *Dissertation Abstracts International, 39,* 6641-A.

Frase, L. T. (1969). Paragraph organization of written materials: The influence of conceptual clustering upon the level and organization of recall. *Journal of Educational Psychology, 60,* 394-401.

Meyer, B.J.F. (1975). *The organization of prose and it's effect on memory.* Amsterdam: North Holland.

Meyer, B.J.F. (1982). Reading research and the composition teacher: The importance of plans. *College Composition and Communication, 33,* 37-49.

Meyer, B.J.F. (1985). Signaling the structure of text. In D. H. Jonassen (Ed.), *Technology of text* (Vol. 2). Englewood Cliffs, NJ: Educational Technology Publications.

Meyer, B.J.F., Brandt, D.M., & Bluth, G.J. (1980). Use of top level structure in text: Key for reading comprehension of ninth-grade students. *Reading Research Quarterly, 16,* 72-103.

Meyer, B. J. F., & Freedle, R. O. (1984). Effects of discourse type of recall. *American Educational Research Journal, 21,* 121-143.

Slater, W. H., Graves, M. F., & Piche, G. L. (1985). Effects of structural organizers on ninth-grade students' comprehension and recall of four patterns of expository text. *Reading Research Quarterly, 20,* 189-202.

11

Implicit Methods for Conveying Structural Knowledge Through Elaboration Theory

DESCRIPTION OF ELABORATION THEORY

Elaboration theory (Reigeluth, 1979, 1983, 1987; Reigeluth & Darwazeh, 1982; Reigeluth, Merrill, Wilson, & Spiller, 1980; Reigeluth & Rogers, 1980; Reigeluth & Stein, 1983) is an instructional model that guides the selection and organization of instructional content and sequences that content according to the particular organization selected. Elaboration theory integrates a number of established cognitive principles of learning into its processes for selecting, sequencing, summarizing, and synthesizing related ideas into "blueprint" for instruction. Several characteristics define elaboration theory.

- Elaboration theory claims that it is important to explicitly state the overall structure of the content being presented. Doing so provides a conceptual scaffolding for comprehending the content. There are three possible ways of structuring ideas. Conceptual organizations (what is) diagram the superordinate, coordinate, and subordinate concepts with the most general concepts in a conceptual hierarchy at the top and the most detailed at the bottom. Procedural organizations (how it works) describe the optimal processes for performing any procedural operations. Theoretical organizations (why it works) present the principles that describe the relationships and the changes in relationships between concepts.

- Elaboration theory presents these structural relationships at an application level using *epitomes*. An epitome is not necessarily the most general or abstract idea, concept, or principle. Rather, it is the simplest, most essential, most representative or fundamental idea that gets presented in a way that shows how it is applied. If you could tell the learner the most important thing about a subject, what would it be? For instance, two of the epitomizing principles of American history include "representative democracy through elected officials" and "economic development through free market (capitalism)."

- Elaboration theory uses analogies to relate new information to existing knowledge structures in the learner. Reigeluth has often used the analogy of the zoom lens on a film or video camera to describe elaboration theory. You start a lesson with a wide-angle view, which allows you to see the whole picture showing all of its parts and the relationships among those parts. You then successively zoom in on parts of the picture, revealing more information about those parts. After zooming in a little to permit study of the subparts, you zoom back out to the wide-angle view to review and integrate the subparts in the context of the whole using summarizers and synthesizers. Continue to zoom in one level to each of the parts of the whole picture or zoom back in further on the same part to a greater level of detail (learning prerequisite sequence). After examining the sub-subparts, zoom back out to the first level of detail to integrate the very detailed information and then back out to the wider angle to show where that information fits. No part of the picture should be viewed unless it has been viewed from the next wider-angled view (higher level) (Reigeluth & Stein, 1983).

- Elaboration theory relates more detailed ideas to more general ideas through summarizers and synthesizers. Summarizers review information at any level of detail, and synthesizers relate it back to more general or inclusive information.

- Elaboration theory progressively elaborates content ideas in more detail around the chosen structure. This progressive process starts with an epitome and repeatedly moves in a level of detail on the content and then summarizes and synthesizes that content by relating it back to the larger whole.

- Elaboration theory permits the learner to determine the sequence in which information is presented when possible.

Each lesson based on elaboration theory includes the following strategy components:

- Elaborative sequence, which arranges the ideas in a unit of instruction based on a single type or structure of content. The sequence is simple-to-complex, with the most essential information presented in advance of more complex and detailed information.
- Learning prerequisite sequence, so that no idea is presented until all prerequisite knowledge is presented.

- Summarizers at the end of each lesson and at the end of each instructional segment that review the ideas taught with salient examples and practice items.
- Synthesizers at the end of each lesson and again at the end of a set of lessons that relate all of the new ideas back to the epitome and the elaborative sequence of ideas.
- Analogies relate new ideas to knowledge and ideas that the learner already possesses, making the instruction more meaningful.
- Cognitive strategies are learning and thinking skills that can be used to interpret a variety of information. These may include organizational or elaborative strategies. These skills can be taught along with content.
- Learner control allows the learner to make decisions about the content, rate, and sequence of learning or the strategy used to learn with at any point.

Most significant for this volume is the elaborative sequence, because it communicates the structural information to the learner. Through the process of summarizing and synthesizing, the learners acquire structural knowledge.

Rationale

Elaboration theory has evolved over the past decade from the work of Charles Reigeluth and his colleagues. It is an instructional design model which specifies:

- the selection of the content to be taught
- the sequencing of that content
- the identification of relationships among the content.

The foregoing design features are intended to enable the student to:

- Develop a cognitive scaffold or network on which to anchor new, more detailed information,
- Understand the relevance or importance of the subject content because it is taught at the application level,
- Provide for better retrieval of information from memory because the content is linked to other content through summarizers and synthesizers,
- Learn the content in the sequence that best corresponds to his/her style of reasoning.

Elaboration theory is founded on a number of well established principles and theories from cognitive psychology. Chief among these is the subsumption theory of Ausubel (1968), which asserts that since knowledge is arranged hierarchically in memory, instruction should recapitulate that arrangement by presenting information in a general-to-detailed sequence. General ideas subsume more detailed knowledge, that is, they provide the structure and the hooks for hanging detailed information, so they need to be presented first as a context for understanding more detailed ideas. The detailed ideas then need to be related back to the broader ideas. Norman's (1973) web learning theory describes memory as a network of interrelated ideas. Both theories agree that information should be presented in an integrated sequence to facilitate encoding of the ideas into memory. Elaboration theory also assumes, as does Gagne (1977), that learners need to learn simpler, prerequisite knowledge before more complex knowledge. These theories form the foundation for elaboration theory, which asserts that instruction should begin with the essential ideas and relate them to what the learner already knows, adding detail in stages, and at each stage, summarizing and relating those ideas back to the more essential ones.

EXAMPLES OF ELABORATION THEORY ORGANIZING STRUCTURES

Figure 11.1 demonstrates an example of a conceptual organizing structure for a course on investments.

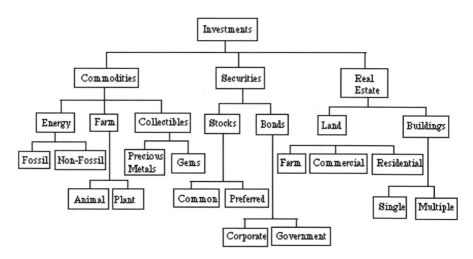

Fig. 11.1. Conceptual organizing structure

Figure 11.2 represents a theoretical organizing structure that organizes instruction on behavioral conditioning.

1. Behavior is controlled by its consequences. Reinforcement or punishment controls the response.
1.1 Organisms avoid aversive conditions. Behavior that is punished ceases to occur.
1.2 Organisms approach desirable conditions. Behavior that is reinforced continues to occur.
1.1.1 Following behavior with an aversive condition causes behavior to cease.
1.1.2 Removing aversive conditions following behavior causes the behavior to be repeated.
1.2.1 Following behavior with a desirable condition causes behavior to be repeated.
1.2.2 Removing desirable conditions following behavior causes the behavior to cease.
1.2.3 Random reinforcement causes superstitious behavior.
1.1.1.1 Punishment should be immediate.
1.1.1.2 Punishment also causes unexpected side effects.
1.2.1.1 Intermittent reinforcement causes increased response rate.
1.2.2.1 Excessive delay in reinforcement causes extinction of behavior.
1.2.2.2 Behavior that is not reinforced eventually ceases.
1.2.1.1.1 The connection between the stimulus and the response must be clear to the organism.

Fig. 11.2. Theoretical organizing structure.

APPLICATIONS OF ELABORATION THEORY

Elaboration theory is a relatively recent instructional development, so published applications are few. To date, elaboration theory has been used to:

• Evaluate textbooks (Reigeluth & Sari, 1980; Sari & Reigeluth, 1982)

• Perform content analysis for sequencing instruction (Reigeluth & Rogers, 1980)

• Design computer-based instruction (Wedman & Ragan, 1986)

• Design instructional texts (Beukhof, 1986; Wedman & Smith, 1989)

PROCEDURE FOR APPLYING ELABORATION THEORY

Elaboration theory starts with some important assumptions that are implicit in its use. If ideas are organized according to their single, implicit conceptual, procedural or theoretical relationships, then that structure can be conveyed to learners. Ideas are presented in a simple-to-complex sequence starting with the most essential ideas and reviewed systematically. As more detailed information is presented it is integrated with more general information. Prerequisite ideas are always presented prior to new ideas. Elaboration theory also assumes that learners should be permitted to control the sequence of instruction. If all of these assumptions are met, then elaboration theory claims that information should be more meaningful to learners, and they should develop more stable knowledge structures. Better knowledge structures in turn yield better understanding and longer term retention.

The following procedure describes only the processes that are used to identify and convey the structural elements of elaboration theory lessons. Other procedures for developing nonstructural lesson elements are not treated here.

1. Establish the goal for the course. Identify the main content elements that are involved in acquiring the goal.

2. Decide which elaborative structure best describes the content, based on the goal of the course: conceptual, procedural, or theoretical. Is the content mostly concepts, procedures, or principles? What level of outcome do you expect? What level of transfer do you expect?

3. Identify the elements in the organizing content. For conceptual content, use some type of concept mapping (see Chapters 6 and 7, for instance). For procedural content, use some type of procedural analysis. For theoretical content, use a technique like causal analysis . List all of the content components.

4. Select an appropriate organizing structure to sequence the list of organizing content. For conceptual tasks, use a taxonomy or matrix to display the content elements. For procedural content, use a flow chart or decision table. For theoretical content, use causal interaction maps (Chapter 14).

5. Write the epitome. From the organizing structure, select the organizing content that will form the epitome lesson (the most essential information) and then identify all other lessons at each level of elaboration. In identifying the epitome, ask yourself if only one idea could be taught, what would it be? For conceptual content, select the least necessary ideas in your organizational structure. These are the details. Select the next least necessary ideas. Do so until you are left with the essential idea. For procedural content, eliminate branches and unnecessary steps in flow chart and combine procedures together to identify the epitome. For theoretical content, use the same procedure as for conceptual content to identify the epitome. Rank-order ideas or put them in a parallel structure (ideas of similar importance together) to determine all levels

of elaboration. This diagram is a chart which identifies the organizing content ideas in the epitome lesson, the organizing and supporting content at each level of elaboration.

6. Describe the supporting content. For each lesson in the elaboration sequence, describe and analyze the supporting content for each lesson. Supporting content is the information that supports the organizing content. It is the meat that is attached to the bones of the organizing structure. It describes in more detail the information in the organizing structure. This and all subsequent processes are beyond the scope of this book. See the reference list for documents describing these processes in greater detail.

7. Sequence the organizing and supporting content. Allocate all of the supporting content and organizing content for each lesson into segments according to the needs of your learners.

8. Write and sequence the organizing content lessons, designate in each lesson the supporting content, the content of lesson summarizers and synthesizers, and the content of the expanded epitomes

9. Sequence the lessons. Determine whether the sequence of organizing content lessons will be fixed or variable and list lesson segments.

EFFECTIVENESS OF ELABORATION THEORY

A number of studies have investigated the effectiveness of elaboration theory for structuring or evaluating textbooks. These studies and others in progress suggest that materials structured according to elaboration theory do produce better conceptual understanding, which in turn enables students to better transfer information. The technique is relatively new, so additional verification will be needed.

- Beissner and Reigeluth (1987) demonstrated that it is possible and desirable to have parallel elaboration sequences based on different organizing structures integrated into a single course. This allows students to progress from simple to complex principles and procedures at the same time and develop both types of schemata while learning.

- Wedman and Smith (1989) found that lessons structured via elaboration theory resulted in the same level of learning as materials structured by hierarchical (prerequisites) analysis, however, the elaboration materials were significantly longer and therefore required more time to use.

- Chao and Reigeluth (1986) found that although the format (visual vs. verbal) of the synthesizer had no effect on remember or application level learning, a complete synthesizer did produce superior remember level performance.

- Carson and Reigeluth (1983) found that a general-to detailed sequence of content produced better learning of relationships than a detailed-to-general sequence, and that positioning the synthesizer at the end of instruction was better than at the beginning.

- Beukhof (1986) demonstrated that elaboration theory benefits learners who need external cues in text most and that learner control benefited students more than text control.

Advantages of Elaboration Theory

- Elaboration theory is based upon well established, cognitive principles of learning.

- Elaboration theory produces coherent and cohesive units of instruction by making the structure of the content obvious.

- Elaboration theory facilitates better conceptual understanding of material.

- Elaboration theory improves retention of information.

Disadvantages of Elaboration Theory

- Elaboration theory involves a difficult and time consuming design process

- Many of the procedures are somewhat inexact and not easily interpretable. This was a major complaint of another cognitively based technique, advanced organizers (see Chapter 19).

- Elaboration theory requires in-depth understanding of subject matter content, deeper than with traditional approaches to design.

REFERENCES

Ausubel, D.P. (1968). *Educational psychology: A cognitive view*. New York: Holt, Rinehart & Winston.

Beissner, K., & Reigeluth, C.M. (1987). *Multiple strand sequencing using elaboration theory*. (ERIC Document Reproduction Service No. ED 314 065)

Beukhof, G. (1986, April). *Designing instructional texts: Interaction between text and learner*. Paper presented at the annual meeting of the American Educational

Research Association, San Francisco, CA (ERIC Document Reproduction Service No. ED 274 313)

Carson, C.H., & Reigeluth, C.M. (1983). *The effects of sequence and synthesis on concept learning using a parts-conceptual structure* (IDD&E Working Paper, No. 8) Syracuse University, School of Education. (ERIC Document Reproduction Service No. ED 288 518)

Chao, C.I., & Reigeluth, C.M. (1986). *The effects of format and structure of synthesizer on procedural - decision learning* (IDD&E Working Paper, No. 22) Syracuse University, School of Education. (ERIC Document Reproduction Service No. ED 289 469)

Gagne, R.M. (1977). *The conditions of learning* (3rd ed.) New York: Holt, Rinehart & Winston.

Norman, D.A. (1973). *Cognitive organization and learning* (Tech. Rep. No. 37). San Diego, CA: University of California at San Diego, Department of Psychology.

Reigeluth, C.M. (1979). In search of a better way of organizing instruction: The elaboration theory. *Journal of Instructional Development, 2,* 8-15.

Reigeluth, C.M. (1983). Meaningfulness and instruction: Relating what is being learned to what a student knows. *Instructional Science, 12,* 197-218.

Reigeluth, C.M. (1987). Lesson blueprints based on the elaboration theory of instruction . In C.M. Reigeluth (Ed.), *Instructional theories in action: Lessons, illustrations, theories and models.* Hillsdale, NJ. Lawrence Erlbaum Associates.

Reigeluth, C.M., & Darwazeh, A.N. (1982). The elaboration theory's procedure for designing instruction: A conceptual approach. *Journal of Instructional Development, 5* (3), 22-32.

Reigeluth, C.M., Merrill, M.D., Wilson, B.G., & Spiller, R.T. (1980). The elaboration theory of instruction: A model for structuring instruction. *Instructional science, 9,* 125-219.

Reigeluth, C.M., & Rogers, C.A. (1980). The elaboration theory of instruction: Prescriptions for task analysis and design. *NSPI Journal, 19,* 16-26.

Reigeluth, C.M., & Sari, F. (1980). From better tests to better texts: Instructional design models for writing better textbooks. *NSPI Journal, 19* (8), 4-9.

Reigeluth, C.M., & Stein, F.S. (1983). The elaboration theory of instruction: In C.M. Reigeluth (Ed.), *Instructional theories and models: An overview of their current status.* Hillsdale, NJ: Lawrence Erlbaum Associates.

Sari, I.F., & Reigeluth, C.M. (1982). Writing and evaluating textbooks: contributions from instructional theory. In D.H. Jonassen (Ed.), *The technology of text: Principles for structuring, designing, and displaying text.* Englewood Cliffs, NJ: Educational Technology Publications.

Wedman, J. F., & Ragan, T.J. (1986). Instructional design for developing computer-based learning materials. *AEDS Journal, 19* (2-3), 124-136.

Wedman, J.F., & Smith, P. L. (1989, February). *An examination of two approaches to organizing instruction.* Paper presented at the annual meeting of the Association for Educational Communications and Technology, Dallas, TX. (ERIC Document Reproduction Service No. ED 308850)

12

Implicit Methods for Conveying Structural Knowledge Through Frames and Slots

DESCRIPTION OF FRAMES AND SLOTS

Marvin Minsky first introduced the notion of using "frames" and "slots" for representing the structure of knowledge (Minsky, 1975). In Minsky's frame theory, a frame is a data-structure for organizing stereotypical events or situations. Each frame has certain information attached to it, which presents expectations for what will happen next, the location of certain items, and so on. For example, one might have a frame about a child's birthday party. When one thinks about a child's birthday party, the appropriate frame is accessed, and certain information will be brought forward. One may expect that at this type of party there will be gifts for the birthday child, a cake with candles, and perhaps party games or some form of entertainment. For each frame there will be categories of information, referred to as slots, which must be filled with specific information for each instance of the frame. Taking the example of the birthday party, there may be a cake slot, which would be filled with information about the type of cake served at a given party. There may also be a games slot, to be filled with information about the types of games played at that party.

Although Minsky's frame theory was meant to explain how the mind works to organize information into knowledge systems, Armbruster and Anderson have applied frame theory to the organization of text. Their work has focused on the identification of generic, content-dependent structures, referred to as frames. Frames provide a general outline for examining a discipline's structure, while slots are the categories of information within the frames. Thus, slots hold the information about the subject area, while frames provide the main organizational structure. For example, this volume organized by a techniques frame, with slots for "description," "examples," "applications," "procedures," "effectiveness," "learner interactions," and "content interactions." To gather an understanding of the techniques included here, information about each of the techniques is entered into these predefined slots, thus providing parallel information about each of the techniques covered.

Frames can be of two main types: static, or dynamic. Static frames are descriptive — they use a listing of properties or attributes of a concept to convey the general ideas about the subject area. Slots within these static frames are the specific properties or attributes that are to be described. There is no particular order in which this content must be presented. For example, if an anatomy textbook were organized according to a "systems" frame, it makes no difference whether the first chapter deals with the cardiovascular system or the neurological system. The order in which slot information is presented is determined by the writer according to his or her preference.

Dynamic frames, on the other hand, have causal or directional relationships between slots. A common dynamic frame that has been identified is the "Goal Frame," which has slots for "goal," "action," and "outcome." This frame has a definite direction, as goals precede actions, and actions necessarily precede outcomes. Thus, the sequence of instruction within a dynamic frame is defined by its slots.

Rationale

The use of frames and slots to organize text material is based on schema theory (Armbruster & Anderson, 1984). A schema refers to the organization of information in an individual's memory structures. According to schema theory a learner will seek to activate prior knowledge to assist in comprehension of new material. When reading text a learner activates his or her schema that is relevant to the text topic and creates a model for understanding the new material based on that prior knowledge. This schema sets up expectations for the type of information that is needed to understand a content area. Thus, comprehension and retention of the new material is enhanced when material in text is organized in a way that is familiar to the learner. Frames and slots were developed as a means of providing coherence in text by using the same organizing structure from one section to the next. Thus, with the first chapter from a text organized with frames and slots, the learner develops a schema for understanding the content area. With subsequent chapters organized in the same manner this schema is reinforced and refined to include more detailed understanding of the content.

EXAMPLES OF FRAMES AND SLOTS

When frames and slots are used to organize text, the headings within text correspond to the various slots of information that is presented. For purposes of presentation here, however, slots and frames are presented in a matrix format.

Art Periods

	Carolingian	Gothic	Byzantine	Renaissance
Major Features				
Time				
Historical Events				
Key Artists				
Impact on Society				

Fig. 12.1. Frame and slots for art periods.

A text on periods or styles of art may include the slots that are shown in Fig. 12.1. The major features or characteristics that distinguish one artistic style from another would be discussed. The text could also address the time period or periods in which this type of art was predominant, as well as any historical events that may have influenced the development of the style. Key artists whose work characterizes the style of interest should be described, and examples of their works of art could be illustrated. Finally, the influences of the art style on society could be discussed.

Diseases of humans, animals or plants might also comprise a frame (Fig. 12.2). Slots for the diseases frame might include the presenting signs and symptoms of the disease, the etiology, or cause of the disease, its prognosis, treatment, and risk factors associated with acquiring the disease. Similarly, a "Drugs" frame could include slots for the purpose of the drug, it's chemical composition, mechanism of action, side effects, and known drug interactions (Fig. 12.3).

Diseases

	Parkinson's Disease	Huntington's Chorea	Friedreich's Ataxia
Etiology			
Signs and Symptoms			
Diagnosis			
Treatment			
Prognosis			

Fig. 12.2. Frame with slots for "Diseases."

APPLICATIONS OF FRAMES AND SLOTS

Frames can be used to organize textbooks or other instructional materials. First, the major concepts that are to be taught must be determined, and the attributes of each concept identified. The attributes then become the slots for the frame, and the frame itself can be identified from the slots. Slots can serve as headings and subheadings within texts, thus explicitly conveying the structure of the content. Likewise, since slots are the main ideas or key points in a piece of instruction, they can serve as a guide for writing introductions and summaries of the text.

Drugs

	Acebutolol	Digoxin	Nitroglycerin	Amiloride
Purpose				
Chemical Composition				
Mechanism of Action				
Side Effects				
Interactions				

Fig. 12.3. Frame with slots for "Drugs."

Use of frames and slots should help learners to organize their thoughts and develop a stable mechanism for thinking about a subject area. The repetition of the same slots throughout a text (or other instructional product) should serve to reinforce the organizational scheme, thus stabilizing the learners' schema.

Frames and their respective slots can be used as class exercises or homework assignments (Armbruster & Anderson, 1985), and can assist in the preparation of test items. As an exercise, students may be asked to fill-in a matrix with appropriate of information. In constructing test items, one could use the boxes in the matrix as a basis for questions, thus ensuring that students are asked about main ideas.

Frames and slots can also be used to evaluate textbooks, to determine whether all of the important content that should be covered on a topic is actually provided in the text (Armbruster & Anderson, 1984). Questions can be developed for each slot in a frame, and the text passage reviewed to determine whether the question is answered. Well organized textbooks should contain information for each of the slots in the frame. If such information is missing, perhaps another textbook should be considered for adoption, or additional instructional materials should be developed to augment the text.

Conveying Structural Knowledge

Frames and slots are primarily used to convey knowledge about a subject area in an organized manner. The use of slot names as headings in the text helps to convey the important categories of information in a content area, a key component of structural knowledge. Generic frames have been identified for Theories (Dansereau, 1985), Structure, Mechanism, Process, Hypothesis-Theory (Lunzer, Davies & Greene, 1980, cited in Armbruster & Anderson, 1985), Systems, Biomes, Technology, People, Goal, Problem/Solution, and Compromise (Armbruster & Anderson, 1985). Use of slots provides learners with a consistent framework for organizing their knowledge in a content area. In addition, structural knowledge is enhanced with the use of matrices which display key information about a content area in a small space. Such matrices can be used as an organizing framework for a course, showing learners how key concepts are similar to or different from concepts previously learned.

Acquiring Structural Knowledge

Frames and slots can provide guidelines for information seeking by students. Again, learners can be given a blank matrix as a homework assignment, with the slots on the matrix indicating the key categories of information which they must find. Alternatively, learners may be required to generate their own slots for a given content area. In this instance, learners must gather information and then organize it themselves, creating their own categories of information. This learning activity can promote learning of relationships between concepts, and can also help to organize content for writing assignments.

PROCEDURE FOR DEVELOPING FRAMES AND SLOTS

1. Determine the content to be conveyed, and the purpose for conveying the information.

2. Is there an existing frame available for organizing this content (for example, theory, structure, process, system introduced earlier)? Each of these frames has associated slots identified, into which a variety of in-

formation from different content areas might fit. If one of these frames matches the intent of the writing, the slots can be used to organize the text.

3. If no suitable generic frame has been identified for the content area you are interested in, create your own frame and slots. Think about the content area and identify the major concepts that must be conveyed for several instances of the major content area. Does the same type of information apply to different instances of the major topic area? If so, name that type of information, and include it as a slot.

4. Continue to identify slots (categories of information on the content area) until all of the relevant categories have been identified.

5. Determine whether there is a logical order or sequence for presentation of the content. Is one category of information prerequisite for understanding information in a subsequent category? Alternatively, one piece of information may seem to fit more appropriately when sequenced before a second piece of information. For example, when discussing styles of art, it makes sense to sequence information about the time in which a particular style was popular prior to discussing any historical events that may have influenced the style. Similarly, in an anatomy and physiology text it makes sense to convey the anatomy of a body system prior to discussing that system's function, because structure often governs function.

EFFECTIVENESS OF FRAMES AND SLOTS

Little empirical research on the effectiveness of frames and slots for conveying structural knowledge can be found in the literature. More extensive research is needed to validate the use of frames and slots to organize text materials. One study, however, does indicate that this method of organizing text is of some value.

- Subjects who were trained to use a frame with its slots to organize information about scientific theories performed significantly better than the untrained group on an essay test over text material on scientific theories (Dansereau, 1985).

Learner Interactions

It is possible that some learners would benefit from the structure provided by the use of frames and slots, while other students are less affected by this organizational method. However, few studies have addressed this issue. In the study of the effectiveness of the Scientific Theories frame in facilitating learning, performance on a standardized vocabulary test was used as a covariate, with nonsignificant findings (Dansereau, 1985). Further research on potential differential effects of this strategy for learners with different abilities is needed.

Content/Task Interactions

Most of the generic frames that have been identified deal with the sciences. For example, Dansereau (1985) identified a frame for scientific theories. The slots that accompany this frame are categories of information that one can acquire about a scientific theory, such as the chief developer of the theory, the history of the theory, a description of the theory, it's consequences, and evidence supporting the theory. These categories of information help a learner organize their thoughts about the various theories learned.

Frames appropriate for use in the social science frames have been developed by Armbruster (1984) and Armbruster and Anderson (1984, 1985). These frames include the Goal and the Problem/Solution frames for structuring history textbooks. Both the Goal and the Problem/Solution frames are dynamic. These frames convey action, or historical events. Other social science frames may be static frames. A Cultures frame, for example, includes slots for Technology, Institutions, Language, and Arts. Content for each of these slots can be included for any different culture being studied (Armbruster & Anderson, 1985).

Little research has been conducted into the effectiveness of frames and slots for the various content areas. Although a number of frames have been developed for different content areas, it is unclear whether the frame approach to organizing instruction is better suited to some content areas than others.

Advantages of Frames and Slots

• Frames and slots provide a method for organizing text passage that helps to ensure that important content is included in the text.

• Slots can serve as headings and subheadings within texts, thus explicitly conveying the structure of the content.

• Frames and slots can help writers organize introductions to, and summaries of text by reminding the writer of the main ideas in text.

• Use of frames and slots should help learners to organize their thoughts and develop a stable mechanism for thinking about a subject area. The repetition of the same slots throughout a text should serve to reinforce the organizational scheme, thus stabilizing the learners' schema.

Disadvantages of Frames and Slots

• Frames and slots provide guidelines for organizing text based primarily based upon hierarchical relationships between ideas. No guidelines are provided in this method for conveying relationships between specific ideas in static frames.

• A limited number of generic frames have been identified. While these frames, and their associated slots, may be of use in some disciplines, this group of frames certainly does not encompass all of the content that may need to be conveyed to learners.

• Little, if any, empirical evidence of the effectiveness of frames in conveying structural knowledge is available. Although this method of organizing text may be theoretically appealing, it is not clear whether the use of frames actually improves student learning.

REFERENCES

Armbruster, B. B. (1984). The problem of inconsiderate text. In G. G. Duffy, L. R. Roehler, & J. Mason (Eds.), *Comprehension instruction*. New York: Longman.

Armbruster, B. B., & Anderson, T. H. (1984). Structures of explanations in history textbooks or so what if Governor Stanford missed the spike and hit the rail? *Journal of Curriculum Studies, 16,* 181-194.

Armbruster, B. B., & Anderson, T. H. (1985). Frames: Structures for informative text. In D. H. Jonassen (Ed.) *Technology of text* (Vol. 2). Englewood Cliffs, NJ: Educational Technology Publications.

Dansereau, D. F. (1985). Learning strategy research. In J. Segal, S. Chipman, & R. Glaser (Eds.), *Thinking and learning skills: Relating instruction to basic research* (Vol. 1). Hillsdale, NJ: Lawrence Erlbaum Associates.

Minsky, M. (1975). A framework for representing knowledge. In P. H. Winston (Ed.), *The psychology of computer vision*. New York: McGraw-Hill.

13

Explicit Methods for Conveying Structural Knowledge Through Semantic Maps

DESCRIPTION OF SEMANTIC MAPS

Semantic maps use categorization of concepts and representation of those concept classifications in a graphical format to convey hierarchical relationships between concepts. The semantic mapping technique was created as a means of increasing learners' vocabulary. With semantic maps, new concepts are related to students' prior knowledge and experiences to increase their understanding of the new words. Semantic mapping is often used as a classroom teaching strategy in which student discussion is used to generate a map of the hierarchical relationships between words. Through these discussions, students are able to link the new concepts to their prior knowledge, thus increasing the meaningfulness of learning.

Semantic maps begin with a main idea word or key concept from a text passage. Words that are related to the main idea are identified and grouped according to common features. These categories of related words are named, forming a three-tiered hierarchy of concepts related to the central theme.

Rationale

While reading comprehension is based on a number of factors, one major factor is understanding of the meaning of words in a text passage. Semantic mapping was developed as a technique for increasing vocabulary, thereby enhancing reading comprehension. This technique was originally based upon research on how people gain an understanding of word meanings. One finding from this research is that readers tend to chunk words into categories as a technique for remembering words. Semantic mapping uses "chunking" or grouping of similar words in order to improve learning of word meanings.

Semantic mapping also uses learners' prior knowledge as a basis for learning new vocabulary and increasing reading comprehension. According to schema theory, learning is enhanced when learners are able to relate new learning to prior knowledge. Learners are encouraged to use prior experience to identify words that are related to the main idea when creating a semantic map. Remembering words from prior experience activates relevant schemata, which provide a framework for understanding the meaning of the text passage.

EXAMPLES OF SEMANTIC MAPS

Semantic maps can be created for almost any content area. Figure 13.1 shows a semantic map of gardens, including examples of different garden types, features of gardens, and major garden styles The semantic map in Fig. 13.2 shows different painters, classified by artistic style. This type of map might be used in an art appreciation course.

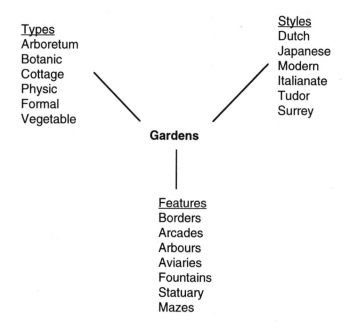

Fig. 13.1. Semantic map about gardens.

Semantic maps on the same topic can be organized in different ways, according to the organization scheme selected by the map maker. For example, Fig. 13.3 shows the topic of Tulips organized by major type of tulip, with examples of different varieties. Figure 13.4 shows the same content area, but this time the varieties are organized by color of the flower. Still another organizational scheme may show different varieties of tulips by the time at which the flowers bloom, as shown in Fig. 13.5. Each of these organizational schemes has a different application. For example, if a gardener is planning a garden and wants to plan exactly which color of tulip belongs where, the organization shown in Fig. 13.4 makes the most sense. Another gardener may know that she wants

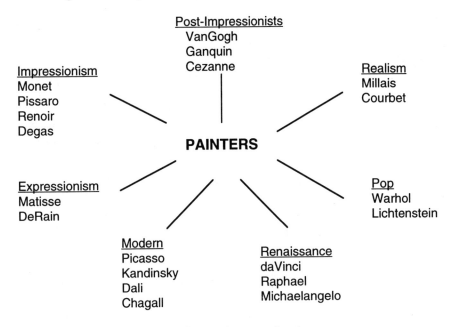

Fig. 13.2. Semantic map of painters.

pink flowers, but wants to plan so that the garden continually blooms in shades of pink throughout the spring, so Fig. 13.5 could help her planning. Finally, Fig. 13.3 would be useful for someone who is learning the distinctions between different types of tulips.

APPLICATIONS OF SEMANTIC MAPS

Semantic mapping has been used primarily as a classroom activity for vocabulary instruction. As such, it can be used before or after reading a passage with new vocabulary words. As a prereading activity semantic mapping serves as an advance organizer (see Chapter 19), identifying important ideas that will be included in the reading. As a postreading activity semantic mapping can serve as a check on the learners' comprehension of the text passage and can help to clarify relationships between ideas.

Semantic maps allow learners to apply their knowledge of the topic area and draw from prior knowledge to enhance their understanding of the topic area. The construction of semantic maps helps learners build more complex cognitive structures, and helps identify hierarchical relationships between ideas (Ward, 1988). Using semantic mapping activities as a prereading exercise serves as an advance organizer, and as a postreading exercise, serves to check students' comprehension of the passage.

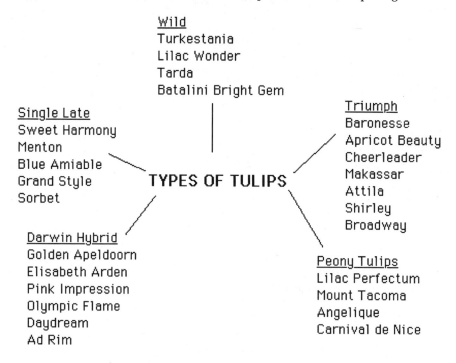

Fig. 13.3. Semantic map of tulips organized by type of tulip.

Representing/Assessing Structural Knowledge

A semantic map that is drawn after reading or studying a text passage reveals the degree to which the learner understands the hierarchical relationships between concepts in the passage. In this manner, semantic maps can serve as a means of assessing learners' structural knowledge. Semantic maps that are developed by an expert reveal that expert's perception of the important concepts in a content area. Since the main ideas in a content area serve as the basis for knowledge structures, this is an important component of structural knowledge. Additionally, the hierarchical relationships between a group of concepts are conveyed in semantic maps, another component of structural knowledge.

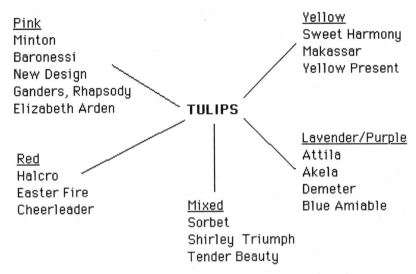

Fig. 13.4. Semantic map of tulips organized by color of tulip.

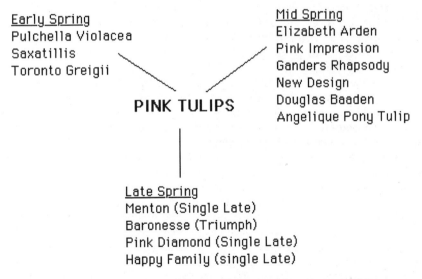

Fig. 13.5. Semantic map of tulips organized by season of bloom.

Conveying Structural Knowledge

Semantic maps convey structural knowledge to the extent that the maps reveal the concepts and the important categories of information about a topic area. In addition, the development of maps relates new concepts to prior knowledge. This process enhances schema development by reinforcing existing relationships and adding new concepts to the established network of concepts in memory.

McClain (1986) suggests using semantic maps as teaching aids in lectures. Rather than following a linear outline she advocates using a semantic map (which she refers to as a "mind map") to organize lectures. Skeleton outlines of semantic maps can also be used as handouts for students to fill in during the course of a lecture. When semantic maps are used as lecture handouts or as overlays for visual aides for lessons, the maps visually convey the hierarchical relationships between ideas. This allows instructors to more efficiently convey not only the meaning of concepts in the lesson, but also the hierarchical relationships between those concepts.

Acquiring Structural Knowledge

Semantic maps have been used for improving vocabulary and increasing reading comprehension in adult learning centers. Ward (1988) notes that in these centers, learners often have little contact with each other or with an instructor, usually spending the majority of their time working independently. Such independent work may encourage learners to minimize their cognitive processing of the text content. By drawing semantic maps in small groups or with an instructor, adult learners are encouraged to relate new concepts to prior knowledge, thereby increasing their comprehension of the content.

The majority of research on semantic mapping has focused on the use of this technique to improve vocabulary and to improve reading comprehension. However, semantic maps may also improve recall of content. In one study of the effect of semantic maps on improving recall, Denner (1986) reports that subjects who constructed an "episodic organizer" (similar to a semantic map) after reading a text passage were better able to recall the text content than subjects who simply read the passage twice or studied a provided map of the content.

Semantic mapping assists learners in acquiring structural knowledge by depicting the hierarchical relationships between concepts. Learners can use semantic maps as a learning strategy to promote acquisition of structural knowledge. Creating semantic maps helps to identify hierarchical relationships between concepts and to clarify meanings of words by relating newly learned words to prior knowledge.

Semantic maps can also be used as a stimulus to writing. Ward (1988) notes that drawing a semantic map helps a learner organize aspects of the topic before writing begins. The map depicts the hierarchical relationships between concepts, thereby helping to structure writing.

PROCEDURE FOR DEVELOPING SEMANTIC MAPS

1. Select the topic to be mapped, and write it on the center of a chalkboard or paper.

2. Identify concepts related to this main idea, and write them on the board (or paper). If drawing a semantic map as part of a classroom activity, have students participate in the identification of related concepts in a brainstorming session.

3. Group related words into categories.

4. Name the categories of related concepts. Again, if map construction is part of a classroom activity, have students generate the titles for each of the groups of related words.

Note: A new class of computer based tools has evolved, known as semantic networking tools, that can facilitate the development of semantic maps. Programs such as SemNet (Fisher, 1990), Learning Tool (Kozma, 1987), TextVision (Kommers, 1989), and Inspiration are powerful mindtools that provide the visual tools to develop semantic maps.

EFFECTIVENESS OF SEMANTIC MAPS

- In a study comparing semantic mapping to two other methods of teaching vocabulary, semantic mapping was found to be superior to a traditional teaching method that uses contextual information to teach word meanings. However, semantic features analysis (Chapter 18) was found to be superior to semantic mapping for teaching vocabulary meanings (Johnson, Toms-Bronowski, & Pittelman, 1982).

- Semantic mapping was found to be significantly more effective in promoting vocabulary acquisition than conventional vocabulary instruction. In addition, these subjects, who participated in the development of semantic maps as a prereading technique also scored higher on reading comprehension measures than subjects who received traditional vocabulary instruction (Jones, 1985).

- Poor readers who received vocabulary instruction using semantic mapping showed significantly higher gains in vocabulary acquisition when compared to other poor readers who did not receive instruction with semantic mapping (Pittelman, Levin, & Johnson, 1985).

- A study of semantic mapping with 5th grade inner city children showed that prereading semantic mapping was more effective in promoting reading comprehension and improved vocabulary than conventional approaches to vocabulary instruction (Jones, 1985).

• Use of teacher-generated semantic maps prior to reading text passages was shown to be effective in increasing three learning disabled children's comprehension of the text material (Sinatra, Berg, & Dunn, 1985).

Learner Interactions

A study using semantic mapping for improving sixth grader's vocabulary showed some cultural differences between rural Native Americans (Menominee), inner city Black, and Caucasian children (Jones, 1985). These differences were primarily in the area of the number of words generated for different semantic maps, and in the number of categories offered for grouping the words on a map. This study indicates that there are some cultural differences between groups that may result in qualitatively different semantic maps (Karbon, 1982).

There is evidence that semantic mapping is effective in improving poor reader's vocabulary (Pittelman et al., 1985). However, research comparing the relative effectiveness of semantic mapping for learners with different abilities or attributes is lacking.

Content/Task Interactions

Semantic maps can be drawn for any subject area in which hierarchical relationships between ideas can be identified. Maps for a variety of content areas have been presented in the literature, but no studies investigating the relative merits of using semantic maps for conveying structural knowledge in different disciplines have been reported.

Semantic maps appear to be most appropriate for tasks that involve learning or classifying concepts. When drawing semantic maps, learners must be able to classify concepts according to key characteristics in order to group words into the categories displayed on the map. Because semantic maps display only hierarchical relationships between ideas, and therefore do not convey causal or quasi-causal relationships, this technique is not well suited for learning tasks that involve principles or procedures.

Advantages of Semantic Maps

• Semantic mapping is easy to learn.

• While most often used as a group activity, semantic mapping can be done individually.

- The main idea is clearly identified on semantic maps, thus reinforcing the hierarchical structures.

- Hierarchical relationships between concepts are made explicit.

Disadvantages of Semantic Maps

- Only hierarchical relationships between ideas are conveyed on a semantic map. While more complex relationships may be identified in the process of creating the semantic map, these relationships are not depicted on the map itself.

- Interrelationships between coordinate concepts are not made explicit on the semantic map.

REFERENCES

Denner, P.R. (1986). *Comparison of the effects of episodic organizers and traditional note-taking on story recall.* Final Rep. Pocatello, ID: Idaho State University. ERIC Document Reproduction Service No. ED 270 731)

Fisher, K.M. (1990). Semantic networking: The new kid on the block. *Journal of Research in Science Teaching, 27*(11), 1001-1018.

Johnson, D. D., Toms-Bronowski, S., & Pittelman, S. D. (1982). *An investigation of the effectiveness of semantic mapping and semantic feature analysis with intermediate grade level children* (Program Report 83-3). Madison, WI: Wisconsin Center for Education Research.

Jones, S. T. (1985). The effects of semantic mapping on vocabulary acquisition and reading comprehension of black inner city students. *Dissertation Abstracts International, 45*, 3061-A.

Karbon, J.C. (1982). *An investigation of the relationships between prior knowledge and vocabulary development with culturally diverse students.* ERIC Document Reproduction Service No. ED 270 722)

Kommers, P. (1989). *Textvision.* Enschede, NL: University of Twente.

Kozma, R. (1987). The implications of cognitive psychology for computer- based learning tools. *Educational Technology, 27*(11), 20-25.

McClain, A. (1986, June). *Improving lectures: Challenge both sides of the brain.* Paper presented at the National Conference of the Association of Optometric Contact Lens Educators, Forest Grove, OR. (ERIC Document Reproduction Service No. ED 274 954)

Pittelman, S. D., Levin, K. M., & Johnson, D. D. (1985). *An investigation of two instructional settings in the use of semantic mapping with poor readers* (Program Report 85-4). Madison, WI: Wisconsin Center for Education Research.

Sinatra, R. C., Berg, D., & Dunn, R. (1985). Semantic mapping improves reading comprehension of learning disabled students. *Teaching Exceptional Children, 4*, 310-314.

Ward, A. M. (1988, May). *Semantic mapping in the adult learning center.* Paper presented at the Annual Meeting of the International Reading Association, Toronto, Canada. (ERIC Document Reproduction Service No. ED 294 150)

14

Explicit Methods for Conveying Structural Knowledge Through Causal Interaction Maps

DESCRIPTION OF CAUSAL INTERACTION MAPS

Many times there are multiple contributing factors that interact to produce a given outcome. Causal interaction maps are graphics that show causal and correlational relationships between both observed and unobserved variables. With causal interaction maps the interactions between variables which lead to a given effect are made explicit in a graphic format.

Causal interaction maps take their form from that used to graphically depict results of causal modeling statistical techniques (Long, 1983). These maps consist of concept words that are enclosed in either a circle or a square. Words enclosed in squares represent variables that are measurable, such as scores on a psychological profile or an achievement test. Encircled concept words represent variables that are not directly measurable, referred to as latent factors. Intelligence is an example of a latent variable. Intelligence cannot be measured directly, but intelligence tests are used to gain a sense of an individual's intellectual abilities.

The outcome variables are linked to factors which impact on them by lines that are used to indicate causal relationships, with arrows to indicate the direction of causality. Straight lines indicate direct causal relationships while curved lines represent indirect, correlational relationships. The variables which affect a given phenomena are arranged hierarchically in causal interaction maps, with the most general variables indicated near the top of the page, and more specific variables nearer the bottom of the page. Multiple interrelationships may be depicted on a single causal interaction map through the use of multiple lines between the variables.

Causal interaction maps can be based on statistical causal modeling procedures such as multiple regression analysis, path analysis, and covariant structure analysis. These statistical techniques are used to produce quantitative models of potential causal relationships between correlated variables that can be depicted in graphical format with causal interaction maps. These statistical techniques allow specification of the strength of the relationships between variables so that link lines may be labeled with the percentage of causality or correlation attributed to that linkage.

EXAMPLES OF CAUSAL INTERACTION MAPS

If learners were studying problem solving ability, it might be useful to speculate the factors that influence this ability. Figure 14.1 shows a causal interaction map which includes some of the variables that may impact problem solving performance. Many factors impact crop productivity. Some of these factors are displayed in a causal interaction map shown in Fig. 14.2.

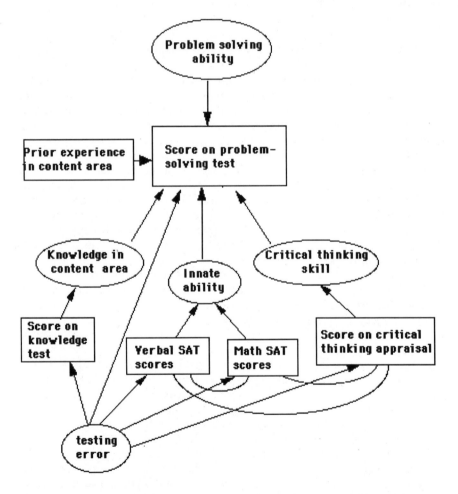

Fig. 14.1. Causal interaction map of factors related to problem solving.

APPLICATIONS OF CAUSAL INTERACTION MAPS

Causal interaction maps can be used for a number of applications to improve learning. Causal interaction maps may serve as a foundation for analyzing the problem solving process. Causal interaction maps can also be used as a graphic depiction of the various forces influencing a problem area. When considering a problem area teachers and learners can consider each of the factors depicted on the map as potential areas for developing solutions.

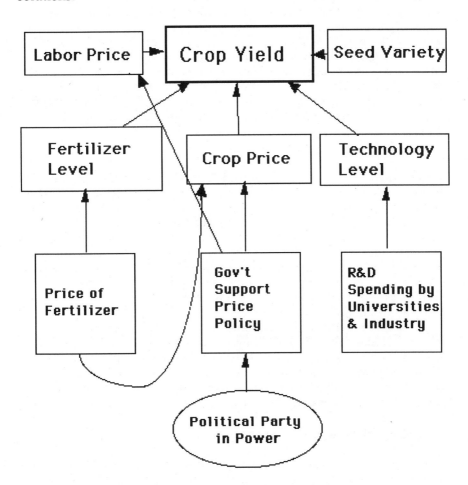

Fig. 14.2. Causal interaction map of factors affecting crop yield.

Jonassen and Dunlap (1991) use causal modeling procedures as the basis for modeling causal reasoning in a hypertext. The graphic representation of these modeling procedures in the form of causal interaction maps can be helpful in visualizing the structure of the content area. In particular, these graphics assist in the identification of decision points and identify consequences of different decisions.

Representing/Assessing Structural Knowledge

Causal interaction maps convey only causal and correlational relationships between concepts. Thus, these maps present a limited view of the relationships between concepts in a content area. While the structural knowledge representation is limited, the causal information that is conveyed in these maps is an important component of structural knowledge. Causal interaction maps depict the map maker's perception of the important variables and their causal and correlational relationships in a content area, so with skilled learners, they may be used to represent their structural knowledge. Learners' maps can be compared to experts' maps to identify differences in perceptions of relationships between variables.

Conveying Structural Knowledge

An instructor may use a causal interaction map as graphic depicting the causal relationships between ideas in a content area as pre- or post-instructional activity. This graphic may be distributed to a class, used as a figure in a text passage, or created on a chalkboard or overhead projection to show content structure. Causal interaction maps generated by experts can serve to clarify relationships and interactions between the factors interacting in a content area. Causal interaction maps can be used by instructors to summarize the major factors affecting a problem area. These maps may be used as pre- or post-instruction organizers (Chapter 19) or as graphics in text.

Expert-generated causal interaction maps may serve as the basis for class discussions regarding the causal relationships. In addition, the degree and bases of correlations between related terms may be discussed in classes. Causal interaction maps that are based on statistical analysis can assist learners and researchers in understanding the structural relationships between the variables in the analysis.

Acquiring Structural Knowledge

Once the format for causal interaction maps is learned, the technique can be used as a learning or study strategy to help organize material. Causal interaction maps can be powerful study tools when used in content areas in which causal relationships are important. After a chapter or unit of study is completed, a learner may draw a causal interaction map to reflect how major characteristics or events in the material interact to cause other events. This type of map may be drawn independently, or may be part of a class assignment.

The process of creating a causal interaction map requires the learner to consider all variables that may impact upon a content area. Structural knowledge is acquired and reinforced when learners determine the direction of causality and identify correlations between variables in a content area. Comparing maps made by learners to maps made by experts may show interesting differences in their perceptions of the content area. Discussions regarding these differences may help to alter learners (and perhaps the expert's) knowledge structures.

Causal interaction maps are also useful brainstorming tools that allow learners to express their thoughts on paper. One example of this application is the use of causal interaction maps to identify variables that should be considered in a research project. In the process of creating a causal interaction map, variables that may impact upon a given outcome are identified. The map making also provides a mechanism for identifying ways to measure the variables and define the limitations of a research project. Limitations are identified by recognizing the multitude of factors that may impact on a given outcome.

PROCEDURE FOR DEVELOPING CAUSAL INTERACTION MAPS

1. Specify the event, phenomena, or outcome of interest. Determine whether this event or outcome can be measured directly or if it needs to be measured indirectly. Write the name of the event of interest at the top of a page of paper. If the event can be directly measured, draw a square around the word(s). If the event cannot be directly measured draw a circle around the word(s). If the event is directly measured move to step 3.

2. If the outcome is not directly measured, consider ways that it could be measured. Write the name of these measurement tools down and draw squares around each. Draw a solid line with an arrow connecting the outcome to the measurement tool. This indicates that the outcome causes (at least in part) performance on that test.

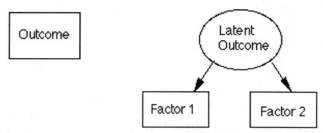

3. Consider what other factors may affect the outcome of interest. Write these on the paper and indicate whether the factors are observed or latent by drawing a square or a circle around the words. Draw straight lines with arrows depicting causal links between the new factor and other factors affecting the variable of interest.

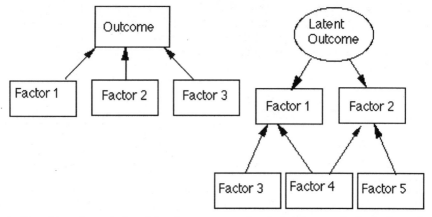

4. Consider the relationships between each of the factors included on the map. Are they correlated in some manner? Draw a curved line between the correlated factors.

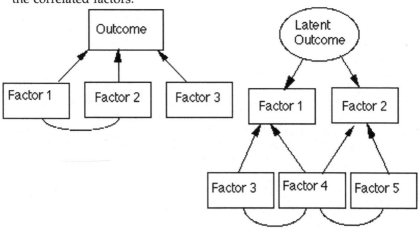

5. Continue to identify factors that may impact upon other factors until all the important factors to be considered are depicted on the map. Draw straight lines between factors with direct causal relationships, and curved lines to connect factors with correlational relationships.

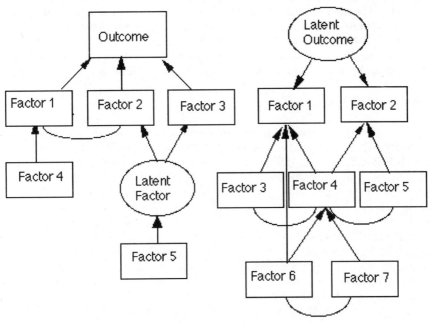

6. If the map is based upon causal modeling procedures, add correlation coefficients and percentages of causation as determined by the statistical analysis.

EFFECTIVENESS OF CAUSAL INTERACTION MAPS

There is no literature available to support the use of causal interaction maps for conveying structural knowledge. However, the maps appear to be useful in identifying and conveying causal relationships between factors, an important element of structural knowledge. Causal interaction maps allow this knowledge to be displayed visually and may supplement the visual information with statistical computations to provide information about the strength of relationships. Thus, while it appears that causal interaction maps would be useful in conveying this type of knowledge, research into the effectiveness of this technique is needed.

Learner Interactions

The effect of different learner aptitudes on ability to use or develop causal interaction maps has not been investigated. It seems, however, that the skills required to generate maps may differ from the skills required to interpret and use the map information. Learners must have a high math aptitude to be able to use the statistical programs to generate percentages of causal relations. However, for interpretation of a predrawn causal interaction map, the learner needs only to be able to understand the meaning of percentages. In addition, both the map drawer and the map interpreter must have the ability to use and interpret spatial relationships.

Content/Task Interactions

By definition, causal relationships are depicted on causal interaction maps. In addition, correlational relations are depicted, but these relationships are not defined in terms of the basis for correlation. Therefore, causal interaction maps are most appropriate for tasks which require utilization of causal relationships. This type of relationship can be used in many disciplines. For example a causal interaction map in literature may depict the multiple causes for the suicide deaths of Romeo and Juliet. In architecture, multiple factors affect the aesthetics and function of buildings, and a causal interaction map may present these relationships in a readily understandable format. Votes in political elections are dependent upon numerous factors, and political analysts may use causal interaction maps to help drive this point home and help to shape policy.

On the other hand, if a learning task involves learning concepts, such as the characteristics of sea urchins, or details such as the batting averages of all left-handed right fielders in the National League, causal interaction maps will be less useful. While causal relationships may be inherent in the structure and function of a sea urchin, the task of simply learning these characteristics does not require an understanding of those relationships.

Advantages of Causal Interaction Maps

• Causal interaction maps depict the multiple variables that may interact to yield a given effect.

• Causal interaction maps are easy to develop and interpret.

• The relative impact of various factors can be identified on the map in terms of percentages of causation, based on statistical analysis.

Disadvantages of Causal Interaction Maps

- Only causal and correlational relationships are depicted on causal interaction maps, limiting the structural knowledge conveyed.

- While correlational relationships are depicted on the map, there is no indication of how the two or more variables are related.

- Causal interaction maps can be based on relatively complex statistical techniques.

- The causal maps that are based on statistical analysis are only as valid as the measurements on which they are based. If the measurement tools used in the data collection are flawed, there may be a misrepresentation of the causal relationships.

REFERENCES

Jonassen, D.H., & Dunlap, J. (1991, November). *Causal modeling for structuring computer-based simulations.* Paper presented at the annual meeting of the Association for the Development of Computer Based Instructional Systems, St. Louis, MO.

Long, J. S. (1983). *Confirmatory factor analysis.* Newbury Park, CA: Sage Publications.

15

Explicit Methods for Conveying Structural Knowledge Through Concept Maps

DESCRIPTION OF CONCEPT MAPS

Concept maps are two dimensional diagrams that illustrate relationships between ideas in a content area. These maps are organized hierarchically, with the broadest, most inclusive concept at the top of the page and subordinate, detailed concepts lower on the page. Concept words are linked by lines that are labeled to identify the type of relationship between the concepts. Although organized primarily in a hierarchical fashion, multiple linkages between concepts can be identified on the maps by using multiple labeled lines to depict how each concept is related to many other concepts.

Rationale

Concept maps are based in large part on the work of Ausubel. According to his Assimilation Theory, learning becomes meaningful only when it is occurs in the context of the learner's prior knowledge (Ausubel, Novak, & Hanesian, 1978; Novak, 1980; Novak & Ridley, 1988). For learning to be meaningful, the learner must actively try to link new information to existing knowledge structures that are related to the new knowledge. This acquisition of new knowledge is accomplished through the learning of new concepts and propositions, and the reformulation (integrative reconciliation) of previously learned concepts as one comes to learn and understand more about the concepts.

Ausubel believes that knowledge structures are organized hierarchically, with more inclusive concepts subsuming more detailed concepts. These concepts are defined and described through propositions, which identify relationships between concepts. Thus, interrelated networks of concepts and propositions are an essential element of human learning. Concept maps are an explicit representation of these integrated knowledge networks. Concept mapping is thought to help the learner activate a meaningful learning set by explicitly relating what she or he already knows to the new information.

EXAMPLES OF CONCEPT MAPS

A concept map related to dairy policy is shown in Fig. 15.1. Figure 15.2 depicts relationships between concepts associated with global climate change.

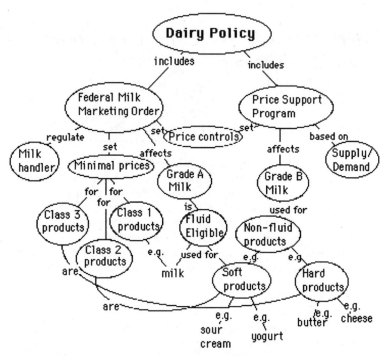

Fig. 15.1. Concept map on dairy policy.

APPLICATIONS OF CONCEPT MAPS

There are numerous applications of concept mapping described in the literature. Learners may use concept maps as an individual learning exercise or study strategy by drawing a map to illustrate concept relationships in a content area. Alternatively, an expert generated concept map can be used as a study guide or to review material.

Concept maps can also be used as a curriculum development tool (Jonassen, Hannum, & Tessmer, 1989; Stewart, Van Kirk, & Rowell, 1979). A concept map of a content area can be used to help identify the areas that need to be included in instruction. Subsequently, the concept map of content covered in a course can serve as the guide for developing traditional test items.

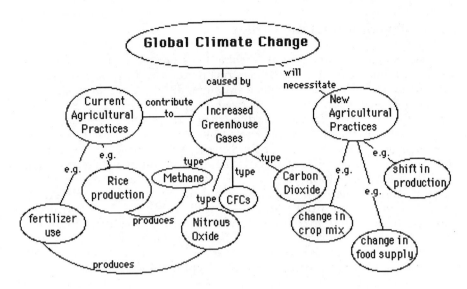

Fig. 15.2. Concept map on global climate change.

Novak and Gowin (1984) indicate that concept mapping can be used to foster creativity by encouraging learners to identify novel relationships between concepts. Concept mapping can also be used as a substitute for outlining as a prewriting strategy, allowing learners to freely associate ideas prior to committing to a rigid, linear structure.

Representing/Assessing Structural Knowledge

Concept maps can be used as a means of representing structural knowledge to serve as the basis for assessing differences between learners' and experts' structural knowledge. Learner's maps can be compared to an instructor's or another expert's map to identify differences in perceptions. Similarly, concept maps generated by learners at different points in a curriculum may be used to identify learners' progression in the attainment of differentiated and organized structural knowledge. Beyerbach (1986) found that learners in more advanced courses in a teacher education program drew concept maps more similar to their instructor's than did subjects in introductory teacher education courses.

Moreira (1979) described the use of concept mapping as a testing strategy. Students were given a list of concepts and instructed to show the relationships between the concepts in a graphical manner. These maps could then be evaluated either through a scoring system developed specifically for concept mapping (Novak & Gowin, 1984) or through a qualitative analysis of the relationships depicted on the map.

Conveying Structural Knowledge

Concept maps are often used as teaching tools. In this regard a map may be used to illustrate the hierarchical structure of main ideas in a single lecture or in an entire unit or course (Moreira, 1979). Concept maps have also served as the basis for computerized mapping of knowledge structures and as the basis for computer based instructional systems (McAleese, 1988).

Concept maps that are generated by experts can be used as pre- or post-instructional summaries of the content area. For example, Bogden (1977) developed concept maps for individual lectures in a genetics course, and used them as a focal point for discussions of content. Some students in this course used the maps as a substitute for formal classroom instruction; others used them as supplements to the traditional instruction and some found them useful as review tools prior to exams. The value of an instructor- (or other expert-) generated concept map is that the ideas that are important to that individual will be explicitly interrelated in a visual manner. Since concept maps show not only which concepts are related, but through the labels also how those concepts are related, concept maps can be used as stand-alone organizers of knowledge structures. However, as Bogden (1977) notes, concept maps are probably most effective when coupled with other instruction.

Acquiring Structural Knowledge

The process of developing a concept map assists learners in acquiring structural knowledge. Evaluations obtained from subjects who used concept mapping in a college-level biology class indicate that concept mapping assists in integrating concepts, organizing material, and increasing retention and comprehension (Heinze-Fry & Novak, 1989). Concept mapping requires the learner to taking an active role in learning rather than being a passive recipient of knowledge. Subjects who used concept mapping noted that the technique helped them understand the material, clarified relationships between concepts, and decreased the amount of time they spent memorizing content.

PROCEDURE FOR DEVELOPING CONCEPT MAPS

Concept mapping was developed as a text mapping strategy, but concept maps may also be developed from memory. The following steps are those designed for use when studying from text.

1. Read through the text passage quickly, noting important ideas. Circle these important concept words.

2. List all of the important words identified when reading through the passage. Rank order these words in order of importance.

3. Select the most important and inclusive concept. Write this concept word at the top of the page and draw a circle around it.

4. Examine the list of concept words and select the most important concept that is related to the first word. Write this word below the main idea and draw a circle around it.

5. Consider the relationship between the two concepts included on the page. Draw a line between these concepts, and write a brief label to indicate how these terms are related.

6. Select another important concept from the list. Write this concept word on the page and circle it.

7. Identify any relationships between the first two words and the new word on the concept map. Draw a line or lines between concepts that are related. Label the line to identify the type of relationship that exists between the two terms.

8. Continue this process until all of the important words are included on concept map. Very detailed information can be included on the map, but should not be circled.

9. Check the concept map to ensure that all relationships between ideas are depicted by labeled lines.

10. Check the organization of the concept map. Does it appear messy and confusing? If so, redraw the map to minimize confusion but retain all lines depicted relationships.

Note: A new class of computer based tools has evolved, known as semantic networking tools, that can facilitate the development of concept maps. Programs such as SemNet (Fisher, 1990), Learning Tool (Kozma, 1987), TextVision (Kommers, 1989), and Inspiration are powerful mindtools that provide the visual tools to develop concept maps.

EFFECTIVENESS OF CONCEPT MAPS

Although much of the literature on concept mapping has been descriptive or qualitative, some experimental studies of the effectiveness of concept mapping have been conducted.

- Subjects who use concept maps to study a text passage demonstrated a greater level of comprehension of the text material than control subjects who studied the same material without using concept maps (Mitchell & Taylor, 1991).

- Subjects who learned concept mapping and practiced its application in a 6-week Biology unit performed better on a standardized achievement test than subjects who were taught the content in a traditional manner without concept mapping (Jegede, Alaiyemola, & Okebukola, 1990).

- Concept mapping appears to reduce anxiety level associated with learning a content area (Jegede et al., 1990). Subjects who used concept maps to study material had significantly lower anxiety scores than subjects who used their usual strategy to study the same material.

- Drawing concept maps of text content appears to increase learners' ability to use that content in solving problems in a physical therapy content area. Subjects who drew concept maps as a study strategy scored higher on a problem solving test than subjects who used their usual study strategy to study a text passage (Beissner, 1992).

- Two groups of subjects were compared for performance on a test of initial recall, retention, and learning efficiency (time required to study) following self-paced instruction in a Biology course. Although no significant differences were found between groups, mean scores favored the group that used concept mapping, especially in a delayed recall test (Heinze-Fry & Novak, 1989).

- Subjects who used concept mapping did not outperform subjects who used an outlining strategy to study a content area on an achievement test (Lehman, Carter, & Kahle, 1985). Although no significant differences between groups was found, it appeared that the group that used concept mapping had a tendency toward higher test scores.

- Following implementation of a mapping program similar to concept mapping, the performance of 11th-grade students on standardized tests improved dramatically. In 1986 only 77% of the students passed standardized Reading Comprehension test, and 85% passed the Written Communications test, but only 47% passed an essay writing test. After implementation of the mapping strategies in social studies and science classes scores on the tests in 1989 had improved to a 99% pass rate for the Reading Comprehension test, a 98% pass rate for the Written Communications test, and a 100% pass rate on the essay writing test. Although this study was not well controlled, the major change in the curriculum was the implementation of the mapping technique, leading administrators and teachers in that district to recommend continued use of the mapping strategy (Peresich, Meadows, & Sinatra, 1990).

Learner Interactions

Concept maps have been used with students from elementary school to graduate school. Novak and Gowin (1984) indicate that this technique is appropriate for all levels of students. Although they have reported that some students have more difficulty learning to use concept mapping than others it is unclear what learner attributes may make concept mapping easy or relatively difficult.

Junior high school learners with high ability as measured by Scholastic Aptitude Test scores appear to benefit more from concept mapping than lower ability learners (Heinze-Fry & Novak, 1989). This advantage may be due to attained competence in the mapping strategy. High ability learners appear to attain competence in concept mapping faster than lower ability learners. Overall, however, skill in concept mapping continues to improve over the course of an academic year (Novak, Gowin, & Johansen, 1983).

In contrast to the Heinze-Fry and Novak study, Stensvold and Wilson (1990) found that 9th-grade students with lower vocabulary scores benefited more from concept mapping than did 9th-grade students with high vocabulary scores. These differences were found on a test of knowledge, comprehension, and application following chemistry laboratory experiment. The differences in outcomes may be due to the level of students involved in the study or the nature of the learning situation. Laboratory experiences are less structured than textbooks, and identification of important concepts and principles from laboratory experiences can be more difficult than learning from text.

Content/Task Interactions

Concept maps have been developed in many different disciplines. The primary area in which published reports of concept map use is in the basic and applied sciences. However, concept maps can be drawn in any content area. Concept mapping has been used in social studies units as well as science classes in a rural Mississippi school district (Peresich et al., 1990).

Concept maps can be drawn on any level of detail, depending upon the proposed use of the map. For example, maps may be drawn very generally, depicting the overall structure of a course or textbook. A more specific concept map can be drawn depicting the content of a unit in a course or a chapter of a textbook. Still more specific maps can be developed for one lecture, or even one part of a lecture, or for detailed content within a chapter of a textbook.

Advantages of Concept Maps

• Concept maps explicitly convey the relationships between ideas in a content area.

• Labeled links on a map convey the type of relationships between concepts.

• Concept mapping is relatively easy to learn.

• Multiple interrelationships between concepts are depicted on concept maps.

Disadvantages of Concept Maps

• Generating a good concept map that depicts all important relationships clearly and neatly requires several redrawings of the map. This is a time-consuming process.

• Concept maps can sometimes be difficult to interpret because of the multiple lines and labels included on maps.

REFERENCES

Ausubel, D. P., Novak, J. D., & Hanesian, H. (1978). *Educational psychology: A cognitive view* (2nd ed.). New York: Holt, Rinehart and Winston.

Beissner, K. L. (1992). Use of concept mapping to improve problem solving. *Journal of Physical Therapy Education, 6,* 22-27.

Beyerbach, B. A. (1986). Concept mapping in assessing prospective teachers' concept development. (ERIC Document Reproduction Service No. ED 291 800)

Bogden, C. A. (1977). *The use of concept mapping as a possible strategy for instructional design and evaluation in college genetics.* Unpublished master's thesis, Cornell University, Ithaca, NY.

Fisher, K.M. (1990). Semantic networking: The new kid on the block. *Journal of Research in Science Teaching, 27*(11), 1001-1018.

Heinze-Fry, J. A., & Novak, J. D. (1989). Concept mapping brings long-term movement toward meaningful learning. *Science Education, 74,* 461-472.

Jegede, O.J., Alaiyemola, F.F., & Okebukola, P.A.O. (1990). The effect of concept mapping on students' anxiety and achievement in biology. *Journal of Research in Science Teaching, 27,* 951-960. 951-960.

Jonassen, D.H., Hannum, W.H., & Tessmer, M. (1989). *Handbook of task analysis procedures.* New York: Praeger Publishers.

Kommers, P. (1989). *Textvision.* Enschede, NL: University of Twente.

Kozma, R. (1987). The implications of cognitive psychology for computer-based learning tools. *Educational Technology, 27*(11), 20-25.

Lehman, J. D., Carter, C., & Kahle, J. B. (1985). Concept mapping, Vee mapping, and achievement: Results of a field study with black students. *Journal of Research in Science Teaching, 22,* 663-673.

McAleese, R. (1988, April). *From concept maps to computer based learning: The experience of notecards.* Paper presented at the annual meeting of the American Educational Research Association, Montreal, Canada. (ERIC Document Reproduction Service No. ED 299 954)

Mitchell, P. D., & Taylor, S. G. (1991, February). *Concept mapping as an aid to computer mediated conversation: An application of conversation theory.* Paper presented to Association for Educational Communications and Technology, Orlando, FL.

Moreira, M. (1979). Concept maps as tools for teaching. *Journal of College Science Teaching, 8,* 283-286.

Novak, J. D. (1980). Learning theory applied to the biology classroom. *The American Biology Teacher, 42,* 280-285.

Novak, J.D., & Gowin, D.B. (1984). *Learning how to learn.* New York: Cambridge University Press.

Novak, J.D., Gowin, D.B., & Johansen, G.T. (1983). The use of concept mapping and knowledge vee mapping with junior high school science students. *Science Education, 67,* 625-645.

Novak, J. D., & Ridley, D. R. (1988). *Assessing student learning in light of how students learn.* Washington, DC, American Association for Higher Education.

Peresich, M. L., Meadows, J. D., & Sinatra, R. (1990). Content area cognitive mapping for reading and writing proficiency. *Journal of Reading, 33,* 424-432.

Stensvold, M. S., & Wilson, J. T. (1990). The interaction of verbal ability with concept mapping in learning from a chemistry laboratory activity. *Science Education, 74,* 473-480.

Stewart, J., Van Kirk, J., & Rowell, R. (1979). Concept maps: A tool for use in biology teaching. *The American Biology Teacher, 41,* 171-175.

16

Explicit Methods for Conveying Structural Knowledge Through Graphic Organizers/Structured Overviews

DESCRIPTION OF GRAPHIC ORGANIZERS

Graphic organizers, otherwise known as structured overviews, are visual aids that are added to text and other instructional materials to communicate the organization of the text passage or the instructional material. Graphic organizers/structured overviews are graphic representations or diagrams consisting of terms connected by unlabeled lines that represent unspecified relationships between concepts. Each major concept that is to be previewed or reviewed is represented by a node. Although definitions vary, a node is generally shown as a box or a circle with a single word inside that represents a concept. Lines connecting these nodes signify relationships between concepts. The lines are unlabeled, and therefore, the exact nature of the relationships between concepts is not supplied to the learner. However, a general framework for information is given to learners with the intent of signaling the structure of the material that is to follow.

The combination of these nodes and links depicts the hierarchical structure of a text or a lesson. Structured overviews take the form of abstract maps of content, and as such appear to be similar to concept maps (see Chapter 15). While originally called structured overviews, this type of diagram was renamed graphic organizer on the recommendation of Ausubel (1978) (Barron, 1980).

Rationale

Barron (1969) developed a method for presenting advance organizers (Chapter 19) in graphic format, showing relationships between terms using explicit graphic links. Barron and Stone (1974) hypothesized that structured overviews work because they cue students to adopt a meaningful learning set by relating new information to prior knowledge. The learning set provides a scaffold for assimilating and comprehending new ideas, in Ausubel's terms. That is, the structured overview provides a foundation for relating and remembering ideas in a text passage or other instructional material.

EXAMPLES OF GRAPHIC ORGANIZERS

Figure 16.1 shows a structured overview that represents the structure of a lesson on descriptive statistics. Figure 16.2 shows a structured overview that represents the structure of a text passage that compares and contrasts informational and persuasive presentations.

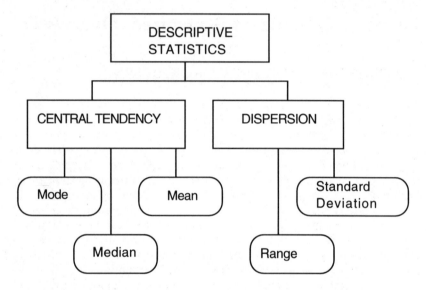

Fig. 16.1. Structured overview of a lesson on statistics.

APPLICATIONS OF GRAPHIC ORGANIZERS

Structured overviews/graphic organizers are primarily used at the onset of an instructional sequence to abstractly convey the relationship between information that is to be learned. As such, they can convey the overall structure of a class session, a course, or an entire curriculum. Graphic organizers are also used at the beginning of text passages with the intent of promoting recall and comprehension of the following text material.

Representing/Assessing Structural knowledge

Structured overviews/graphic organizers are most commonly associated with the areas of writing and reading (Barron, 1990). Generally, graphic organizers are used to convey the structure of books, articles, and papers.

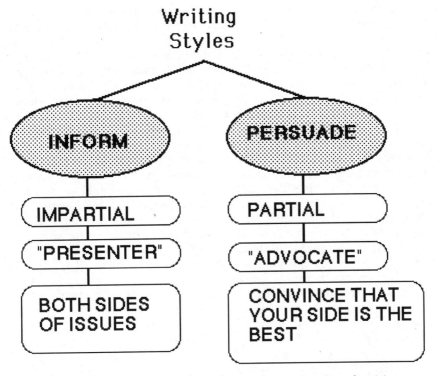

Fig. 16.2. Structured overview of comparison of styles of writing.

Structured overviews represent the general names of concepts and the fact that some concepts *are* related.

• Graphic organizers/structured overviews may also be learner-generated, where learners create the nodes and identify the nature of the relationships.

• In instruction, they may be used to help teachers to organize their thoughts and to give learners an overview of the oncoming lesson.

• Graphic post organizers can be used at the conclusion of a lesson or at the conclusion of a text passage for the purpose of reviewing material. Student-created graphic organizers can be useful in allowing students to elaborate or meaningful encode information.

Conveying Structural Knowledge

The function of structured overviews/graphic organizers is to convey the organization of subject matter or text presentation. Numerous studies support the idea that organization of information helps facilitate recall of information (Glynn & DiVesta, 1977). The use of structured overviews and graphic organizers helps to facilitate the acquisition of structural knowledge by showing the organization of the material to the learner.

Most principles of cognitive psychology assume that information is learned and recalled better when it is organized. Whether or not students should be actively engaged in this organization of material, or whether it is the responsibility of instructors and instruction to supply this organization, has been the primary distinction between respectively, discovery learning and expository teaching. Structured overviews and graphic organizers that are presented and prepared by instructors appear to support expository teaching to convey structural knowledge and aid comprehension.

A learner peruses the graphic organizer at the beginning of instruction or at the beginning of reading a text passage, with the intent of previewing the material and preparing *ideational scaffolding* for the ideas that are to come. This process communicates the author's or teachers conception of the information structure. Although the connections between concepts may not be explicitly shown in the organizer, the intent is to signify relationships in a more general way, by simply showing concepts that are related. Hierarchical relationships can also be shown by using a graphic organizer; graphic organizers can convey subordinate and superordinate relationships pictorially, without the extra cognitive processing of explicitly labeling these relationships.

Acquiring Structural Knowledge

Learners can identify the general structure of the subject matter through graphic organizers, which facilitates recall and comprehension. However, the addition of processing instructions along with the graphic organizer has been shown to greatly facilitate learning with some classes of students. Processing instructions are explicit directions to the learner to reexamine the graphic organizer from time to time within the instruction or the text passage. While some students may naturally use this strategy, significant improvements in recall have been shown when processing instructions were included. Although this strategy is not effective for all types of learners, for good readers, using this strategy in conjunction with structured cueing almost doubled recall (Bernard, 1990).

PROCEDURE FOR DEVELOPING GRAPHIC ORGANIZERS

One of the advantages of structured overviews is that they are quick to develop.

1. Identify the key conceptual elements in the course, class, or text passage. These should be listed on a page.

2. Arrange the concepts in a hierarchical arrangement. The layout of the items should be manipulated such that related items are near each other and connected with lines. Hierarchical organizations should clearly show the superordinate and the subordinate relationships. Concepts that do not fit into the hierarchy are not organizationally important and so should be discarded.

EFFECTIVENESS OF GRAPHIC ORGANIZERS

Although there is some inconsistency in the research, graphic organizers have generally shown a small facilitative effect in promoting learning. A meta-analysis by Moore and Readence (1984) showed that there was a small effect size in using graphic organizers to learn from text.

- Barron (1972) found no differences in performance when he compared structured overviews with prose organizers and no organizers.

- Students who were provided with structured overviews outperformed a control group on a comprehension and production of hierarchies tasks (Eggen, Kauchuk, & Kirk, 1978).

- Amerine (1986) found that science students comprehended more when their lesson was preceded with a structured overview.

- Boothby and Alvermann (1984) found that students who were shown structured overviews recalled more from social studies passages immediately as well as on delayed tests.

- Learners who received extensive training in the use of structured overviews performed better than students who received less training or students who received only traditional instruction (Alverman & Boothby, 1984).

Learner Interactions

Graphic organizers were believed to supplant the learner's organizational strategies; that is, they were believed to help the learner to understand the structure of the subject matter by supplying the learner with a previously created structure. Recent research suggests that with good readers, this occurs. However, with poor readers, the graphic organizer does not appear to supply organization, and instead might actually interfere other organizational cues within a text (Bernard, 1990). This might suggest that only good readers can benefit from graphic organizers, and that graphic organizers may interfere with the efforts of poor readers by requiring additional cognitive processing.

- Similarly, more mature students (university level) seem to derive more benefit from graphic organizers than do lower grade levels (Moore & Readence, 1984).

- Average readers seem to be unaffected by the absence or presence of processing instructions.

Content/Task Interactions

- Student-or instructor-created graphic organizers, used at the end of instruction seems to be more useful than inserting teacher-created graphic organizers at the beginning of instruction (Moore & Readence, 1984)

- Graphic organizers help students to learn vocabulary knowledge, perhaps by focusing attention upon specific areas.

Advantages of Graphic Organizers

- Used with good or more mature readers, and with processing instructions and other structural cures included, graphic organizers can produce significant improvements in recall of information.

- Using post organizers at the end of instructions seems to serve an elaborative function that enables learners to better encode information.

- Under these circumstances, graphic organizers are effective ways to improve learning by conveying the structure of the information.

- Structured overviews are relatively easy to construct. There are no symbol systems or complex instructions to learn.

- The inclusion of processing instructions that specifically explain to students how to use the graphic organizer may help students who do not naturally know how to effectively use a graphic organizer.

Disadvantages of Graphic Organizers

- The hierarchical nature of the relationships in structured overviews limits the kinds of ideas that can be represented.

- The absence of labels between concepts limits the ability to depict interrelationships.

- Some students see the pictorial representation as irrelevant to learning goals.

- Some students lack the metacognitive skills that can enable them to profit from graphic organizers.

- In some cases, such as poor readers, the inclusion of graphic organizers may confuse the students and may actually detract from learning. However, in the absence of other methods of conveying the structure of the information to the learner, even poor readers can benefit from graphic organizers.

REFERENCES

Amerine, F.J. (1986). First things first. *Clearing House, 59*, 396-397.

Ausubel, D.P. (1978). *Educational Psychology: A cognitive view.* New York: Holt, Rinehart, and Winston.

Barron, D.D. (1990). Graphic organizers and the school library media specialist. *School Library Media Activities Monthly.* Vol. VII. (1).

Barron, R.F. (1969). The use of vocabulary as an advanced organizer. In H.L. Herber & P.L. Sanders (Eds.), *Research on reading in the content area, First year report.* Syracuse, NY: Syracuse University Press.

Barron, R.F. (1972). The effects of graphic organizers and grade level upon the reception learning and retention of general science content. In F.P. Greene (Ed.), *Investigations related to mature reading* (21st Yearbook of the National Reading Conference). Milwaukee, WI: National Reading Conference.

Barron, R.F. (1980). *A systematic research procedure, organizers, and overviews: An historic perspective.* (ERIC Document Reproduction Service No. ED 198 508)

Barron, R.F., & Stone, V. F. (1974). Effect of student-constructed graphic post organizers upon learning vocabulary relationships. In P. L. Nacke (Ed.), *Interaction: Research and practice for college-adult reading.* Twenty-third Yearbook of the National Reading Conference. Clemson, SC: National Reading Conference.

Bernard, R.M. (1990). Effects of processing instructions on the usefulness of a graphic organizer and structural cuing in text. *Instructional Science, 19*, 207-217.

Boothby, P.R., & Alvermann, D. E. (1984). A classroom training study: The effects of graphic organizer instruction on fourth graders' comprehension. *Reading World, 23*, 325-339.

Eggen, P. D., Kauchak, D. P., & Kirk, S. (1978). The effect of hierarchical cues on the learning of concepts from prose materials. *Journal of Experimental Education, 46*(4), 7-11.

Glynn, S. M., & DiVesta, F.J. (1977). Outline and hierarchical organization as aids for study and retrieval. *Journal of Educational Psychology, 69*, 89-95.

Moore, D.W., & Readence, J.E. (1984). A quantitative and qualitative review of graphic organizer research. *Journal of Educational Research, 78* (1), 11-17.

17

Explicit Methods for Conveying Structural Knowledge Through Cross Classification Tables

DESCRIPTION OF CROSS CLASSIFICATION TABLES

Cross Classification tables represent a method for explicitly conveying the structure of information. Specifically, cross classification tables are best used for the purpose of comparing and contrasting several different objects with similar attributes or criteria. A cross classification table is a matrix of rows and columns with the names of objects across the columns and with object attributes featured as rows.

Rationale

Cross classification tables can be seen as an artifact of frame theory (Minksy, 1975), schema theory (see for example, Rumelhart, 1980), or script theory (Schank & Abelson, 1977). That is, each theory posits a cognitive structure that is built primarily by experience and that contains slots for specific types of information. Rumelhart and Norman (1981) among others, have forwarded ideas that analogical reasoning functions because of the parallel nature of the attributes/slots of a schema. A cross classification table makes these slots highly explicit by labeling them as attributes. In teaching structural knowledge, it is assumed that the learner can readily learn these attributes/slots and that explicit teaching of the attributes helps to facilitate recall.

EXAMPLES OF CROSS CLASSIFICATION TABLES

The first example of a cross classification table, shown in Fig. 17.1, compares several different Computer-based training formats, according to their varying attributes. The second example of a cross classification table in Fig. 17.2 compares the attributes of several different types of audiences for a speech on nutrition.

	CBT	Simulation	Hypertext/ Hypermedia
General Educational Strategy	Expository: tutorials	Discovery: games	Discovery: research
Design Approach	Instructional systems design	Interactive, artistic, creative	Electic: bits and pieces coordinated in friendly interface
Graphics Usage	When instructionally appropriate	Integrated within the game or simulation	As available and retrievable

Fig. 17.1. Cross classification table.

APPLICATIONS OF CROSS CLASSIFICATION TABLES

Cross classification tables are perhaps best used to explicitly convey the similarities and differences between several objects. Many text books use a compare and contrast format for organizing the subject matter. A cross classification table can more explicitly enable a learner to learn and recall this material (Jones, Amiran, & Katims, 1985). In addition to increasing recall of compare and contrast features, cross classification tables may be modified so that learners may specifically try to infer relationships and form conclusions when dealing with compare and contrast material. This presumably facilitates deeper processing and enables learners to not only understand the overall structure of the material, but also to begin to recognize relationships that occur both within columns and across rows.

Representing/Assessing Structural Knowledge

As a means of assessing structural knowledge, cross classification tables are less subjective than a traditional compare and contrast essay test item. However, it is possible to recall the information in the table and not necessarily comprehend the underlying relationships and what they mean. In terms of assessing the recall of structured information, however, cross classification tables are an unambiguous and easily scored method of testing. In addition, using cross classification tables enables "teachers and researchers to separate entirely the scoring or organization from the scoring of content." (Jones et al., 1985).

	Basic Nutrition Dos and Don'ts	Sports Nutrition / 14-16 yr. old inner city youths	The Mind and Nutrition: / Faculty	New B S Degree in English / Students
Amount of Hands-on Knowledge vs. Experience				
Amount of Theoretical Knowledge				
Amount of "Dinner Table" Knowledge				
Interest Level of Perceived Relevance				
Attitude Toward Presenter				
English Language Ability				
Attention Span				

Fig. 17.2. Cross classification table.

Conveying Structural Knowledge

Cross classification tables are used most commonly as prewriting organizers. That is, before writing a compare and contrast essay, the learner may more efficiently organize his or her energies by constructing a cross classification table. In like manner, answering essay questions has been shown to be facilitated by using these tables (Jones et al., 1985).

Cross classification tables can be used in expository instruction, as a means of summarizing information, such as at the end of chapters or units. They can also be used by giving students a blank matrix and requiring them to take notes in a systematic fashion.

In a discovery learning approach, cross classification tables can be used as a means of guided discovery. That is, students can be given a matrix with rows and columns filled in and can be asked to research these areas to complete the table. A further discovery function of cross classification tables might be to give students only the names of the objects, and to encourage students themselves to determine the attributes that are of interest in comparing and contrasting objects. Jones et al. (1985) note that this is a weakness in cross classification tables.

Acquiring Structural Knowledge

Used as notetaking aids, cross classification tables may not necessarily produce the rich relationships that are desired in teaching structural knowledge. For example, recalling the framework attributes and even the specific content of the matrix does not necessarily guarantee that the learner is able to go beyond a simple recall task.

The addition of inferences and summaries into a table may force the learner to process the information more deeply. While the ability to recall the overall structure of the material may be seen as a prerequisite to learning structural knowledge, it should not be seen as an equivalent to it.

PROCEDURE FOR DEVELOPING CROSS CLASSIFICATION TABLES

Two types of content can be taught using cross classification tables: the comparison between objects or the instantiation of varying conceptual attributes. For example, Fig. 17.2 shows an example in which the important learning occurred in the *rows*; that is, the table was used as a way of comparing and contrasting varying instantiations of this collection of attributes (which, incidentally, are questions of interest in performing an audience analysis).

In contrast, Fig. 17.1 gives an illustration of learning subject matter in which the important learning occurs across the *columns*. That is, the terminal objective is to develop structural knowledge relating to types of computer-based training. The specific attributes are only important as long as they enable the comparison and contrast of the various types of computer-based training. Note that not all possible similarities or contrasts are included, only those that are of educational value.

A second major decision needs to be made in terms of how a cross classification table will be used functionally in instruction. For example, will the table be used as part of an expository sequence, or as part of a discovery sequence? These issues determine in what manner the cross classification table is constructed.

In order to develop *expository tables*:

1. If both the objects and attributes are of primary interest (such as comparing and contrasting the Viet Nam Conflict and The Persian Gulf War) then create a matrix with objects as the column headings.

2. Select a list of attributes by which the objects may be compared and contrasted.

3. Place these attributes as row headings.

4. Fill in the matrix and present to students.

If the attributes are the most important features of the instruction, then develop attribute tables. In order to develop *attribute tables*:

1. List the features as the row headings.

2. Select a variety of objects that instantiate the attributes, and place the object names as column headings.

3. Fill in the matrix and present to students.

Student-produced tables may be done similarly by leaving the matrix incomplete and by requiring students to complete it. A discovery method with less guidance might leave the attributes columns to be supplied by students (if the objects are of primary importance) or leave the columns to be filled by students (if learning about instances of the attributes are of importance).

EFFECTIVENESS OF CROSS CLASSIFICATION TABLES

There is a limited body of research specifically relating to cross classification tables. However, some general research results, which were fundamental in developing these ideas, are cited.

Advantages of Cross Classification Tables

- Cross classification tables help to organize information, which facilitates recall of subject matter better than unorganized information (Frase, 1969).

- Given unorganized information, students can organize it into cross classification tables which helps to facilitate recall (Jones et al., 1985).

178 Conveying Structural Knowledge

- Training in the development of cross classification tables enable students to produce higher quality essays (Jones et al., 1985).

- By drawing inferences and writing conclusions based on a cross classification table, presumably students are engaged in deeper levels of processing of the information. (Craik & Lockhart, 1972)

Disadvantage of Cross Classification Tables

- It is possible to recall the comparison and contrast schema, yet not have the rich cognitive structure to which it corresponds. That is, students can learn the form and the content, yet be unable to draw rich conclusions form the data.

REFERENCES

Craik, F.M., & Lockhart, R.S. (1972). Levels of processing: A framework for memory research. *Journal of Verbal Learning and Verbal Behavior*, 11, 671-684.

Frase, L.T. (1969). Paragraph organization of written materials. The influence of conceptual clustering upon level of organization. Journal of Educational Psychology, 60, 394-401.

Jones, B.F., Amiran, M., & Katims, M. (1985). Teaching cognitive strategies and text structures within language arts programs. In J.W. Segal, S.F. Chipman, & R. Glaser (Eds.), *Thinking and Learning Skills*. Hillsdale, N.J: Lawrence Erlbaum Associates.

Minksy, M. (1975). A framework for representing knowledge. In P.H. Winston (ed.) *The Psychology of Computer Vision*. New York: McGraw- Hill.

Rumelhart, D.E. (1980). Schemata: The building blocks of cognition. In R.J.Spiro, B.C. Bruce, & W.F. Brewer (Eds.), *Theoretical issues in reading comprehension: Perspectives from cognitive psychology, linguistics, artificial intelligence, and education*. Hillsdale, NJ: Lawrence Erlbaum Associates.

Rumelhart, D.E., & Norman, D.A. (1981). Analogical processes in learning. In J.R. Anderson (Ed.), *Cognitive skills and their acquisition*. Hillsdale, NJ: Lawrence Erlbaum Associates.

Schank, R.C., & Abelson, R.P. (1977). *Scripts, plans, goals and understanding*. Hillsdale, NJ: Lawrence Erlbaum Associates.

18

Explicit Methods for Conveying Structural Knowledge Through Semantic Features Analysis

DESCRIPTION OF SEMANTIC FEATURES ANALYSIS

Semantic features analysis is a technique that relies upon categorical analysis of words to increase vocabulary and comprehension (Johnson et al, 1982; Johnson et al, 1984). Designed as a classroom technique, semantic features analysis (SFA) is intended to activate learners' prior knowledge as the learners relate new vocabulary terms to their own prior experiences. This technique has been used before or after reading from a text as a means of increasing comprehension and vocabulary. Through activities that surround the generation and completion of a semantic features analysis, learners also build structural knowledge in a content area.

To create a semantic features analysis, the general topic of instruction is selected, and words related to the topic are identified and listed in a column. Then features shared by some or all of the words are listed in a row across the top, forming a grid. Within this grid the relationships between the concepts and features are indicated with a "+" or a "-" in each of the boxes, a "+" indicating that a concept has a particular feature, and a "-" indicating that it does not. In a classroom setting this technique can be used with the teacher providing some new vocabulary words (in the column) with students using prior experience to identify other words that are related to the general topic.

Rationale

Like semantic mapping (Chapter 13), semantic features analysis is based on the logical premise that understanding word meanings enhances reading comprehension. Semantic features analysis focuses on the understanding of the similarities and differences between concepts in order to increase understanding of reading materials. This technique uses a structured approach to identifying characteristics of concepts using a matrix or grid format. Thus, subtle differences between words can be identified through completion of the SFA grid.

Semantic features analysis provides for activation of students' prior knowledge to enhance learning of vocabulary and reading comprehension. Schema theory indicates that relating new learning to prior knowledge helps learners develop a context for comprehending text. In addition, linking new words to words already in a learner's vocabulary assists in understanding the meaning of the new words. Students' contributions to the column of words in a SFA help to activate their prior knowledge about the general topic, and thereby enhance acquisition of the new words meanings and increase understanding of text.

EXAMPLES OF SEMANTIC FEATURES ANALYSIS

Figure 18.1 depicts a semantic features analysis of different forms of government.

	Economic Democracy	Political Democracy	Private Property	Dictatorship/Autocractic	Free Market	Welfare State
Communism	+	+	-	-	-	+
Socialism	+	-	-	+	-	+
Nazism	-	-	+	+	-	-
Capitalism	-	+	+	-	+	-

Fig. 18.1. Semantic features analysis of different forms of government.

Key features of different tulips are depicted in Figs. 18.2 and 18.3. Figure 18.2 depicts features of individual tulips, while Fig. 18.3 shows general features of types of tulips.

	Very Late Spring	Early Spring	Mid Spring	Low Growing	Med. Height	Tall Height	Oval Shaped Flower	Indoor Facing	MATLED Leaves	Lily Flowering	Multi-colored
Lilac Perfectum	–	–	–	–	+	–	–	–	–	–	–
Red Shrine	–	–	–	–	–	+	–	–	–	+	–
Pink Diamond	–	–	–	–	+	–	–	–	–	+	–
Shirley Triumph	–	–	+	–	+	–	+	+	–	–	–
Olympic Flame	–	–	+	–	–	+	+	–	–	–	+
Toronto	–	–	+	–	–	–	–	–	+	+	–
Johan Strauss	+	–	–	–	–	–	–	–	–	+	–

Fig. 18.2. Semantic features analysis of features of individual tulips.

	Huge Flower	Tall Stems	Oval Shape	Short	Medium Tall	Early	Mid Spring	Late Spring	Mottled Leaves	Forcing	Perennialization
Single Late	+	+	+	-	-	-	-	+	-	?	+
Triumph	-	-	+	-	+	-	+	-	-	+	+
Darwin Hybrid	+	+	+	-	+	-	+	-	-	?	+
Single Early Tulips	-	-	+	+	-	+	-	-	-	-	-
Greizi	-	-	-	-	+	-	+	-	+	-	-

Fig. 18.3. Semantic features analysis of general features of types of tulips.

APPLICATIONS OF SEMANTIC FEATURES ANALYSIS

Semantic features analysis has been shown to be effective in increasing students' vocabulary and comprehension of text. It can be used either as an in-class strategy with student participation in the construction of the semantic features matrix, or as an individual assignment. As an in-class activity, learners participate in discussions regarding the meaning of words, and jointly complete the SFA matrix. Alternatively, an empty matrix may be given as a homework assignment, with the learner instructed to complete the matrix.

Representing/Assessing Structural Knowledge

A completed SFA matrix represents key features of concepts, thereby depicting the degree of similarity between main ideas, but does not show relationships between those ideas. It is possible to determine by looking at an SFA whether concepts share similar attributes and how they differ.

A modified SFA can depict the degree of relatedness between concepts, thus further representing structural knowledge. In this application, rather than showing whether a concept possesses certain features, the SFA may consist of a row of terms in a matrix with other related terms. Completion of the grid would involve determining the degree to which each pair of concepts are similar or dissimilar using Likert scale values. This version of an SFA provides additional information about knowledge structures.

Either version of SFA can also be used to assess structural knowledge. Individual assignments to complete SFAs to depict the features of key concepts may result in very different matrices. Review of the SFAs can help to determine whether a learner understands the subtle differences between similar concepts. This type of diagnostic matrix can explicitly convey the degree to which learners know the key features of a group of concepts. Similarly, learners may be required to complete a matrix showing the degree of relatedness between terms. Such a matrix could be compared to an expert's matrix, showing any discrepancies between expert and learner. This type of comparison may then be used as the basis for further instruction.

Conveying Structural Knowledge

Semantic features analysis can be used to convey structural knowledge to learners in at least two ways. First, the terms included on an SFA give some idea of the important concepts in a content area. An instructor typically selects these important concepts based up their own knowledge in the content area and their own belief about the important ideas to be learned. Thus, the selection of terms for inclusion on the SFA cues learners to the important relationships in the subject area. The identification of main ideas is an important component of structural knowledge because knowledge structures are organized around key concepts.

Second, a completed SFA matrix clearly shows the relationships between concepts and their features. Completed SFAs may be given to learners or used as figures in text to summarize key features of concepts. Such SFAs not only depict the ideas that are important in the content area, but also shows how these ideas are related, whether by the features that are shared or by the degree of relatedness to other key ideas.

Acquiring Structural Knowledge

Because thinking is accomplished primarily through words, and our understanding of a content area is expressed through words, acquisition of vocabulary is an important component of structural knowledge. Groups that used semantic features analysis to promote acquisition of vocabulary learned more vocabulary words than groups that were taught vocabulary either with semantic mapping or by analyzing the context in which words were presented (Johnson et al., 1982). SFA promotes learning of vocabulary, and also helps learners make fine distinctions between words or concepts (Beyersdorfer & Schauer, 1989).

Aside from improving vocabulary comprehension the process of completing a SFA, especially in a classroom setting, involves relating the new concept words to prior knowledge. By linking the new concepts to previously learned concepts, learners build integrated knowledge structures. With these more integrated structures, future learning is made more efficient and meaningful.

PROCEDURE FOR DEVELOPING SEMANTIC FEATURES ANALYSIS

Semantic features analyses have been used as prereading and postreading activities to promote vocabulary acquisition and reading comprehension. Although semantic features analysis has been used primarily in association with reading assignments, it is possible to create these analyses for use without reading assignments. In an effort to make these procedures applicable to more settings, the procedure described here has slight modifications from previous instructions for creating an SFA (Anders, Bos, & Filip, 1983; Johnson et al., 1982). The procedures described are for use of SFA as a classroom activity, but can be modified for individual use.

1. Select the topic for the SFA. If the goal of the activity is improved vocabulary, select a topic in which a number of vocabulary words are interrelated. Preferably, a text passage that contains the key ideas or content that is to be learned can be selected for reading either before or after the SFA is completed.

2. Think about the topic area, or read through the text passage to identify the major ideas associated with the topic. List a word or short phrase that represents each main idea.

3. Select from this list the most important (superordinate) concepts, and then identify the features that are common to some or all of the concepts.

4. Create a relationship matrix with the more general, superordinate concepts represented in columns and the potential features of concepts represented in rows. Leave several blank columns and rows to allow learners to add additional concepts to the matrix.

5. Copy the matrix and distribute to learners and use an overhead transparency or blackboard representation of the matrix for instructional uses during the discussion.

6. Begin a discussion of the SFA topic by defining or describing each of the superordinate concepts. Encourage learners to relate these concepts to their own experiences and to share these experiences in the discussion. Add additional superordinate concepts suggested by learners in the course of the discussion.

7. Continue the discussion with a brief definition or description of each of the features. Again, encourage interaction from learners regarding these concepts, and add any additional pertinent subordinate concepts to the matrix as they are suggested by the learners.

8. Either as a class or as an individual assignment, have learners determine the relationship between each superordinate concept and the features depicted in the matrix. Have them mark a "+" if the subordinate concept is positively related to the superordinate concept and a "-" if the subordinate concept is negatively related to the superordinate concept. A "0" marks that the subordinate is not related to the superordinate concept, and a "?" indicates that the relationship between the two concepts is unclear. If conducted as a group activity, try to have students reach consensus on the relationships between concepts as consensus is reached.

As an alternative to using features of superordinate concepts to organize a SFA grid, the grid may be constructed using related concepts. Then a Likert-type rating scale can be used to indicate the degree to which terms are related (Johnson & Pearson, 1978). A "5" may indicate a very strong, positive relationship between the concepts, while a "4" would indicate a positive relationship and "3" a neutral relationship. Rating two concepts as a "2" would then indicate that the concepts were negatively related, while a "1" would indicate a very negative relationship. This type of rating scale requires closer scrutiny of the relationships between concepts than simple use of plus or minus signs, and therefore should be used with more sophisticated learners (Johnson & Pearson, 1978).

9. After the matrix has been completed, have learners refer back to reading materials or other references to clarify uncertain relationships between concepts. After reading or reviewing these materials, the matrix can be modified to reflect new learning.

EFFECTIVENESS OF SEMANTIC FEATURES ANALYSIS

- A modified semantic features analysis was found to improve the quality of students' essays following classroom activities designed to elaborate on the essay theme (Beyersdorfer & Schauer, 1989).

- In research with learning disabled students Anders and Bos (1986) have found that semantic features analysis is more effective in promoting vocabulary acquisition and reading comprehension than traditional vocabulary instruction.

- Semantic features analysis was found to be superior to semantic mapping and a traditional vocabulary instruction technique in building the vocabularies of 4th, 5th, and 6th grade students (Johnson et al., 1982).

Learner Interactions

Little research has been conducted into the efficacy of semantic features analysis for learners with different abilities. One study demonstrated that the technique was superior to a standard vocabulary technique for improving learning disabled high school students' comprehension of a text (Anders & Bos, 1986). However, there is no indication that this technique is more valuable for these students than other nondisabled students.

Given the format of semantic features analysis, it seems likely that learners with high analytical ability would be able to learn and use semantic features analysis easily. Because the product of semantic features analysis is a completed matrix, spatial ability is not required for learning from this technique.

Content/Task Interactions

Concepts from any discipline can be displayed in a semantic features analysis. While some content areas may be more conducive to semantic features analysis, there have no studies investigating the effectiveness of this technique in different content areas.

Semantic features analysis provides a powerful mechanism for conveying similarities and dissimilarities between concepts. Creation or completion of a semantic features analysis matrix requires the learner to distinguish between related concepts based upon key characteristics. Therefore, this technique appears to be particularly well suited to learning tasks that focus on distinguishing between concepts.

Semantic features analyses show only whether a concept displays or does not display a certain characteristic. Since more complex relationships between concepts are not displayed in the matrix format, the format does not lend itself well to the learning of principles or procedures.

Advantages of Semantic Features Analysis

• Semantic features analysis can be used effectively to convey the characteristics or features of a large number of concepts.

• The format allows easy comparison of concepts on the basis of the features selected for inclusion.

• SFAs can be modified to show the degree to which terms are related, providing more complete information about content structures.

Disadvantages of Semantic Features Analysis

• Multiple interrelationships between concepts are not conveyed in the grid. The relationships that are represented are categorical, limiting representation to the features of the concepts listed but not the way that the concepts themselves are interrelated.

• Semantic features analyses are relatively difficult to construct. Development of the matrix with identification of pertinent characteristics of concepts is time consuming.

REFERENCES

Anders, P.L., & Bos, C.S. (1986). Semantic feature analysis: An interactive strategy for vocabulary development and text comprehension. *Journal of Reading, 29*, 610-616.

Anders, P. L., Bos, C. S., & Filip, D. (1983, November). *The effect of semantic features analysis on the reading comprehension of learning disabled students.* Paper presented at the Annual Meeting of the National Reading Association, Austin, TX. (ERIC Document Reproduction Service No. ED 237 969)

Beyersdorfer, J.M., & Schauer,D.K. (1989). Semantic analysis to writing: Connecting words, books, and writing. *Journal of Reading, 32*, 500-508.

Johnson, D.D., & Pearson, P. D. (1978). *Teaching reading vocabulary.* New York: Holt, Rinehart and Winston.

Johnson, D.D., Pittelman, S.D., Toms-Bronowski, S., & Levin, K.M. (1984). An investigation of the effects of prior knowledge and vocabulary acquisition on passage comprehension (Program Report 84-5). Madison, Wisconsin: Wisconsin Center for Education Research.

Johnson, D. D., Toms-Bronowski, S., & Pittelman, S. D. (1982). *An investigation of the effectiveness of semantic mapping and semantic feature analysis with intermediate grade level children* (Program Report 83-3). Madison, Wisconsin: Wisconsin Center for Education Research.

19

Explicit Methods for Conveying Structural Knowledge Through Advance Organizers

DESCRIPTION OF ADVANCE ORGANIZERS

Advance organizers consist of introductory material that is presented in advance of instruction at a higher level of abstraction, generality, or inclusiveness than the information presented in the instruction. The inclusion of advance organizers in learning materials prevents the learner from having to discover the ideas that will make the information meaningful. Organizers show the learner how to relate the new material to what he or she already knows or what area of the content domain the ideas should be included in, rather than having to discover that context for themselves. Organizers provide learners with the appropriate context for understanding the ideas in a text passage. Advance organizers are typically at a higher level of generality or inclusiveness than the material to be learned. They are presented in advance of the instructional message, regardless of how it is presented (e.g., text, video, computer lesson, etc.). Typically the length of advance organizers is 10% to 15% percent of the length of the primary instructional message.

Advance organizers serve a variety of functions during instruction. Organizers are presented during instruction in order to:

- provide advance ideational scaffolding for new material at an appropriate level of inclusiveness,
- deliberately introduce relevant and abstract concepts into the learner's cognitive structure to enhance incorporability and stability of new, more specific and detailed ideas,
- increase discriminability of the new material presented in the learning passage from similar and/or conflicting ideas already in the learner's cognitive structure,
- provide anchoring points in the learner's cognitive structure for understanding and relating new ideas, and
- bridge the gap between what is known and what is to be learned.

It is important to distinguish between organizers and other instructional strategies. For instance, organizers are NOT:

- overviews or abstracts;
- summaries of main ideas of an instructional sequence;
- necessarily at a higher level of abstraction;
- meant to simply eliminate specific information and detail.

Classes of Organizers

There are two primary types of advance organizers that are designed to accomplish the same general purpose but do so in different ways.

Expository Organizers. Expository organizers are used when material being studied is unfamiliar, and no concepts are known by the target learners to which new ideas can be anchored. That is, there are no existing terms to which new material can be related. Expository organizers are therefore more abstract. They provide contextual ideas to which the new material can be anchored. In effect, the designer is saying to the reader, "In the bigger picture, this is where this information fits, this is how to make sense of it."

The rationale for using expository organizers is expressed in the concept of *ideational scaffolding*, which means providing an appropriate conceptual foundation or skeleton for relating the new material. Just as you cannot add a new room onto your house until you have built the frame (foundation), you cannot add meaningful concepts to memory without an appropriate conceptual foundation.

Comparative Organizers. Have you ever struggled with a problem or a unit of novel information, unable to "get a handle on it"? When the intellectual light bulb lit up, you were suddenly able to understand the problem or the information. Your sudden understanding probably resulted from your being able to relate the problem in terms of another problem that you had encountered previously or in terms of ideas or constructs with which you were already familiar. Thinking about the new material in familiar terms made the problem meaningful. Comparative organizers are designed to access those familiar constructs in advance of learning. They stimulate recall of ideas with which the learners should be familiar. So, comparative organizers are used when learners are familiar with material to which new concepts can be anchored. They must clearly and explicitly delineate similarities and differences between the familiar, contextual material that is already known by the learners and the new material to be learned.

The conceptual rationale for comparative organizers is the concept of *integrative reconciliation*, which states that consistently relating new material back to concepts that already exist in the learner's cognitive structure in essence explains new ideas in terms of old ideas.

Rationale

The rationale for advance organizers were developed and published over a period of years by David Ausubel and associates (Ausubel, 1960, 1962, 1963, 1968; Ausubel & Fitzgerald, 1961; Ausubel, Robbins, & Blake, 1957; Ausubel & Youseff, 1963. Ausubel believed that learning can be characterized along two dimensions — rote versus meaningful learning and reception versus discovery learning (see Fig. 19.1).

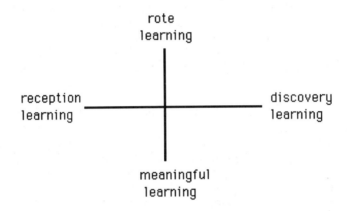

Fig. 19.1. Dimensions of learning.

The type of learning in which an individual engages is determined by the individual's purpose for learning and the way he or she interacts with instructional materials and sequences. On the first dimension, rote learning consists of remembering discrete, isolated units that are not related to already known ideas. Meaningful learning, on the other hand, occurs when ideas can be related to ideas that already exist in the learners' cognitive structures. Reception learning results when all of the substance necessary for learning is presented to the learner, so the learner is not required to relate new ideas to prior knowledge. In reception learning, cognitive activity is limited to assimilating the new material and integrating it with what is known. Discovery learning occurs when all material necessary to solve a problem is not presented, and the learner is required to reorganize available information and call upon prior learning for the problem's solution.

Subsumption Theory.   Advance organizers are grounded in subsumption theory.   Subsumption theory assumes that rote learning is less resistant to forgetting, because it is not anchored to any cognitive context. Therefore, information becomes meaningful insofar as we are able to relate it to something we know.

Our cognitive structures, according to Ausubel, are organized hierarchically with broader, more inclusive concepts at the top subsuming less inclusive subconcepts, which in turn subsume more concrete and specific concepts and instances.   Through this process of *progressive differentiation*, we elaborate our knowledge bases from greater to lesser inclusiveness, each idea in the hierarchy linked to the next higher step through a process known as subsumption.

If we assume that content or subject matter is also hierarchically organized, then what is known about any subject can also be conceived of as a pyramid, with the most abstract or inclusive classes of knowledge subsuming less inclusive classes of knowledge on down to individual instances. So, new material becomes meaningful to the extent that it can be subsumed under relevant existing concepts.

To the degree that we can incorporate material into our existing cognitive structure, that is, conceptually anchor it to what we know, that new material will be more meaningful.   In so doing, that material will become more stable and therefore less susceptible to forgetting. Stabilization of new ideas into the learner's cognitive structure is the key idea in subsumption theory. Meaningful learning does not entail the mere absorption of ideas but rather the stable incorporation of ideas into one's prior knowledge structure. If relevant subsuming concepts are not available in the learner's cognitive structure, the learner will attempt to relate it to the most appropriate concepts available, providing less than optimal anchorage and resulting in less learning and retention.

EXAMPLES OF ADVANCE ORGANIZERS

Table 19.1 describes a number of advance organizers along with the topic of the presentation.

APPLICATIONS OF ADVANCE ORGANIZERS

Mayer (1979a) contends that meaningful learning depends on reception of the material to be learned, availability in the learner of a meaningful set of past experiences (assimilative context), and activation of that context during learning. The key to assimilation theory is the integration of the new information with the learner's prior knowledge. The organizer must en courage the learner to actively integrate the new material with the old. He concluded that organizers will work only:

- when a learner does not possess or normally use an assimilative context for learning new material;

Topic of Presentation	Organizer Topic	Type of Organizer
Metallurgical properties of carbon steel	Major similarities and differences between metals and alloys, their respective advantages, disadvantages, and reasons for making/using alloys	Expository
House wiring and flow of electricity	Plumbing and the flow of water through pipes	Comparative
Supply and demand	Principles of Keynesian economics -- you can charge what the market will bear	Expository
Endocrinology of pubescence	Uniformity and variability of primary and secondary sex characteristics	Expository
Intelligent tutoring systems	Classes of artificial intelligence including microworlds, knowledge based systems, and intelligent CAI	Expository
Buddhism	Comparing doctrines of Buddhism to Christianity	Comparative
Making beer	Fermentation of grains for creating alcohol	Expository

Table 19.1. Examples of advance organizers.

- when material is potentially conceptual and unfamiliar to the learner, thereby lacking the necessary organization for incorporation;
- when the learner lacks related knowledge or abilities;
- when the organizer provides a high-level context for learning;
- when tests of learning measure breadth of transfer rather than recall.

Based on several of his own studies, Mayer (1979b) concluded that organizers will most effectively facilitate learning when:

- far transfer of knowledge (as opposed to near transfer recall) is required,
- organizers are presented prior to learning for transfer materials (near transfer facilitated by postorganizer);
- conceptual information is presented that relates material to other ideas (retention of detail facilitated by postorganizers);
- low-ability subjects fail to possess or use an assimilative context;
- textual material is unorganized;
- discovery method is employed to produce far transfer learning; and
- organizer is presented prior to task requiring storage and integration of premises (postorganizer group retained presented organization).

PROCEDURE FOR DEVELOPING ADVANCE ORGANIZERS

1. Determine if organizers are appropriate. Before you begin constructing organizers, you should first determine if they are necessary or appropriate. Advance organizers are appropriate (Ausubel, 1963; Bransford & Johnson, 1973) in these situations:

   • Use organizers when material is novel, when readers are not likely to have encountered the concepts before. Organizers are not needed for familiar material.
   • Use organizers when the material is difficult, when you anticipate that readers will have difficulty understanding the material.
   • Do not use organizers for short passages with only a single theme they are not necessary.
   • Use organizers when the reader's ability is limited. Facilitating the construction of an ideational framework for understanding is the basis for organizers and the weakness of lower-ability learners.
   • If the text passage for which you are writing and organizing is well-organized, with built-in organizers, adjunct organizers are not necessary.

2. Define the type of organizer to be used. Once you have decided that organizers will facilitate learning and/or retention, you need to determine the more appropriate type of organizer to use — expository or comparative. In order to do this, ask yourself:

   • What conceptual models can be used to compare the information presented in the passage?
   • Are the learners familiar enough with that information to use it as a conceptual model? Such a determination may be based on evidence of prior learning (e.g., pretest, courses completed).
   • If relevant conceptual structures (ideas to which new material may be related) are available, write a comparative organizer.
   • If no relevant conceptual structures are available, write   an expository organizer.

3. Write the organizer.

   (a)   Analyze text passages, scripts, or storyboards to identify the main topic.
   (b)   Enumerate the main points of the passage, script, or storyboard.
   (c)   Determine the appropriate level of inclusiveness, that is what points should be abstracted?
   (d)   Write the organizer. It should be relatively short (50-500 words) or approximately 10% to 15% percent of the length of the lesson.

(e) Try interspersing organizers throughout the passage or script. For instance, try beginning each section of the passage with one to two sentence organizers (Rickards, 1976).

(f) Occasionally, formulate organizers in question form rather than standard, expository form, or write organizers in different forms Mayer (1979a), such as:

- concrete models or diagrams of content (see structured overviews, Chapter 16)
- analogies
- examples
- sets of higher order rules
- discussions of main themes in general terms.
- illustrations (Royer & Cable, 1976)
- maps (Dean & Kulhavy, 1979).

(g) Avoid writing organizers that are:
- factual presentations
- summaries
- outlines
- directions to attend to specific portions of text.

4. Evaluate the organizer. Mayer (1979b) presented a checklist for evaluating the potential effectiveness of your organizer.

(a) Does the organizer require the learner to generate some or all of the logical relationships in the material to be learned? That is, will the learners be thinking about the material or just memorizing it? Will they be integrating the new material with the old?

(b) Does the organizer provide a means for relating the new material to the learner's existing, familiar knowledge?

(c) Is the organizer learnable and understandable to the learners? Like analogies, organizers are useful only if the learner understands them.

(d) Would the learners usually fail to identify an use organizing information (what Mayer calls *assimilative set*) because of inexperience or time pressures. If so, an organizer is likely to be more effective.

EFFECTIVENESS OF ADVANCE ORGANIZERS

Ausubel, who conceived of advance organizers and the subsumption theory on which they are based, published most of the early research on their effectiveness (Ausubel, 1960; Ausubel & Fitzgerald, 1961, 1962; Ausubel & Youseff, 1963; Fitzgerald & Ausubel, 1963). Almost all of these assessed the effectiveness of organizers using novel subjects with undergraduate students. All of the studies reported that organizer groups recalled and re-

effectiveness of organizers using novel subjects with undergraduate students. All of the studies reported that organizer groups recalled and retained more than control groups, who were usually presented with an historical overview. Although statistically significant, the advantages for organizer-preceded passages were not very large. Ausubel's results were not regarded as adequate substantiation of subsumption theory by many researchers (Faw & Waller, 1976).

Reasons for the inconsistent showing of organizers are numerous. One of the primary reasons that organizers may not work is because learners do not use them effectively (Kloster & Winne, 1989)   Hartley and Davies (1976) attributed the inconsistencies to the problem of generating and recognizing advance organizers, a claim that Ausubel (1978) vehemently denied. Mayer (1979b), in a series of studies, suggested that the wrong questions were assessing the wrong variable. The strongest criticism to date was provided by MacDonald-Ross (1979), who concluded that the entire theoretical framework for organizers was unsound and that organizer research exemplified, "the tendency of weakly grounded empirical research to produce more confusion, the more experiments are conducted" (p. 252). He claimed that subsumption theory, based on hierarchical models of memory and of subject matter structure, is inaccurate and that the most logical structure of cognition is heterarchical, not hierarchical. His concerns were echoed by McEneany (1990) who claimed that fundamental notions of subsumption theory were questionable thereby raising doubts about the generalizable use of organizers. Barnes and Clawson (1975) concluded that they simply do not work.

Hartley and Davies (1976) summarized the results of several years of research by concluding that:

- Organizers seem to facilitate learning and retrieval, although a number of studies failed to support this conclusion.
- The effects of organizers seem to be specific and cannot be generalized.
- Organizers need not be prose passages; effective organizers have taken the form of games, models, and visuals.
- Organizers need not necessarily be presented in advance of instruction in order to be effective. Postorganizers have also facilitated learning.

More recent reviews of research have used the technique known as meta-analysis, where researchers aggregate and compare studies based on effect sizes which are comparisons based upon the standard deviation (Glass, 1977). A meta-analysis of 132 studies (Luiten, Ames, & Ackerson, 1980) concluded that organizers do in fact facilitate both learning and retention. Stone (1983) conducted a meta-analysis on different characteristics of organizers and learning conditions finding that:
- overall, advance organizers facilitate recall and retention
- illustrated organizers are more effective
- nonsubsuming organizers are more effective than hierarchical ones

- expository organizers are more effective than comparative
- concrete organizers are more effective than abstract.

Learner Interactions

The nature of advance organizers predicts that they will most benefit learners with lower levels of prior knowledge. While most of the research has focused on the cognitive effects of organizers, few have looked for learner interactions. The review of research conducted by Hartley and Davies (1976) reported that:

- Organizers generally benefit older, more intellectually capable learners than younger, less able students.
- For the less able learners, expository organizers are more effective than comparative.

Stone's (1983) meta-analysis provided some conflicting evidence, when she reported that :

- Organizers are more effective at the junior high school level than elementary, high school or college, and
- Females seem to benefit more from them than males.

Content/Task Interactions

Stone (1983) reported that :

- organizers were more effective for factual and formula type content rather than generalized knowledge;
- organizers appear to be more effective in the science and mathematics content areas.

It is reasonable to expect that organizers would be most effective for conceptually rich material that does not require very far transfer.

Advantages of Advance Organizers

- In the correct circumstances, organizers will aid comprehension and retention of ideas.

- Organizers facilitate generative processing by requiring learners to relate new information to prior knowledge.

- Organizers are a popular instructional strategy and the subject of extensive research (Newell, 1984).

Disadvantages of Advance Organizers

• Using organizers requires more time to be spent on learning.

• Organizers may interfere with learners' normally successful strategies.

• Organizers are less likely to aid far transfer of learning.

• Organizers are difficult to operationalize for designers. The process for constructing organizers is not systematized or well understood.

REFERENCES

Ausubel, D.P. (1960). The use of advance organizers in the learning and retention of meaningful verbal material. *Journal of Educational Psychology, 5*, 267-272.

Ausubel, D.P. (1962). A subsumption theory of meaningful verbal learning and retention. *Journal of General Psychology, 66*, 213-224.

Ausubel, D.P. (1963).*The psychology of meaningful verbal learning.* New York: Grune & Stratton.

Ausubel, D.P. (1968). *Educational psychology: A cognitive view.* New York: Holt, Rinehart, & Winston.

Ausubel, D.P. (1978). In defense of advance organizers A reply to the critics. *Review of Educational Research, 48*, 251-257.

Ausubel, D.P., & Fitzgerald, D. (1961).The role of discriminability in meaningful verbal learning and retention. *Journal of Educational Psychology, 52*, 266-274.

Ausubel, D.P., & Fitzgerald, D. (1962). Organizer general background, and antecedent learning variables in sequential verbal learning. *Journal of Educational Psychology, 53*, 243-249.

Ausubel, D.P., Robbins, L.C., & Blake, E. (1957). Retroactive inhibition and facilitation in the learning of school materials. *Journal of Educational Psychology, 48*, 334-343.

Ausubel, D.P., & Youseff, M. (1963). The role of discriminability in meaningful parallel learning. *Journal of Educational Psychology, 54*, 331-336.

Barnes, B., & Clawson, E. (1975). Do advance organizers facilitate learning? Recommendations for further research based on an analysis of 32 students. *Review of Educational Research, 45*, 637-659.

Bransford, J.D., & Johnson, M.K. (1973). Considerations of some problems of comprehension. In W. Chase (Ed.), *Visual information processing.* New York: Academic Press.

Dean, R.S., & Kulhavy, R.W. (1979, April). *The influence of spatial organization in prose learning.* Paper presented at Annual Meeting of American Educational Research Association, San Francisco.

Faw, H.W., & Waller, T.G. (1976). Mathemagenic behaviors and efficiency in learning from prose materials. Review, critique, and recommendations. *Review of Educational Research, 46*, 239-265.

Fitzgerald, D., & Ausubel, D.P. (1963). Cognitive versus affective factors in the learning and retention of controversial material. *Journal of Educational Psychology, 54*, 73-84.

Glass, G. (1977). Integrating findings: The meta-analysis of research. *Review of Educational Research, 53*, 352-379.

Hartley, J., & Davies, I.K. (1976). Pre-instructional strategies: The role of pretests, behavioral objectives, overviews, and advance organizers. *Review of Educational Research, 46,* 239-265.

Kloster, A.M., & Winne, P. (1989). The effects of different types of organizers on student's learning from text. *Journal of Educational Psychology, 81,* 9-15.

Luiten, J., Ames, A., & Ackerson, G. (1980). A meta-analysis of the effects of advance organizers on learning and retention. *American Educational Research Journal, 17,* 211-218.

MacDonald-Ross, M. (1979). Language in texts. In L.S. Shulman (Ed.), *Review of research in education* (Vol. 6). Itasca, IL: Peacock.

Mayer, R.E. (1979a). Twenty years of research on advance organizers: Assimilation theory is still the best predictor of results. *Instructional Science, 8,* 133-167.

Mayer, R.E. (1979b). Can advance organizers influence meaningful learning? *Review of Educational Research, 49,* 371-383.

McEneany, J.E. (1990). Do advance organizers facilitate learning? A review of subsumption theory. *Journal of Research and Development in Education, 23* (2), 8-96.

Newell, J. (1984). Advance organizers: Their construction and use in instructional development. In R. Bass & C. Dills (Eds.), *Instructional development: The state of the art* (Vol 2). Dubuque, Iowa : Kendall/Hunt Publishing. Co

Rickards, J.P. (1976). Interaction of position and conceptual level of adjunct questions on immediate and delayed retention of text. *Journal of Educational Psychology, 68,* 210-217.

Royer, J.M., & Cable, G.W. (1976). Illustrations, analogies, and facilitative transfer in prose learning. *Journal of Educational Psychology, 68,* 205-209.

Stone, C.L. (1983). A meta-analysis of advance organizer studies. *Journal of Experimental Education, 51,* 194-199.

Part IV

Structural Knowledge Learning Strategies:

Chapter 20   Pattern Notes
Chapter 21   Spider Maps
Chapter 22   Frame Games
Chapter 23   Networks
Chapter 24   Node Acquisition and Integration Technique

INTRODUCTION

In this last section, we explore learning strategies that facilitate the acquisition of structural knowledge (see Fig. IV.1). Learning strategies are mental operations that the learner may use to acquire, retain, and retrieve different kinds of knowledge, in this case, structural knowledge. Learning strategies are generalizable skills that enable learners to take an active, constructive role in generating meaning for information by accessing and applying prior knowledge to new material. Learning strategies are intended to increase the number of links between presented information and existing knowledge which is an essential aspect of structural knowledge. Learning strategies may be applied to knowledge acquisition in different content domains. They typically entail complex cognitive transformations and elaborations that are required by specific learning strategies. Examples of commonly used learning strategies include paraphrasing, creating images, generating questions, cognitive mapping, comparison-contrasts, and so on. In these activities, information is transformed and elaborated to make it more meaningful for the learner. Researchers (Tessmer & Jonassen, 1988) have argued for the explicit teaching of cognitive learning strategies or the embedding of those strategies in instruction to foster deeper, more meaningful thinking from students.

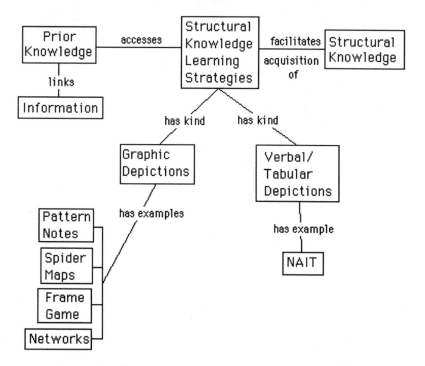

Fig. IV.1. Structural knowledge learning strategies.

The learning strategies described in this final section are designed to foster structural knowledge acquisition. Like the other techniques described in this volume, they are intended to focus learners' attention on the interrelationships between ideas in the content domain being studied. Although most of the methods described in this book have some implication as learning strategies (as described in each chapter under the Acquiring Structural Knowledge section), the primary and explicit purpose of these techniques is to function as learning strategies. The first four strategies, pattern notes, spider maps, frame game, and networking, are graphic techniques. These techniques are very similar in purpose and function. In fact, at least three of them could be substituted for each other with no probable change in process or product. The final technique, the node acquisition and integration technique, uses a tabular format. However, they all focus on concepts and interrelationships.

REFERENCE

Tessmer, M., & Jonassen, D.H. (1988). Learning strategies. In N.D.C. Harris (Ed.), *World yearbook of education*. London: Kogan Page.

20

Structural Knowledge Learning Strategies: Pattern Notes

DESCRIPTION OF PATTERN NOTES

Pattern noting is a self-report technique for associating ideas together and displaying the arrangement of the ideas. The pattern usually starts with a central theme which is blocked in the center of the page. The central idea may be the main topic of a report, lecture, or the subject being analyzed for instruction. The pattern noter then free associates about the idea, thinking of all of the ideas s/he can that are related to the idea. These ideas are linked to the central topic. Each of those ideas are also free associated with ideas linked to them by lines, so that the pattern noter develops an enlarging web of ideas. When the pattern is large enough, the noter then looks at all of the ideas and interconnects related ideas by direct lines.

Pattern noting is a notetaking technique that was developed by Buzan (1974) for organizing and displaying information in a relational manner. Buzan referred to them as "brain patterns," however they are referred to more commonly as pattern notes. Buzan observed that information is normally recorded in regular verbal notes in a linear manner, because we listen to lectures or read materials in a linear sequence. If we accept the cognitive principle that the organization of ideas in memory constitutes a network of interrelated and integrated concepts, then our organizational devices (notes, outlines, etc.) should be similarly structured (Buzan, 1974).

So, pattern notes (see Fig. 20.1 for an example of a pattern note on the functions of pattern noting) function as a spatial word association task where the distance between ideas on the pattern generally represents their semantic distance between each other in memory, reflecting their degree of relatedness in one's knowledge structure. Each idea is displayed on the page with lines (representing relationships) linking it to a central idea and to other related ideas.

Examples of Pattern Notes

Pattern notes can be generated for any topic. Figure 20.1 shows a pattern note on pattern noting.

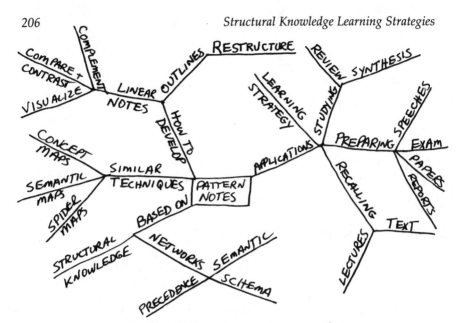

Fig. 20.1. Pattern note on pattern noting.

The pattern note in Fig. 20.2 was drawn by a high school student during an experiment (Jonassen, 1987). It was completed in 1 1/2 minutes.

APPLICATIONS OF PATTERN NOTES

Pattern notes can be used for a variety of purposes (see Fig. 20.1 for a graphic description). For instance, pattern notes are useful for notetaking from books, lectures or other learning materials (Buzan, 1984). They are also used for "getting ideas together" (organizing) papers or reports or for studying for an exam (Fields, 1982). Pattern noting also comprises a general organizational strategy for helping learners learn by reflecting the organization of ideas in memory and acting as a memory retrieval aid (Jonassen, 1984). This is especially useful if learners classify the nature of the links that they create. Research has shown that pattern notes may also be used to map cognitive structure, discussed in Chapter 1 (Jonassen, 1987).

Representing/Assessing Structural Knowledge.

Jonassen (1987) showed that pattern notes are an efficient and effective means for assessing cognitive structure (structural knowledge). He compared the pattern notes developed by students to free word associations, the benchmark method for assessing cognitive structure (Preece, 1976). Using multidimensional scaling, he showed that the structures of the pattern notes were nearly identical to the structures of the word associations.

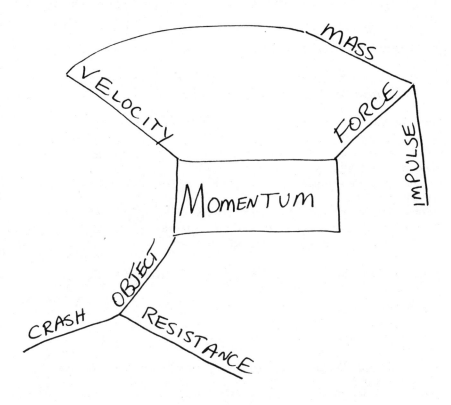

Fig. 20.2. Pattern note from experiment.

Have students generate pattern notes at different points during instruction, emphasizing the growth and development of the schemata related to the ideas being covered. Be sure that they classify the links as well as generate the pattern (Jonassen, 1984). It is important that learners understand the relationship between the ideas.

Conveying Structural Knowledge

Pattern notes that are created by the teacher or lecturer may be used as advanced graphic organizers (see Chapters 16 and 19) of content to be taught. By illustrating all of the ideas contained in a lesson and how they interrelate to each other and to other units of instruction, learning of those ideas can be facilitated. The pattern note should be referred to at the beginning of the lesson and periodically throughout the lesson as a synthesizer,

"These are the ideas that we have covered, and notice how they are related...."

Acquiring Structural Knowledge

Pattern noting is an excellent learning/study strategy for helping students acquire knowledge. The following activities will support learning:

* Rearranging the linear flow of ideas in a lecture or book into a content map;
* Use pattern notes for organizing information while studying for an exam, especially an essay exam;
* Generate pattern notes as a retrieval tool, when sitting in the exam trying to get started;
* Substitute pattern notes for other network tools, such as network analysis (PERT, critical path, precedence diagrams), topical networks, algorithms, and conceptual networks

PROCEDURE FOR DEVELOPING PATTERN NOTES

Assumptions

Pattern notes have been shown to be an effective and accurate means of externalizing (mapping) cognitive structure, that is, the arrangement of ideas in memory (Jonassen, 1987). They have also been shown to the be an effective noting technique for representing the organization of subject matter content. Therefore, we assume that pattern notes are an effective means for representing and displaying the organization of knowledge and subject content.

1. Identify main topic. Start with a blank sheet of paper, chalkboard, or other display surface. Clarify the main topic for consideration. What is the most essential concept being considered? This may be the skill you are analyzing or the main content area that you are inventorying. Write that topic in capital letters in the middle of the page and draw a box around it.

```
┌─────────┐
│ Main    │
│ Topic   │
└─────────┘
```

2. Identify primary issues. Now clear your mind. On the back of the sheet of paper or on the edge of the page, quickly write down the first 5-10 things that come to your mind when you think of the main topic. This is a free association task. Select the more important of those related topics. Which are the key issues related to the main topic? Write those

words alongside or around the topic. Draw a line underneath each issue joining it to the main topic. Can you think of additional topics?

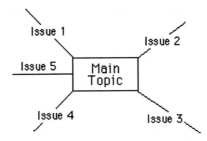

3. Identify subissues. Repeat step two for each of the issues. That is, for each issue, write down a list of words, check them, and then draw a line underneath each word and connect it to the end of the line underneath the issue.

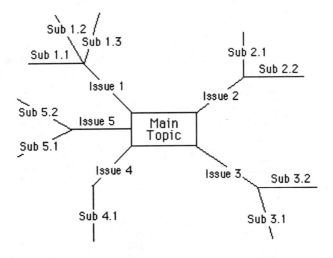

4) Identify sub-subissues. Repeat step three for each of the subissues that you can think of. Decide now if your pattern needs more development or elaboration. If you have not adequately described the subject domain, add additional layers of detail.

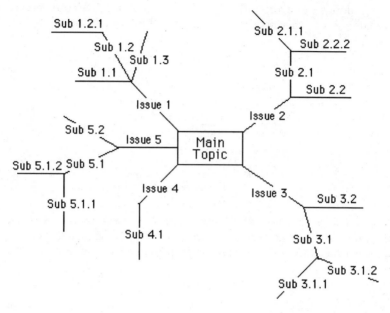

5. Compare each of the issues, subissues, and sub-subissues with each other. See if there are inter-inkages. That is, are words in different parts of the pattern related to each other? If they are, draw lines between the words.

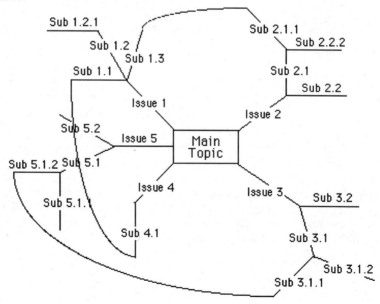

Note: A new class of computer based tools has evolved, known as semantic networking tools, that can facilitate the development of pattern notes. Programs such as SemNet (Fisher, 1990), Learning Tool (Kozma, 1987), TextVision (Kommers, 1989), and Inspiration are powerful mindtools that provide the visual tools to develop pattern notes.

EFFECTIVENESS OF PATTERN NOTES

Practically no empirical verifications of pattern noting exist. The technique is supported by a lot of anecdotal evidence. It is generally recognized as an effective notetaking technique and study strategy. It has been verified as a means for mapping cognitive structure, that is, it was compared with the results of free word associations (the benchmark method for assessing cognitive structure) and found to produce the same structures (Jonassen, 1987).

Advantages of Pattern Notes

- The main idea in a pattern note is clearly defined and explained in terms of related ideas.

- The relative importance of each idea is spatially identified.

- The relationships (links) between concepts are clearly recognizable.

- Pattern notes improve recall and retrieval of information.

- Pattern notes are a useful instructional strategy for introducing new content.

- Pattern noting is a simple technique that is easier to use than other mapping techniques.

Disadvantages of Pattern Noting

- Pattern noting is not easily accomplished by nonspatial thinkers

- Pattern noting does not normally involve labeling links, however this can be done easily (Jonassen, 1984).

REFERENCES

Buzan, T. (1974). *Use both sides of your brain.* New York: E.P. Dutton.
Fields, A. (1982). Getting started: Pattern notes and perspectives. In D.H. Jonassen (Ed.), *The technology of text: Principles for structuring, designing, and displaying text.* Englewood Cliffs, NJ: Educational Technology Publications.

Fisher, K.M. (1990). Semantic networking: The new kid on the block. *Journal of Research in Science Teaching, 27*(11), 1001-1018.

Jonassen, D.H. (1984). Developing a learning strategy using pattern notes: A new technology. *Programmed Learning and Educational technology, 21*(3), 163-175.

Jonassen, D.H. (1987). Assessing cognitive structure: Verifying a method using pattern notes. *Journal of Research and Development in Education, 20*(3), 1-14.

Kommers, P. (1989). *Textvision.* Enschede, NL: University of Twente.

Kozma, R. (1987). The implications of cognitive psychology for computer- based learning tools. *Educational Technology, 27*(11), 20-25.

Preece, P.F.W. (1976). Mapping cognitive structure: A comparison of methods. *Journal of Educational Psychology, 68,* 1-9.

21

Structural Knowledge Learning Strategies: Spider Maps

DESCRIPTION OF SPIDER MAPS

Spider maps represent a technique that was developed by Hanf (1971) as an alternative to traditional notetaking from text. In spider mapping the main idea of the text passage is written in the center of a page and related subordinate concepts are drawn on lines connected to the central idea. Additional lines with increasingly detailed content can be added to the drawing, with the end product looking similar to a spider web. Spider maps can be seen as simplified pattern notes (see Chapter 20), as the format for representing ideas and relationships is similar. Spider maps differ from pattern notes in that only hierarchical relationships between ideas are depicted in spider maps, whereas in pattern notes relationships between coordinate concepts are depicted.

The spider mapping strategy was originally developed as a means of noting the structure of a passage of text. However, it can also be used as a general mapping strategy by including content from prior knowledge or multiple sources when generating the spider map, thus representing content structure.

Rationale

Hanf (1971) identified three main benefits of spider mapping. First, spider mapping assists in the development of critical thinking by freeing learnersto select important ideas and organize them into a meaningful pattern, and integrating ideas into a relevant whole without the constraints of formal, linear writing. Second, mapping improves reasoning skills by requiring learners to organize and analyze thoughts. Finally, spider mapping improves memory by organizing details in relation to main ideas.

When main ideas are recalled, the details are also more likely to be recalled as part of the integrated knowledge structure. Although Hanf did not relate spider mapping to schema theory in her presentation of the technique, spider mapping is certainly consistent with this theory.

EXAMPLES OF SPIDER MAPS

Figure 21.1 shows a spider map of types of rocks. This map might be used for a unit in which students learn about different types and characteristics of rocks. Landscaping plants are depicted in spider map format in Fig. 21.2.

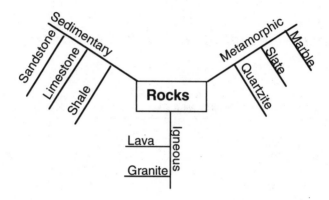

Fig. 21.1. Spider map of rocks.

APPLICATIONS OF SPIDER MAPS

Spider maps can be used as a prewriting activity to help learners generate ideas about a topic area, and to organize those ideas in place of a linear outline. Drawing a map assists learners in identifying key topics in a subject area, and provides a mechanism for identifying links between those topic areas. Drawing maps in this manner may help writers organize their ideas and serve as a stimulus to writing. Maps help not only inexperienced writers in organizing their thoughts, but are also used by more experienced writers when planning their writing (Buckley & Owen, 1981).

Representing/Assessing Structural Knowledge

Spider maps depict the relationships between ideas in a content area. When drawing a spider map a the map maker must make decisions about how to organize the map and what type of content to include on the map. Thus, spider maps depict the map maker's ideas about a what is important in a content area, and the hierarchical relationship between these ideas. In this manner, the map maker's structural knowledge is represented by the spider map. However, representing structural knowledge is not their explicit purpose.

In instructional settings, the maps generated by learners can be reviewed by an instructor as a basic check on the learner's understanding of the relationship between ideas in the content area. Areas of inaccuracy in understanding may be identified in this manner, allowing for corrective instruction of the misunderstandings.

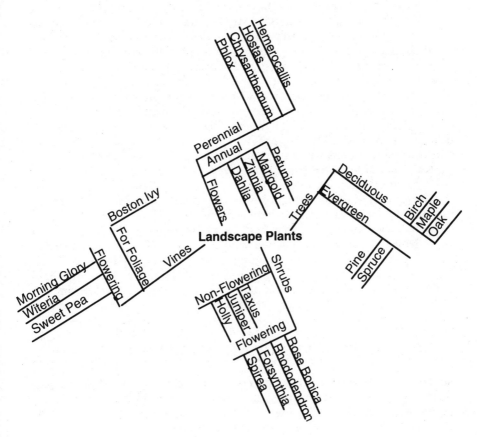

Fig. 21.2. Spider map of landscaping plants.

Conveying Structural Knowledge

Spider maps generated by instructors can be used to help organize lectures. Copies of the maps can be presented to learners as organizers for the instruction. Likewise, spider maps can be used as figures in text to help synthesize material. A series of spider maps may be used as figures, depicting the material that has been covered in the text, and how that material relates to previously covered material. As more material is covered in the text, subsequent spider maps would convey this additional information in more complex maps.

Acquiring Structural Knowledge

Spider maps can be useful for note taking, transforming linear text or lectures into a more organized representation of structure. Mapping content from text ensures that learners identify relationships between ideas as notes are taken. Once a learner has gained proficiency in spider mapping he or she may begin to use the technique to map the content from a lecture, thus providing a more integrated representation of the material covered than would be possible with linear notes.

Spider maps can also be used to promote comprehension as a study strategy. Learners may take a passage of text and map the relationships between ideas to promote understanding. Because text is usually organized in a linear manner, mapping provides a method for depicting the relationships between ideas in a more holistic format. This reorganization of content from notes or text is hypothesized to promote recall of the material, thus improving learning.

The process of constructing a spider map requires learners to determine the hierarchical relationships between concepts, thus helping to build structural knowledge. One may begin a mapping process by identifying a large group of concepts associated with the main idea. Then the learner must organize those ideas by grouping similar concepts, naming or labeling these groups , and depicting the relationships between the ideas in a graphical manner. The organization of the ideas, and then structuring the ideas into a unified whole, helps the learner to build knowledge structures in the content area.

PROCEDURE FOR DEVELOPING SPIDER MAPS

Spider maps can be drawn as an classroom activity, with students participating in brainstorming sessions to identify ideas related to the main topic. Alternatively, spider mapping can be undertaken by an individual. In either case, the basic steps in spider mapping are:

1. Select the main idea for the spider map and write it in the center of the page. Draw a circle, square, or some other geometric shape around the main idea.

2. Brainstorm ideas related to the main idea. Write these concepts down.

3. Categorize the concepts, grouping similar concepts and labeling the groups.   These labels will serve as the first level of subordinate con-

cepts. Identify and categorize all concepts that are important to the central topic and need to be included in the map.

4. Begin with one group of concepts. Write the label for that group on a line leading out from the main idea.

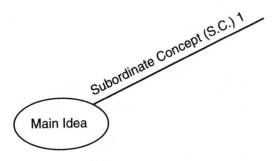

5. List subordinate concepts or ideas on lines leading out from the secondary concepts.

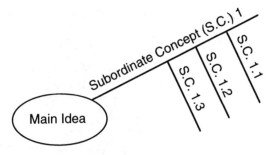

6. Add additional levels of detail to the map by including more lines leading out from the higher levels of the map.

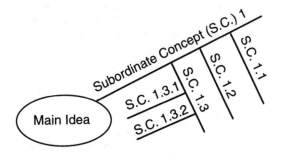

7. Continue to add additional secondary and tertiary concepts to the map until all of the important content is included. Review the map to ensure that correct hierarchical relationships are depicted.

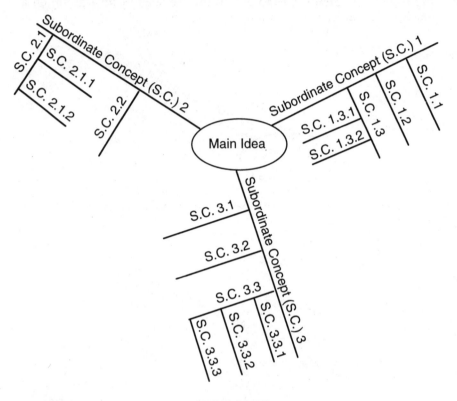

EFFECTIVENESS OF SPIDER MAPS

While spider mapping appears to be an effective means for conveying content structure, controlled studies of the effectiveness of spider maps have not been conducted. Persons who use this technique have suggested that it is an effective study technique to help synthesize knowledge and an effective strategy for organizing writing (Hanf, 1971; Buckley & Owen, 1981).

Learner Interactions

No research on the relationships between learner attributes and spider mapping has appeared in the literature. Like other graphic representational strategies, spider mapping skill may be most easily acquired by learners with strong visual/spatial abilities.

Content/Task Interactions

Spider maps can be constructed for any content area. Content areas with strong hierarchical structures would appear to be best represented by this technique, although no data are available to support this claim.

Advantages of Spider Maps

• Spider mapping is easy to learn.

• The spider map format provides an easily understandable format for depicting hierarchical relationships in a content area.

• Spider mapping requires recall, organization and structuring of concept relationships, thereby improving future recall of the content.

Disadvantages of Spider Maps

• Spider maps depict hierarchical relationships between ideas, but do not depict relationships between coordinate concepts. Thus, a limited picture of the structure of the content is provided with these maps.

REFERENCES

Buckley, M.H., & Owen, B. (1981). *Mapping the writing journey.* Curriculum Publication No. 15. California University, Berkeley School of Education. (ERIC Document Reproduction Service No. ED 225 191).

Hanf, M.B. (1971). Mapping: A technique for translating reading into thinking. *Journal of Reading, 14,* 225-230.

22

Structural Knowledge Learning Strategies:
Frame Games

DESCRIPTION OF FRAME GAMES

The Frame Game is a structural knowledge learning strategy that requires the learner to determine the relationships among important concepts, principles and procedures in a content domain, most often a chapter in a textbook. In fact, it was developed as a textbook supplement by Clifford (1981), entitled "Ed Syke: The Frame Game." Clifford's model of the Frame Game included only concepts and the relationships between them. We believe that the game can be effectively extended to include procedures and principles. The Frame Game combines the advantages of chunking or grouping with visual patterns in order to improve learning. In the game, each relationship pattern is represented with an arrangement of geometric shapes and signs (see Fig. 22.1). Students are presented with a list of important concepts in each textbook chapter and are required to fit the concepts into the blocks. This requires that students figure out which concepts have which relationships to which other concepts.

Although Clifford conceived of only seven types of relationships, we have identified ten basic patterns of relationships for the Frame Game (see Fig. 22.1 for examples of these relationships). Other relationship types might emerge as the Frame Game is applied to new domains.

- *Superordinates/Subordinates/Coordinates Pattern*: A set of terms demonstrating a hierarchical relationship (e.g., computers, mainframe computers, mini-computers, personal computers, Macintosh II ci).
- *Sequence Pattern*: Two or more terms that are related to each other by their order (e.g., spring, summer, fall, winter). The first term in the sequence is placed in the top box; the last, in the bottom box.
- *Parts-Whole Pattern*: Two or more terms, with all but one term being parts of that term.
- *Associates Pattern*: A key term with several terms related to it. Associates might be examples of a class (e.g., fruit: apple, plum, orange, pear) or attributes of a concept (e.g., apple: stem, core, peel, meat). Note that the geometrical shape changes to accommodate the number of parts.

We gratefully acknowledge the help of Peggy Cole on this chapter. She was the primary author.

- *Equals Pattern*: Two terms that can be used interchangeably (e.g., autumn, fall).
- *Opposites Pattern*: Two terms that have opposite meanings (e.g., night, day).
- *Similarity Pattern*: Two terms that are closely related but not interchangeable (e.g., skin, rind).

- *Cause-Effect Pattern*: Two terms or groups of terms, the first of which causes the second (e.g., too much alcohol causes drunkenness; icy roads and careless driving cause accidents).
- *Influence Pattern*: Two terms or groups of terms, the first of which can influence or contribute to the second (e.g., clouds influence the temperature; freezing rain contributes to hypothermia). (Note: This pattern might be considered a variation of the cause-effect pattern.)
- *Analogy Pattern*: An even-numbered set of terms (usually 4) arranged in pairs, with each pair having a similar relationship (e.g., steering wheel is to car as handle bars are to bicycle).

EXAMPLES OF FRAME GAME

A Frame Game can be created for any well defined domain. Figure 22.1 illustrates the ten basic types of relationships that a game can represent. Figure 22.2 shows a completed Frame Game for a chapter in an introductory psychology textbook for college undergraduates. Figure 22.3 shows the game as students would receive it for a homework assignment.

APPLICATIONS OF FRAME GAME

The Frame Game was originally designed as a textbook study strategy to promote comprehension. As such, it requires students to think about the relationships among the concepts introduced in each chapter of the textbook. Furthermore, it provides visual cues for chunking the material, both of which are hypothesized to promote recall of the material. The Frame Game constitutes a generalized structural knowledge learning strategy that may support learning from textbooks, lectures, or any type of material.

There are a variety of methods for integrating the Frame Game in different instructional settings.

1. *Modeling*: During discussions, lead the students in constructing frames and providing explanations of the relationships. Or after class discussion of the related chapter, lead students in solving the Frame Game for the whole chapter.
2. *Discussion guide*: After class discussion of the related chapter, have the students work collaboratively (3 or 4 students) to solve the Frame Game and provide explanations of the relationships. Provide feedback.

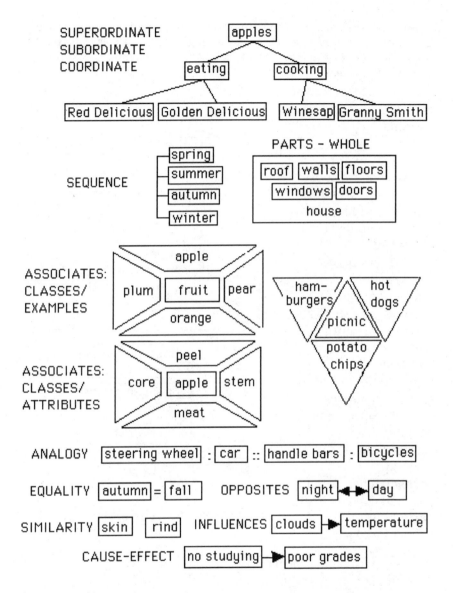

Fig. 22.1. Relationship patterns in the frame game.

3. *Homework*: After class discussion of the related chapter(s), distribute copies of the game to each student for homework. Provide feedback.
4. *Competitive races*: Have students individually or collaboratively play the game in class.

5. *Interactive courseware*: The Frame Game could readily be embedded in
    computer-assisted instruction and testing. Varying levels of help could
    provide a review of the types of relationships, examples, and hints for
    solving a particular relationship.

associative learning
chaining
classical conditioning
cognitive learning
conditioned response
conditioned stimulus
discriminated response
discriminated stimulus
extinction
fixed interval
fixed ratio
generalization
habituation
law of contiguity
law of effect
learning
negative reinformcement
operant conditioning
partial reinforcement schedule
punishment
reinforcement
shaping
unconditioned response
unconditioned stimulus
variable interval
variable response

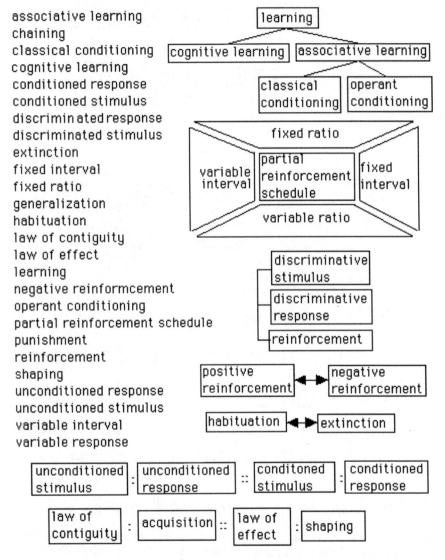

Fig. 22.2. Completed frame game.

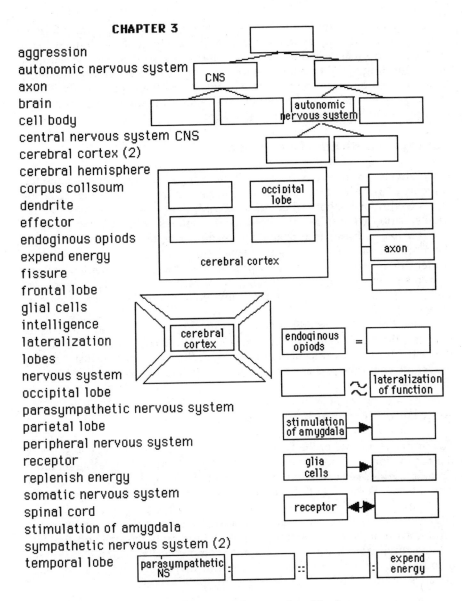

CHAPTER 3

aggression
autonomic nervous system
axon
brain
cell body
central nervous system CNS
cerebral cortex (2)
cerebral hemisphere
corpus collsoum
dendrite
effector
endoginous opiods
expend energy
fissure
frontal lobe
glial cells
intelligence
lateralization
lobes
nervous system
occipital lobe
parasympathetic nervous system
parietal lobe
peripheral nervous system
receptor
replenish energy
somatic nervous system
spinal cord
stimulation of amygdala
sympathetic nervous system (2)
temporal lobe

Fig. 22.3. Frame game top be completed by learner.

Representing/Assessing Structural Knowledge

The Frame Game may be effectively used to assess structural knowledge acquisition similarly to the verbal tests described in Chapter 9. It depicts the relationships between concepts, principles, and procedures in a well structured domain. In completing the game, the learner must organize information and match it to an expert's graphic representation of the domain. The student's performance in the game allows the instructor to assess the learner's understanding of the relationships among elements in the domain. Discrepancies between the student's answers and the expert's provide the opportunity for the instructor to probe the logic of the student's answers and to provide additional instruction if necessary.

Conveying Structural Knowledge

Alternatively, an instructor may distribute completed copies of the game for students to use as an graphical advance organizer (for example, Fig. 22.2) before a lecture or textbook chapter. Likewise, the Frame Game may be distributed prior to a lecture with the students completing them as the information is revealed during lecture and discussion. Although such organizers lack the motivational value of the games, they are an attractive alternative when student or instructor time is at a premium. Organizers benefited college students in an introductory psychology course (Jonassen, Cole, & Bamford, 1992). Furthermore, students in the study tended to prefer the organizers to the games.

Instead of using the Frame Game as an organizer, the instructor might complete the Frame Game *during* instruction. This technique not only allows the instructor to convey structural knowledge, it also allows the instructor to model the cognitive processes required to structure knowledge and to solve the game.

Acquiring Structural Knowledge

The primary purpose of the Frame Game is as a learning strategy to support the acquisition of structural knowledge. The process of completing a Frame Game requires learners to determine the relationships among the important concepts in a knowledge domain. The learner must identify the type of relationship a given set of frames represents (e.g., in Fig. 22.3, the cause-effect relationship depicted for "stimulation of amygdala"), and then search memory (or if this is not a test, notes or text) to recall or identify the effect of stimulating the amygdala. If the Frame Game is comprehensive, completing it will help the learner build a comprehensive knowledge structure of the domain which is reinforced with a graphic representation.

PROCEDURE FOR DEVELOPING AND USING FRAME GAMES

1. Identify the content area. This may include a chapter in the textbook or a series of lectures.

2. Identify the key terms, concepts, principles, and procedures that relate to the course/unit objectives. In textbooks, lists of concepts are often included with the textbook or in the teacher's edition of the book. At first, you may have many more concepts than you can use (see steps 8-10.).

3. Identify the relationships among the concepts, principles and procedures.

4. Construct sets of frames which represent the relationships most important in mastering the objectives.

5. Complete one frame/slot in each set of frames. Complete a frame/slot in one of the lower levels of hierarchical relationships; if the analogy is particularly difficult, complete one slot in *each* of the pairs of terms in an analogy.

6. Estimate the amount of time that it will take for learners to complete the sets of frames. (The amount of time may increase significantly as the difficulty of the material and the number of terms in the exercise increase.)

7. Construct an alphabetized list of all the terms used in the exercise and a template of the sets of frames. If a term is used more than once, put the number of times used in parentheses after the term (e.g., see "cerebral cortex" in Figs. 22.2 and 22.3). The frames should be large enough for learners to write the names of the terms. (Although no research has been conducted on this issue, it is hypothesized that writing and seeing the actual term in the frames will facilitate learning the relationships, particularly for visually-oriented learners).

8. Make sure students understand the 10 basic types of relationships before having them use the Frame Game with the course material. If necessary, provide instruction and have them practice on familiar material first. With usage, this will cease to be a problem.

EFFECTIVENESS OF FRAME GAMES

Logically, the Frame Game appears to be an effective motivational and learning strategy. However, there is little empirical support for using this strategy versus an organizer-instructional strategy (providing students with completed games).

• Jonassen, Cole, and Bamford (1992) compared the effects of the Frame Game learning strategy versus instructor-completed-frames on college students in an introductory psychology course. Although both frame treatments appeared to facilitate learning structural knowledge, there was no significant difference in test scores between the two types of frames treatments.

Learner Interactions

• Jonassen, Cole, and Bamford (1992) found no interactions between learner-generated or instructor-provided frames with field independence.

It is likely that the information processing required by the Frame Game is so intense and deep, that it will wash out any individual differences effects.

Content/Task Interactions

A Frame Game can be constructed for any well defined content domain. The Frame Game has been utilized in introductory psychology courses by its author, but no studies investigating the relative merits of using the Frame Game to convey structural knowledge in other disciplines have been reported.

The Frame Game appears to be most appropriate for tasks that require students to perceive the relationships among declarative or procedural knowledge. Before beginning the Frame Game, learners should already understand the concepts of superordination, subordination, coordination, cause-effect, influence-effect, sequence, parts, whole, similarity, equality, opposite, and analogy. In completing the Frame Game, learners must be able to identify salient attributes of concepts, principles and procedures and perceive the relationships among them. This technique is not well suited for learning tasks involving conditional knowledge (that is, knowledge about when and where to apply declarative and procedural knowledge) or ill-defined domains.

Advantages of the Frame Games

• The game can be used to illustrate types of relationships among concepts, principles and procedures.

• Completing the game requires learners to actively process information; they cannot be passive. Completing the game makes the relationships among the elements of the explicit, thereby promoting learning and future recall.

• The game is versatile. It can be used as a large-group, small-group, or individual activity. It can be used as a study strategy, a motivational activity (individual or group competition), or an assessment tool. It lends itself to print medium or interactive courseware.

Disadvantages of the Frame Games

• The game may require training for students to understand the 10 basic relationships and the geometric representations. It may thus reduce the amount of time otherwise available for instruction in the content area. Because each game is time consuming, inclusion of all the important concepts, principles and procedures is not feasible.

- The game requires considerable motivation (a) to master a new study strategy and (b) to complete each game. Great care must be taken to provide adequate incentives and to demonstrate the value of learning the relationships among the elements of the domain.

- The game may interfere with their preferred learning strategies (often rote memorization). Adequate time and instructional support must be provided for students to incorporate the necessary learning strategies into their repertoire. This may take several months (Duffy & Roehler, 1989).

- The game does not lend itself to conditional knowledge (i.e., knowledge about when and where to apply declarative and procedural knowledge).

- Construction of each game can be very time consuming.

REFERENCES

Clifford, M. (1981). "Ed Syke: The frame game." Supplement to *Practicing educational psychology*. New York: Houghton Mifflin.

Duffy, G. G., & Roehler, L. R. (1989). Why strategy instruction is so difficult and what we need to do about it. In C.McCormick, G.Miller, & M.Pressley (Eds.), *Cognitive strategy research: From basic research to educational applications* (pp. 133-154). New York: Springer-Verlag.

Jonassen, D. H., Cole, P., & Bamford, C. (1992). Learner-generated vs. instructor-provided analysis of semantic relationships. In *Proceedings of selected research presentations*. Washington, D. C.: Association for Educational Communications and Technology, Research and Theory Division.

23

Structural Knowledge Learning Strategies: Networks

DESCRIPTION OF NETWORKS

Networking is a text graphing technique that was developed as part of an overall study strategy program for college students (Dansereau, 1978). The entire study strategy program consists of primary and support strategies. Primary strategies are those techniques that directly assist the learner in identifying and understanding the important and difficult material in a content area. Support strategies are those strategies that are used to set an appropriate mood and environment for learning. Networking was developed as a primary study strategy that incorporates the best aspects of three techniques: paraphrasing, question-answer, and imagery into an overall study strategy (Dansereau, 1978). These three strategies have been shown to produce positive results in student performance when used as study strategies.

The process of networking was developed to promote recall and comprehension of content by requiring learners to remember text material and reorganize it into a non-linear format. Networking produces a spatial organization of concepts or topics into node-link maps where the relationships between concepts are identified. Completed networks are diagrams of words connected to other words by labeled lines. It employs linkages to describe the relationships between nodes. While the "nodes" of a network can be any concept or "idea" word, there are predefined links that are used when networking. The current networking technique includes six types of links that can be used to identify the relationships between concepts. Two links describe hierarchical relationships between concepts. "Part of" indicates that the content in a lower node is a component of the content in the upper node. "Type of" links indicate that the content in the lower node is an example or member of the category expressed in the higher node. A chain link, "leads to" indicates that the content in one node leads to, precedes or results in the content in the second node. Other links show cluster relationships between nodes. The "analogy" link shows that the content in one node is analogous to or similar to the content in another node. Another type of link shows that the content in one node is a "characteristic" or attribute of content in another node. Finally, the "evidence" link shows that the content in one node provides support or proof of content in the second node. Dansereau and his colleagues also developed a more complicated system composed of 13 types of links by expanding on the four classes stated earlier (Dansereau, 1978). Students have found the use of a 6-link system to lack sufficient detail, and the use of the 13-link system difficult to remember and apply. Subsequent research has found the use of a 6-link system to be effective and a good compromise between specificity and generality (Dansereau & Holley, 1982).

Rationale

Networking is based on the network models of memory such as that proposed by Quillian (1968). According to this model, memory is composed of *nodes* (concepts or ideas) that are related to other nodes by named relationships (*links*). See Chapter 1 for more discussion. The networking technique spatially represents semantic networks with concept words linked to other concept words with labeled lines. It is speculated that the use of networking will increase the number of connections between concepts so as to increase understanding, retention, and retrieval of material. By using the networking strategy learners actually draw representations of memory networks.

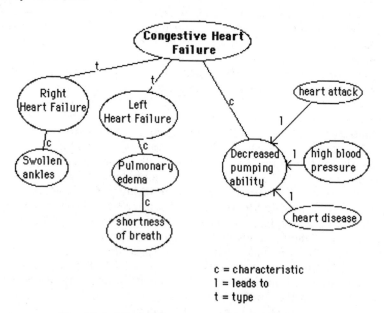

c = characteristic
l = leads to
t = type

Fig. 23.1. Network on congestive heart failure.

Networking is also supported by learning theories regarding cognitive processing. According to the depth of processing theory, recall of content is enhanced if that content is encoded in such a way as to reinforce the meaning of the content rather than its superficial characteristics.

Networking uses meaningful processing because it requires learners to identify which concepts from a content area are related and to indicate the type of relationship between those concepts.

EXAMPLES OF NETWORKS

Figure 23.1 shows a simple network of information about congestive heart failure and it's pharmacological management. Figure 23.2 is a network of concepts related to carbohydrates.

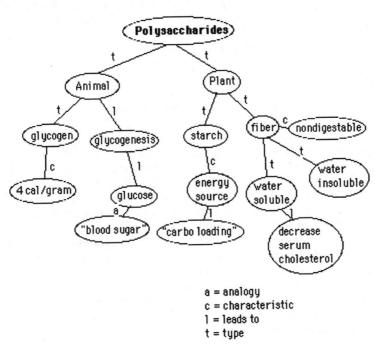

a = analogy
c = characteristic
l = leads to
t = type

Fig. 23.2. Network on carbohydrates.

APPLICATIONS OF NETWORKS

Dansereau and his colleagues have suggested multiple applications of networking (Dansereau, McDonald, Collins, Garland, Holley, Diekhoff, & Evans, 1979). Networks have also been used as a problem solving tool. Networking has been found useful as a tool for organizing, manipulating, and visually representing the problem space to facilitate individual or group problem-solving (Dansereau, 1978).

Potential applications of networking includes its use as a tool for evaluating content and content organization in text. The use of networking in this context would aid in analyzing whether the text is logically organized and whether relationships between ideas are unambiguous. Networking may also provide an index of comprehensibility based on the ease and/or accuracy with which text can be mapped (Dansereau & Holley, 1982).

Representing/Assessing Structural Knowledge

Dansereau suggests that networks may applied to learner assessment. The ability to identify main ideas and express the relationships between ideas in a graphic format, as required in networking, logically seems to be related to reading comprehension. Therefore, it has been suggested that learners' success in drawing clear and accurate networks from a text may give some indication of their reading comprehension ability (Dansereau et al., 1979).

A learner-generated network can serve as a representation of that learner's structural knowledge in a content area. These networks may be reviewed by an instructor to give some idea of the degree to which a learner understands the structural relationships between concepts in a content area. To date no measurement tool has been developed to quantify quality of a network or the degree of similarity between learner's network and an expert's network. However, simple visual inspection of a learner's and an expert's networks may show areas of deficiency in a learner's structural knowledge. Such a comparison may be used as the basis for further instruction or tutorial work.

Because networks so closely resemble the graphics depicting networking models of memory it is easy to assume that the learner's network accurately conveys their structural knowledge. However, the accuracy of a learner's networks is dependent upon his or her mastery of the networking strategy. Learners who do not fully understand the use of networking may draw fairly simplistic networks when, in fact, their knowledge structures are well-developed.

Conveying Structural Knowledge

Networks can be developed by instructors as an alternative to outlining. Although lectures themselves are linear and therefore logically conducive to outlining, networks of a lecture may remind the instructor of links that should be made between ideas as the lecture progresses. Networks drawn by the instructor can be distributed to the class as an advance organizer or post-organizer for a lecture or series of lectures. When used in this manner the networks are referred to as "knowledge maps" (Rewey, Dansereau,

Skaggs, Hall, & Pitre, 1989). Networking can also be used as an outlining technique for preparing presentations or for organizing a response. An instructor may draw a network as a visual aid while giving a lecture which reviews content in an area. In this manner the instructor would model the technique of networking while spatially and verbally representing the content that was just covered in a lesson or series of lessons.

Networks developed by experts in a content area can be used as figures in text or as lecture handouts. Expert-developed networks can be used either before or after instruction to depict the relationships between main ideas in the content area. These networks can serve as an advance organizer of the content to be covered, or as a review of the material in a lesson or unit. Expert generated maps were found to promote recall of main ideas and superordinate ideas (Rewey et al, 1989). These expert-generated networks have the advantage of being both more accurate than learner-generated maps, and more time-efficient, as learners do not have to spend time learning the networking technique and developing their own network maps.

Acquiring Structural Knowledge

Its most common use is as a study technique to reorganize text material to assist recall and comprehension of content. The completed networks may help learners "see the whole picture" rather than concentrating on memorization of detailed content. Networking is designed as a study strategy to promote acquisition of structural knowledge. This process is facilitated by first requiring the learner to identify the important concepts in a content area and then identify the relationships between those concepts. The process of concept and relationship identification directly builds structural knowledge. Learners can use the networking technique to study course material by reorganizing content from a textbook or class notes into a network. The completed network can then be used as a review tool to reinforce learning.

PROCEDURE FOR DEVELOPING NETWORKS

While networking was designed as a strategy for learning from text, networks can also be developed from content learned in another medium or from memory. In any case, the steps for constructing the network are the same.

1. Select the content area, text passage or other instructional materials to be networked.

2. Identify the important concepts in the content area. If necessary, read through or review the materials on the topic. These are represented spatially as the nodes.

3. Begin with the most important concept. Write the concept word on a sheet of paper and draw a circle around it.

4. Select a second concept that is related to the first. Write it on the paper and encircle it. Draw a line between the two concepts.

5. Consider the manner in which the two concepts are related. Is one a "part" of the second? Are the two concepts analogous? Does one concept logically lead to the second concept? Review the six types of links used in networking (type (of), part (of), leads to, analogy, characteristic, evidence) and select the link that best describes the relationship between the two concepts.

6. Label the link by using the first initial of the relationship type ("t" for type, "p" for part, "a" for analogy, "l" for leads to, etc.)

7. Select another concept from the content area, write it on the paper and encircle it. Determine whether this third concept is related to the first concept and the second concept. Draw a line between each of the concept words that are related and label the line according to the type of relationship.

8. Continue this process until all of the important concepts from the content area/text are included on the network graphic.

9. Review the network to ensure that all relationships between ideas have been transformed into links between nodes. Make sure that all links have been labeled with the relationship type.

10. Reorganize the network if necessary to make it more visually appealing and to minimize long lines between nodes. Be certain that all links and nodes are retained when redrawing the network.

11. Retain the network to review prior to testing on the content area.

EFFECTIVENESS OF NETWORKS

While networking has been subjected to a number of studies of its effectiveness, most of the research has used outcome measures requiring recall of main ideas and recall of details. Since recall is presumed to be facilitated by an integrated knowledge network, these studies give some insight into the effectiveness of networking in conveying structural knowledge.

Dansereau et al. (1976) explored the effectiveness of imagery (drawing), paraphrasing, and questioning as study strategies for textbook materials. The results (mean performance) in order from best to worst on a delayed essay test were: paraphrase, imagery, question-answer, and control (students using their own study strategies). The prose material used for these studies has generally been relatively short (1500 words or less). When dealing with longer bodies of information, research suggests that an organizing framework or schema is necessary for complete understanding and may aid in retention. It was therefore conjectured that for long bodies of material, reorganizing the information into a meaningful framework may be more effective than the simple use of paraphrasing, imaging, and questioning.

• Students who received training in the 3-link version of networking did not outperform control subjects on immediate and delayed recall after reading and studying a text passage. Three links were not as comprehensive as necessary for mapping text material (Holley & Dansereau, 1984).

• Using the 13-link model of networking, no differences were found between networking and a control group that did not receive training in the networking technique. This time, while students were found to be responsive to using the strategy, the number of linkages was found to be too cumbersome for students to use (Holley & Dansereau, 1984).

• The 6-link network was developed, and tested within the context of a broader study strategy curriculum (Dansereau, Collins, McDonald, Holley, Garland, Diekhoff, & Evans 1979), and as a separate strategy (Holley, Dansereau, McDonald, Garland, & Collins, 1979; Holley &

Dansereau, 1984). With this 6-link model and approximately 6 hours of training, networking students outperformed control group students on recall of main ideas of a passage (Holley et al., 1979).

• When subjects received training emphasizing recall of both main idea and detail and were able to practice the technique for 7 weeks before testing, there was improved performance on recall of both main ideas and details (Dansereau, Brooks, Holley, & Collins, 1983).

• There is anecdotal support for using networks to promote problem solving. Students who used networking in a graduate psychology seminar indicated that it was a helpful problem solving tool (Dansereau, McDonald et al., 1979).

• Subjects who received expert-prepared networks referred to as "knowledge maps" scored higher on tests of recall of main and intermediate level ides as compared to subjects without access to such networks (Rewey et al., 1989).

Learner Interactions

• Students with high verbal aptitude were able to use a less structured networking technique with good results, while low verbal aptitude students using a less structured networking method did not perform any better than control groups (Holley & Dansereau, 1984). The less structured method involved students generating their own link labels, rather than using the 6 prespecified 6-link labels. Thus, low verbal ability students appear to benefit from a more structured study strategy, while higher ability students are able to benefit from less structured strategies.

Research regarding the effectiveness of networking on learners with different aptitudes has been limited to consideration of subjects' verbal aptitude as measured by standardized vocabulary test scores and achievement as measured by grade point average. Learners with low verbal aptitude appear to benefit from the structured networking technique which uses six types of links, while learners with higher aptitude in this area performed better when they were free to generate their own labels for links. It appears that the higher ability subjects felt constrained by the 6-link system, which may have interfered with their usual study methods. In contrast, lower ability learners who presumably had less effective study methods to begin with, appear to benefit from the more structured networking method (Holley and Dansereau, 1979, 1984).

Networking appears to be more effective for low achieving students than for high achieving students. Low achieving students who used networking to study a text passage performed as well on tests of recall of detailed content as high achieving students who used networking to study the same passage. In fact, high achieving subjects who used their usual study methods performed better on the test of recall of details than high achieving subjects who used networking to study the passage. It is speculated that high achieving students have well developed study strategies prior to learning networking, and that the networking strategy may interfere with their usual, effective study methods (Holley et al., 1979).

There is some speculation that learners with high reading comprehension should be able to learn to network more readily than subjects with lower reading comprehension (Holley, & Dansereau, 1984). However, there has been no research to validate this claim. In addition, it would appear that learners with spatial abilities would both learn networking more readily and benefit more from it's use than learners with lower spatial abilities. Again, this area has not been investigated.

Content/Task Interactions

There are no apparent content limitations for networking, which was designed as a content-independent spatial strategy. Networks have been developed for statistics, psychology, nursing, ecology and numerous other fields of study. However, Dansereau et al. (1979), found that the use of networking had a greater impact on student performance on short-answer portions of comprehension /retention tests than on multiple-choice portions

From the available research on network effectiveness, it is clear that networking promotes recall, and that the level of detail recalled is related to the training that learners receive on the networking strategy. Thus, it appears that if a content area requires attention to details learners must be trained to include detailed information on their network maps. Conversely, if the content area is one in which general themes or principles must be learned, learners must be instructed in use of more global networking strategies. Networking does not appear to be effective in improving both recall of main ideas and details simultaneously. If both details and main ideas are required in a content area some other strategy may be more effective.

The use of networking may have a greater impact when used with difficult material (Dansereau et al., 1979). There is some theoretical and anecdotal support for using networking to promote problem solving, but this has not been demonstrated through controlled research studies. In fact, there has been no experimental research reported on the effectiveness of networking for promoting learning outcomes other than recall and comprehension of content.

Advantages of Networks

• Networking is a theory-based spatial strategy.

- The overall structure of content area is conveyed in networks.

- Networking is a well-researched technique with demonstrated effectiveness in promoting recall and comprehension of information.

- Networks include labeled links which explicitly convey the types of relationships between concepts. Therefore, networks can be used as stand-alone representations of knowledge structures. These links aid in retrieval of information.

- Networking is readily adaptable to many instructional uses.

- Networking provides needed structure for low verbal aptitude students.

Disadvantages of Networks

- Skill in networking requires 6 hours or more of training.

- The categories of links used to label relationships between concepts are not intuitive, but rather must be specifically learned.

- Predefined links are not exhaustive — other types of relationships exist that are not subsumed by these links.

- Outcomes from networking are dependent upon the type of training provided (details versus main ideas).

- Research on effectiveness of networking is limited to college student populations, so it may not be generalizable to other learner populations.

- High verbal aptitude students perform better with less structured techniques.

REFERENCES

Dansereau, D. F. (1978). The development of a learning strategies curriculum. In H. F. O'Neil, Jr., (Ed.), *Learning strategies*. New York: Academic Press.

Dansereau, D.F., Brooks, L.W., Holley, C.D., & Collins, K.W. (1983). Learning strategies training: Effects of sequencing. *Journal of Experimental Education, 51,* 102-108.

Dansereau, D. F., Collins, K. W., McDonald, B. A., Holley, C. D., Garland, J. C., Diekhoff, G. M., & Evans, S. H. (1979). Development and evaluation of a learning strategy training program. *Journal of Educational Psychology, 71,* 64-73.

Dansereau, D. F,. & Holley, C. D. (1982). Development and evaluation of a text mapping strategy. In A. Flammer & W. Kintsch (Eds.), *Discourse Processing*. Amsterdam: North Holland.

Dansereau, D. F., McDonald, B. A., Collins, K. W., Garland, J. C., Holley, C. D., Diekhoff, G. M., & Evans, S. H. (1979). Evaluation of a learning strategy system. In H. F. O'Neil, Jr., & C. D. Spielberger (Eds.), *Cognitive and affective learning strategies.* New York: Academic Press.

Holley, C.D., & Dansereau, D.F. (1984). Networking: The technique and the empirical evidence. In C. D. Holley & D. F. Dansereau (Eds.), *Spatial learning strategies: Techniques, applications and related issues.* New York: Academic Press.

Holley, C.D., Dansereau, D.F., McDonald, B.A., Garland, J.C., & Collins, K.W. (1979). Evaluation of a hierarchical mapping technique as an aid to text processing. *Contemporary Educational Psychology, 4,* 227-237.

Quillian, M. R. (1968). Semantic meaning. In M. Minsky (Ed.), Semantic information processing. Cambridge, MA.: M.I.T. Press.

Rewey, K.L., Dansereau, D.F., Skaggs, L.P., Hall, R.H., & Pitre, U. (1989). Effects of scripted cooperation and knowledge maps on the processing of technical material. *Journal of Educational Psychology, 81,* 604-609.

24

Structural Knowledge Learning Strategies: Node Acquisition and Integration Technique

DESCRIPTION OF NODE ACQUISITION AND INTEGRATION TECHNIQUE

The node acquisition and integration technique (NAIT) is a structured, nonspatial learning strategy. NAIT was designed to assist learners in organizing memory networks to promote recall of information Diekhoff, 1977). *Nodes* represent the key concepts that are learned (acquired) and integrated with other key concepts. NAIT is similar to the networking strategy (see Chapter 23) both in theory and in construction, and both techniques were part of the overall learning strategy system developed by Dansereau and his colleagues at Texas Christian University. Although similar in theory, these strategies differ considerably in their tangible products. While networks are spatial diagrams of the relationships between ideas, NAIT results in completion of worksheets which are linear in nature. Although the product is linear, the process of NAIT involves identification of key concepts, and the definition of the concepts through their relationships to other concepts.

The primary emphasis of NAIT is on the links between concepts in memory. The same six types of links used in networking are also used in NAIT to define relationships between ideas. Dansereau indicates that when the type of link between concepts is emphasized those links can be used as retrieval cues (Dansereau, McDonald, Collins, Garland, Holley, Diekhoff, & Evans 1979). For example, when attempting to recall some information about the history of baseball, a learner can search memory according to the type of link between ideas. Does the learner want to recall a *characteristic* of a particular baseball player or commissioner? Perhaps the information desired is a chain, such as the contention that one event *led to* (or caused) another event. Alternatively, one might be trying to recall something that was a *type of* another concept such as the name of a baseball player who played third base for the Baltimore Orioles. Each of these links can be used to assist the learner in searching through memory for the information desired.

Identification of information on these types of relationships is used to develop definitions of individual concepts. In addition, NAIT provides a means of building connections between concepts through the completion of comparison worksheets. These worksheets require the learner to compare pairs of concepts based on their relationships to other concepts.

In addition to building connections between concepts in a given area, NAIT provides a mechanism for relating new knowledge to prior knowledge. This is accomplished through the completion of an elaboration section of the worksheet. In this section, the learner thinks of examples of the key concepts, identifies terms that are related to the concepts, and considers potential applications of the concepts. In this manner new knowledge is linked to prior knowledge to assist in recall of content.

In some ways NAIT is similar to Frames/Slots (see Chapter 12). Frames and Slots are used primarily to assist in the writing of text, but can also be used as an adjunct learning strategy exercise by having learners complete a worksheet by providing information on key aspects of a topic area. NAIT begins with a similar framework, but instead of identifying categories of information about a subject area, the learner organizes information according the relationships between concepts.

Rationale

NAIT is based on networking models of memory, and consistent with depth of processing models of memory (Diekhoff, Brooks, & Dansereau, 1982). According to the networking models of memory, memory is organized in nodes that represent concepts, linked to other nodes in memory in some meaningful manner. The more links that are established between concepts and within networks of concepts, the better probability that the concepts will be recalled. NAIT requires learners to identify relationships between newly learned concepts and to relate new content to prior knowledge, thus establishing multiple links between concepts in memory. The depth of processing theory of information processing proposes that learning is enhanced when content is deeply or meaningfully processed. Deep processing is contrasted with more superficial processing such as repetition of key words or noticing incidental features about words, such as rhyming words. NAIT uses *deep* types of processing by requiring learners to consider how concepts are related to other new concepts, and by specification of the similarities and dissimilarities between pairs of concepts.

EXAMPLES OF NODE ACQUISITION AND INTEGRATION TECHNIQUE

A completed NAIT worksheet for the concept Aerobic Exercise is shown in Fig. 24.1. Note that the categories of links are similar to those used in networking, and that an additional section of the worksheet is devoted to elaborations on the key concept by listing of related terms. A comparison worksheet for Aerobic and Anaerobic exercise is shown in Fig. 24.2, and a comparison worksheet for annuals and perennials is shown in Fig. 24.3.

KEY Concept : <u>Aerobic Exercise</u>

Characteristic: Sustained exercise; Oxygen consumption balanced, fats and carbohydrates metabolized
Antecedent: Warm-up, stretching
Leads to: Cardiac conditioning; weight loss
Evidence: No lactate accumulation; talk test
Type: "Aerobics" classes, jogging, swimming
Part of: General exercise
Elaboration: Cardiac rehabilitation program, Step classes

Fig. 24.1. NAIT for the concept aerobic exercise.

APPLICATIONS OF NAIT

NAIT was developed as a learning strategy that aids in the analysis of concepts, producing more complete concept definitions and has it's primary use in that area. However, in addition to using NAIT as an individual study strategy, it is also useful for classroom exercises, perhaps in a cooperative learning environment. In this manner pairs or small groups of

Key Concepts: <u>Aerobic Exercise</u>   <u>Anaerobic Exercise</u>

	Similarities	**Differences**
Characteristic		
	Forms of exercise.	Metabolism Purpose of exercise.
Antecedent		
	Warm ups/stretching	
Leads to		
	Increased fitness level for exercise.	Outcomes depend on purpose
		Improved cardiac conditioning in aerobic exercise.
Evidence		
	Increased heart rate	Lactic acid (yes in anaerobic)
Type		
		High intensity vs moderate intensity
Part of		
	General exercise	
Summary		

Summary
     Aerobic exercise burns fat and carbohydrates, results in minimal lactic acid build up, includes exercises like swimming, jogging, "aerobics" classes. Anaerobic exercise burns carbohydrates and proteins, results in lactic acid build up, and includes high exertion exercises like sprinting, and body building.

Fig. 24.2. A comparison worksheet for the concepts aerobic exercise and anaerobic exercise.

Key Concepts: <u>Annuals</u>   <u>Perennials</u>

Similarities	Differences
Characteristic flowers, multitude of colors sizes, varieties	length of blooming season Propagation
Antecedent Good soil, warm temperatures drainage, sun exposure (most)	Perennials need winter hardiness Perennials may have tuber vs seeds
Leads to Flowers	Annuals - all spring and summer Perennials - partial season of bloom
Evidence Repetitive bloom year to year?	
Type geraniums, begonias	Perennials: peonies, daylillies Annual: petunias, marigolds
Part of Plants, flowering.	
Summary Primary similarity is that both are flowering, non-woody plants. Annuals provide flowers through the season, but last only one year. Perennials grow back from year to year but bloom for shorter periods than annuals.	

Fig. 24.3. A comparison worksheet for annual and perennial flowering plants.

students could complete the worksheets together, providing their own prior knowledge and experience to enhance elaborations on the key concepts.

This technique has been shown to be an effective learning/study strategy promoting a more meaningful understanding of concepts. Likewise, completion of the NAIT worksheets can be used as a whole classroom activity, with an instructor leading discussions to assist in the completion of the sheets. The same worksheets could serve a useful purpose as a homework assignment or some other graded assignment or test. The completion of such worksheets can provide the instructor with a measure of the learner's comprehension of key concepts and their relationships to other concepts.

The Node Acquisition and Integration Technique's use of definition and comparison worksheets could be implemented in computer courseware (Jonassen, 1988) allowing learners to input information concerning the relationships for key concepts, as they work through a program.

Representing/Assessing Structural Knowledge

Completed NAIT worksheets can be used as a method of representing and assessing a learner's structural knowledge. Testing relationships and comparisons between concepts tests a higher level and more meaningful understanding than having students simply define concepts. Worksheets can be reviewed for their accuracy and for the comprehensiveness of relationship analysis. Inaccuracies in content in the completed worksheets can identify weaknesses in the learner's knowledge structures. The instruction preceding such assessment, must also be at a level where students are encouraged to actively construct meaning for themselves.

Conveying Structural Knowledge

Expert-completed NAIT worksheets could be used to summarize key points and to highlight key relationships between concepts. These worksheets could be distributed to learners at the completion of a learning unit, perhaps for comparison to student-completed worksheets. Alternatively, the expert-completed NAIT worksheets may be used to generate class discussion on the content area. The expert-generated and completed comparison worksheets not only convey accurate information about the relationships between concepts, but also highlight that expert's impression of the most important concept pairs to contrast. Students can also be taught heuristics for identifying important concepts as they are encountered or prior to reading. The teacher can also use similar formats as outlines when presenting or discussing new material. This type of information can help to reinforce those relationships in the learners' own cognitive structures.

Acquiring Structural Knowledge

Node Acquisition and Integration Technique was specifically designed to promote the learning of relationships between main ideas in a content area. This technique has it's greatest use as a study strategy to promote acquisition of this type of learning. The emphasis on defining concepts in terms of their relationships to other concepts helps to reinforce the learning of an integrated knowledge network rather than memorization of isolated definitions of terms. Learners can use this technique independently to study course material, or the worksheets can be incorporated into class assignments to be completed on an individual or group basis.

NAIT may be used in the following ways to support learning:

- identifying the relationships for key concepts in a text, lecture, or any other form of information presentation (e.g., CAI);
- rearranging the information to compare/contrast concepts;
- using the structure (skeleton) as an aid to retrieving information stored in memory;
- used as a tool for analysis prior to using other structural tools such as constructing concept maps.

PROCEDURE FOR DEVELOPING NAIT

1. Select key concepts. This step may be completed by the instructor or by learners themselves. If learners identify key concepts independently, they may use cues from a text passage such as highlighted, underlined or italicized words to identify the important concepts.

2. Develop and produce NAIT worksheets (Fig. 24.4). The links used in networking (characteristic, type, part, antecedent, leads to, and evidence) can be used as categories on the worksheet. Alternatively, new types of links can be identified according to the material to be studied. Add an additional category, *elaboration*, for building links between key ideas and prior knowledge.

3. Guide definition. Develop the relationship-guided definitions of the concepts. As information is encountered which relates to the key concept in any of the above ways, the learner completes the worksheets by identifying key characteristics of the key concept, identifying an antecedent event, identifying important parts of the concept, and so on.

4. Elaborate on the key concept by identifying other terms/concepts that are related to the main idea. In addition, identification of examples of the

key concept and possible applications of the concept help to link the new information to prior knowledge.

Key Concept

Characteristics / Description

Antecedents

Consequences / Influences

Evidence

Subsets

Supersets

Elaboration

Fig. 24.4. NAIT worksheet.

5. Guide comparisons. To compare and contrast concepts, the two concepts are entered side-by-side on a comparison worksheet (Fig. 24.5). Learners compare and contrast pairs of concepts by completing comparison worksheets. Select the pairs of concepts that have the most important similarities or differences. Diekhoff, Brooks and Dansereau (1982) suggest developing a matrix which represents all possible pairs of concepts. Then pairs that are just off the matrix diagonal should be selected for comparison. As an alternative to completion of a full worksheet on comparisons, these authors suggest that learners may simply summarize the similarities and differences between the concepts in paragraph format.

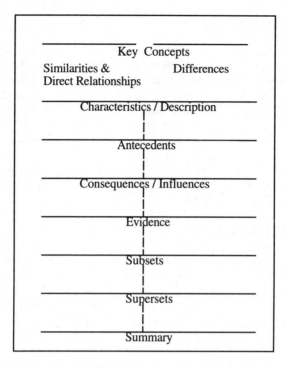

Fig. 24.5. Comparison worksheet.

EFFECTIVENESS OF NAIT

- NAIT was not found to be an effective study strategy for recall of content as tested by multiple choice and short answer tests. The first test was given prior to any study strategy training, the second followed training in general learning strategies such as goal setting and mood setting, and the third was given following training in NAIT. Subjects showed no improvement in test scores from the second to the third test, indicating that NAIT was not useful in improving test performance (Dansereau et al., 1979).

- College students who used NAIT to study a text passage on psychology outperformed students who used their usual study strategy in defining key terms and describing the relationships between key terms in the passage. The test questions were similar to the items on NAIT worksheets, perhaps giving some advantage to subjects who used NAIT over other study strategies (Diekhoff et al., 1982).

Learner Interactions

There is no literature available regarding the effects of individuals' characteristics on a learner's ability to use NAIT or benefit from the use of this strategy. Because NAIT requires some writing and interpretation of relationships learned from text, it seems logical to expect that learners with high verbal ability will find NAIT easier to learn and use. Since NAIT is a nonspatial learning strategy, those learners who have difficulty with spatial relations may find this technique easier to use than the spatial strategies such as networking.

In that NAIT is a structured learning strategy, future research should investigate whether low verbal ability students are aided more than high verbal ability students.

Content (Task) Interactions

NAIT has been used primarily with introductory material from the social sciences (Diekhoff et al., 1982). It also appears to be useful in the basic sciences. While there is no evidence to support the use of this technique in the humanities, it may be a useful learning strategy in these areas as well. Modification of the worksheets to include other types of relationships between concepts may increase the flexibility of this learning tool.

Advantages of Node Acquisition and Integration Technique

- NAIT presents an alternative method for building knowledge structures that is nonspatial. This may be advantageous to learners with limited spatial learning ability.

- NAIT is theory based and appears to show promise in improving learner's acquisition of structural knowledge.

- Worksheets are easy to construct and categories of links may be modified to fit specific content areas.

- Learners produce more varied and complete definitions of important concepts.

- NAIT assists students in gathering information which may be scattered throughout a passage.

- Learners integrate new information.

- NAIT aids in identifying what is most important in a passage.

Disadvantages of Node Acquisition and Integration Technique

- The process of completing NAIT worksheets can be tedious and time-consuming.

- While NAIT intuitively appears to be a useful learning strategy, research conducted on the effectiveness of NAIT has had conflicting results.

- Research on the effectiveness of NAIT has been confined to college student populations. It is unclear whether this technique can be used effectively by less mature learners.

- Because NAIT is a linear study strategy, concepts are compared to other concepts in pairs. This limits the integration of one concept to multiple other concepts. Networking and other spatial strategies allow for multiple relationships between concepts, allowing more integration.

REFERENCES

Dansereau, D.F., McDonald, B.A., Collins, K.W., Garland, J, Holley, C.D., Diekhoff, G.M., & Evans, S.H. (1979). Evaluation of a learning strategy system. In. H.F. O'Neil & C.D. Spielberger (Eds.), *Cognitive and Affective Learning Strategies*. New York: Academic Press.

Diekhoff, G. M. (1977). *The node acquisition and integration technique: A node-link based teaching/learning strategy*. Presented at the Annual Meeting of the American Educational Research Association, New York, NY. (ERIC Document Reproduction Service No. ED 138 570)

Diekhoff, G.M., Brooks, P.J., & Dansereau, D.F. (1982). A prose learning strategy training program based upon network and depth-of-processing models. *Journal of Experimental Education, 50*, 180-184.

Jonassen, D. H. (1988). Integrating learning strategies into courseware to facilitate deeper processing. In D. H. Jonassen (Ed.), *Instructional designs for microcomputer courseware*. Hillsdale, NJ: Lawrence Erlbaum Associates.

Author Index

Abelson, R., 3, 19, 173, 178
Ackerson, G., 196, 199
Acton, W. H., 33, 35, 76, 78, 79, 80
Adelson, B., 66, 70
Aidinejad, H., 75, 80
Alaiyemola, F. F., 160, 162i
Alvermann, D. E., 169, 171
Amerine, F. J., 169, 171
Ames, A., 196, 199
Amiran, M., 174, 175, 176, 178, 178
Anders, P. L., 183, 185, 186
Anderson, J. A., 12, 17
Anderson, J. R., 9, 17
Anderson, T. H., 16, 17, 126, 129, 130, 132, 133
Armbruster, B. B., 16, 17, 101, 113, 126, 129, 130, 132, 133
Ausubel, D. P., 16, 17, 118, 123, 155, 162, 191, 194, 195, 196, 198
Bamford, C., 226, 227, 229
Barnes, B., 196, 198
Barron, D. D. , 166, 171
Barron, R. F., 16, 18, 165, 166, 169, 171
Bartlett, B. J., 110, 111, 113
Baxter, J. A., 45, 48, 49, 50, 51, 52
Beissner, K., 121, 123
Beissner, K. L., 160, 162
Berg, D., 198, 142, 143
Berg, W., 67, 69, 70, 71
Bernard, R. M., 168, 170, 171
Beukhof, G., 119, 122, 123
Beyerbach, B. A., 157, 162
Beyersdorfer, J. M., 183, 185, 186
Blake, E., 191, 198
Bluth, G. J., 110, 111, 113
Bogden, C. A., 158, 162
Boothby, P. R., 169, 171
Bos, C. S., 183, 185, 186
Brandt, D. M., 110, 111, 113

Bransford, J. D., 194, 198
Breedin, S. D., 77, 79, 80
Breen, T. J., 62, 71, 73, 81
Brezin, M. J., 17, 18
Brooks, L. W., 238, 240
Brooks, P. J., 244, 250, 251, 252, 253
Brown, L. T., 40, 41, 42, 43, 64, 66, 71
Brown, P., 17, 18
Buckley, M. H., 214, 218, 219
Buzan, T., 205, 206, 211
Cable, G. W., 195, 199
Carson, C. H., 122, 123
Carter, C., 160, 162
Champagne, A. B., 5, 18
Chao, C. I., 122, 123
Chi, M. T., 10, 18
Chi, M. T. H., 4, 19
Clancy, W., 11, 18
Clawson, E., 196, 198
Clifford, M., 221, 229
Cocchiarella, M. J., 5, 19
Cole, P., 226, 227, 229
Collins, A. M., 7, 18
Collins, K. W., 17, 18, 233, 234, 237,238, 239, 240, 241, 243, 251, 253
Cooke, N. J., 77, 79, 80
Cooke, N. M., 62, 71, 73, 76, 77, 78, 79, 80, 81
Cox, D. L., 37, 41, 43, 68, 69, 71
Craik, F.M., 178, 178
Curran, T. E., 37, 41, 43, 68, 69, 71
Dansereau, D. F., 17, 18, 129, 131, 132, 133, 231, 232, 233, 234, 237, 238, 239, 240, 241, 243, 244, 250, 251, 252, 253
Dansereau, D. F., 234, 235, 238, 241
Darwazeh, A. N., 113, 123
Davenport, D. M., 76, 80
Davies, I. K., 196, 197, 198
Dean, R. S., 195, 198

Dearholt, D. W., 73, 74, 76, 77, 78, 79, *80*
Demaio, J. C., 62, *71*, 73, *81*
Denner, P. R., 140, *143*
Desena, A. T., 5, *18*
Diekhoff, G. M., 4, 16, 17,*18*, 38, 39, 41, 42, *42*, *43*, 66, 67, 69, 70, *70*, *71*, 92, 93, 95, *95*, 233, 234, 237, 238, 239, *240* , 243, 244, 250, 251, 252, *253*
Diekhoff, K. B., 16, *18*, 38, 39, 41, *43*, 66, 67, 69, *71*
Dietze, A. G., 59, *60*
DiVesta, F. J., 168, *171*
Duffy, G. G., 228, *229*
Dunlap, J., 147, *153*
Dunn, R., 198, 142, *143*
Durso, F. T., 62, *71*, 73, 74, 76, 77, 78, 79, *80*, *81*
Eggen, P. D., 169, *171*
Erickson, G., 17, *18*
Evans, S. H., 17, *18*, 233, 234, 238, 239, *240*, 243, 251, *253*
Faw, H. W., 196, *198*
Feltovich, P. J., 10, *18*
Fenker, R. M., 14, 15, *18*, 39, *43*, 62, 65, 66, 68, *71*
Fields, A., 205, 206, *211*
Filip, D., 183, *186*
Fillenbaum, S., 59, *60*
Fisher, K. M., 141, *143*, 159, *162*, 210, *211*
Fitzgerald, D., 191, 195, *198*
Frase, L. T., 109, *113*, 177, *178*
Freedle, R. O., 110, 111, *113*
Gagne, R. M., 118, *123*
Garland, J. C., 17, *18*, 233, 234, 237, 238, 239, *240*, 241, 243, 251, *253*
Garskoff, B. E., 30, *35*
GeeslinW. E., 33, *35*, 61, 65, 68, *71*
Gentner, D., 94, *95*
Gentner, S., 6, 7, *19*
Gick, M. L., 94, *95*
Gill, R. T., 10, *18*
Gillan, D. J., 77, 79, *80*

Glaser, R., 10, *18*
Glass, G., 196, *198*
Glynn, S. M., 168, *171*
Goldsmith, T. E., 33, *35*, 62, *71*, 73, 76, 78, 79, *80*, *81*
Goodman, M. S., 6, 9, *18*
Gordon, S. E., 10, *18*
Gowin, D. B., 16, *19*, 157, 161, *163*
Graves, M. F., 110, *113*
Guilford, J. P., 33, *35*
Hall, R. H., 234, 235, 238, *241*
Hanesian, H., 155, *162*
Hanf, M. B., 16, *18*, 213, 218, *219*
Hannum, W. H., 156, *162*
Hartley, J., 196, 197, *198*
Heinze-Fry, J. A., 158, 160, 161, *162*
Hirschman, E. C., 45, 50, 51, *51*
Holley, C. D., 17, *18*, 232, 233, 234, 237, 238, 239, *240*, *241*, 243, 251, *253*
Holmes, M., 66, *71*
Holyoak, K. J., 94, *95*
Houston, J. P., 30, *35*
Jegede, O. J., 160, *162*
Johansen, G. T., 161, *163*
Johnson, D. D., 141, 142, *143*, 179, 183, 184, 185, *186*, *187*
Johnson, M. K., 194, *198*
Johnson, P. E., 37, 41, *43*, 68, 69, *71*
Johnson, P. J., 33, *35*, 76, 78, 79, *80*
Jonassen, D. H., 15, 16, 17, *18*, *19*, 70, *71*, 77, *80*, 90, 93, 94, *95*, 147, *153*, 156, *162*, 202, 203, 206, 207, 208, *211*, *211*, 226, 227, *229*, 248, *253*
Jones, B. F., 174, 175, 176, *178*, *178*
Jones, L. K., 51, *51*
Jones, S. T., 141, 142, *143*
Kahle, J. B., 160, *162*
Karbon, J. C., 142, *143*
Katims, M., 174, 175, 176, 178, *178*
Kauchuk, D. P., 169, *171*

Kaye, K., 15, 20, 41, *43*, 65, 69, *71*
Kelly, G. A., 5, *18*
Kirk, S., 169, *171*
Klopfer, L. E., 5, *18*
Kloster, A. M., 196, *199*
Kommers, P., 141, *143* , 159, *162*,
   211, *211*
Kozma, R., 141, *143*, 159, *162*,
   210, *211*
Kruskal, J. B., 61, *71*
Kulhavy, R. W., 195, *198*
Lakoff, G., 10, *18*
Larkin, J. H., 10, *18*
Lehman, J. D., 160, *162*
Leinhardt, G., 45, 48, 49, 50, 51,
   52
Levin, K. M., 141, 142, *143*, 179,
   186
Lin, Y. G., 35, *35*, 83, 86, 87, 88, *88*
Lockhart, R.S., 178, *178*
Loftus, E. F., 7, *18*
Long, J. S., 145, *153*
Luiten, J., 196, *199*
Luria, A. R., 46, *51*
MacDonald-Ross, M., 196, *199*
Magoon, A. J., 16, *18*
Mandler, J., 6, 8, 9, *18*
Martys, N., 30, *35*
Mayer, R. E., 192, 193, 195, *199*
McAleese, R., 158, *163*
McClain, A., 140, *143*
McDermott, J., 10, *18*
McDonald, B. A., 17, *18*, 233, 234,
   237, 238, 239, *240*, *241*, 243,
   251, *253*
McDonald, D. R., 77, *80*
McDonald, J. E., 73, 77, 79, *80*
McDonald, J. L., 69, *71*
McEneany, J. E., 196, *199*
McKeachie, W. J., 35, *35*, 83, 86,
   87, 88, *88*
McKeithen, K. B., 84, 88, *88*
Meadows, J. D., 161, *163*
Merrill, M. D., 113, *123*
Meyer, B. J. F., 16, *19*, 101, 102,
   107, 109, 110, 111, 112, *113*

Meyer, D. E., 75, *80*
Miller, G. A., 45, 46, 48, 50, *52*
Minsky, M., 12, *19*, 125, *133*, 173,
   178
Mitchell, A. A., 4, *19*
Mitchell, P. D., 160, *163*
Moore, D. W., 169, 170, *171*
Moreira, M., 157, 158, *163*
Nagy, P., 4, 14, *19*, 34, *35*
Naveh-Benjamin, M., 35, *35*, 83,
   86, 87, 88, *88*
Newell, J., 197, *199*
Norman, D. A., 6, 7, 9, *19*, 93, *95*,
   118, *123*, 173, *178*
Novak, J. D., 16, *19*, 155, 157, 158,
   160, 161, *162* , *163*
Okebukola, P. A. O., 160, *162*
Ortony, A., 3, 6, *19*
Osgood, D. W., 4, *19*
Owen, B., 214, 218, *219*
Paap, K. R., 77, *80*
Pearson, P. D., 184, 185, *186*
Peresich, M. L., 161, *163*
Peterson, C., 4, *19*
Pettey, G. R., 69, *71*
Piche, G. L., 110, *113*
Pitre, U., 234, 235, 238, *241*
Pittelman, S. D., 141, *143*, 179,
   183, 185, *186,187*
Plate, T. A., 77, *80*
Polanyi, M., 4, *19*
Preece, P. F. W., 4, 15, *19*, 30, 32,
   33, 34, *35*, 37, *43*, 53, 56, 57,
   59, *60*, 89, *95*, 206, *211*
Price, J. M., 66, *71*
Quillian, M. R., 7, *19*, 232, *241*
Ragan,T. J., 119, *123*
Rapoport, A., 58, 59, *60*
Readence, J. E., 169, 170, *171*
Reigeluth, C. M., 16, *19*, 113, 116,
   119, 121, 122,*123*
Reitman, J. S., 41, 42, *43*, 83, 84,
   86, 87, 88, *88*
Rewey, K. L., 234, 235, 238, *241*
Rickards, J. P., 195, *199*
Ridley, D. R., 155, *163*

Rigney, J., 1978, 17, *19*
Rips, L. J., 63, *71*
Robbins, L. C., 191, *198*
Robertson, W. C., 10, *19*
Roehler, L. R., 228, *229*
Rogers, C. A., 113, 119, *123*
Rowell, R., 197, 156, *163*
Royer, J. M., 195, *199*
Rueter, H. H., 41, 42, *43*, 83, 84, 86, 87, *88*
Rumelhart, D., 3, 6, *19*
Rumelhart, D. E., 6, 7, *19*, 93, *95*, 173, *178*
Ryle, G., 3, *19*
Sari, F., 119, *123*
Sari, I. F., 119, *123*
Schank, R., 3, *19*, 173, *178*
Schauer, D. K., 183, 185, *186*
Schooler, L. J., 9, *17*
Schvaneveldt, R. W., 62, *71*, 73, 74, 75, 76, 77, 78, 79, *80, 81*
Scott, W. A., 4, *19*
Shavelson, R., 14, 15, *19*
Shavelson, R. J., 4, 9, 14, 15, *19*, 33, *35*, 61, 65, 68, *71*
Shepard, R. N., 61, *71*
Shoben, E. J., 63, *71*
Simon, D. P., 10, *18*
Simon, H. A., 10, *18*
Sinatra, R. C., 198, 142, *143*
Sinatra, R., 161, *163*
Skaggs, L. P., 234, 235, 238, *241*
Slater, W. H., 110, *113*
Smith, E. E., 63, *71*
Smith, P. L., 119, 122, *123*
Spiller, R. T., 113, *123*
Squires, D. A., 5, *18*
Stanners, R. F., 40, 41, 42, *43*, 64, 66, *71*
Stein, F., 16, *19*, 113, 116, *123*
Stein, M. K., 45, 48, 49, 50, 51, *52*
Stensvold, M. S., 161, *163*
Stevens, A. L., 6, 7, *19*
Stewart, J., 197, 156, *163*
Stone, C. L., 196, 197, *199*
Stone, V. F., 165, *171*

Taylor, S. G., 160, *163*
Tennyson, R. D., 5, *19*
Tessmer, M., 17, *19*, 156, *162*, 202, *203*
Thro, M. P., 9, *20*, 65, *71*
Toms-Bronowski, S., 141, *143*, 179, 183, 185, *186, 187*
Tucker, D. G., 35, *35*, 83, 86, 87, 88, *88*
Tucker, R. G., 62, *71*, 73, *81*
Van Kirk, J. 197, 156, *163*
Waern, Y., 56, 59, *60*
Wainer. H., 67, 69, *70, 71*
Wallendorf, M. R., 45, 50, 51, *51*
Waller, T. G., 196, *198*
Wang, S., 90, 93, 94, *95*
Ward, A. M., 137, 140, *143*
Wedman, J. F., 119, 122, *123*
Wigginton, P., 41, *43*
Williams, S. K., 51, *52*
Wilson, B. G., 113, *123*
Wilson, J. T., 161, *163*
Winne, P., 196, *199*
Wittrock, M. C., 16, *20*
Youseff, M., 191, 195, *198*
Zweig, A., 8, 9, *20*

Subject Index

Advance organizers, 165
  advantages of, 197
  classes of, 190
  description of, 189-90
  disadvantages of, 197
  effectiveness of, 195-6
  examples of, 192-3
  procedure for developing, 194-5
  rationale for, 191-2
Analogies, 116
  applications of, 94
  description and examples of, 934
  procedure for developing, 94
Assimilation theory, 155
Blueprint, for instruction, 115
Card sort,
  advantages of, 51
  content (task) interactions, 51
  description of, 45-6
  disadvantages of, 51
  effectiveness of, 50-1
  examples of, 46-7
  for acquiring structural knowledge, 49
  for assessing structural knowledge, 48
  for conveying structural knowledge, 48-9
  learner interactions, 50-1
  procedure for developing, 49-50
  rationale for, 45-6
Causal interaction maps,
  advantages of, 153
  content (task) interactions, 152-3
  description of, 145-6
  disadvantages of, 153
  effectiveness of, 152
  examples of, 146-7
  for acquiring structural knowledge, 148-9
  for assessing structural knowledge, 148
  for conveying structural knowledge, 148
  learner interactions, 152
  procedure for developing, 149-52
Causal modeling, 145
Causation content structures, 38, 104
Cognitive maps, 42
  compared with course grade, 65
  correspondence of student's and teachers, 65
Cognitive strategies, 117
Cognitive structure, 4-5, 10, 37, 84-5,
  convergence with content structure, 65
  correspondence of student's and teachers, 65
Collection content structures, 103-4
Comaprative organizers, 190
Comparison content structures, 105-6
Concept maps,
  advantages of, 162
  as curriculum development tool, 156
  as organizer, 158
  content (task) interactions, 161
  description of, 155
  disadvantages of, 162
  effectiveness of, 159-61
  examples of, 156-7
  for acquiring structural knowledge, 158

for assessing structural
knowledge, 157
for conveying structural
knowledge, 158
in solving problems,160
learner interactions,161
procedure for
developing,158-9
Conceptual organizations, 115
Conceptual scaffolding, 115, 117
Connected graphs, 83
Connectionist models, 11
Constructivist approach, to
learning, 16
Content selection, using
similarity ratings, 39
Content structures,
advantages of, 112
as writing plans, 101
content (task) interactions,
111-2
description of, 101-2
disadvantages of 112
effectiveness of, 109-10
examples of, 102-6
for acquiring structural
knowledge, 108
for assessing structural
knowledge, 107
for conveying structural
knowledge, 107
learner interactions, 110-1
procedure for developing,
108-9
rationale for, 102
Controlled word association,
rationale for, 25-7
Conveying structural knowledge,
explicit methods, 15-6, 135-99
graphic organizer of, 98
implicit methods, 15-6, 101-33
introduction, 98-9
Critical thinking, 213
Cross classification tables,
advantages of, 178-9
as guided discovery, 176

as notetaking aid, 176
description of, 173
disadvantages of, 179
effectiveness of, 177
examples of, 173-5
for acquiring structural
knowledge, 176
for assessing structural
knowledge, 174-5
for conveying structural
knowledge, 175-6
procedure for developing,
176-7
rationale for, 173
Declarative knowledge, 3-4, 9, 12
Description content structures,
102-3
Descriptive writing plans, 102
Dimensional representations,
advantages of, 69-70
content (task) interactions 69
description of, 61-2
disadvantages of, 70
effectiveness of, 68-70
examples of, 62-4
for acquiring structural
knowledge, 67
for assessing structural
knowledge, 63-6
for conveying structural
knowledge, 66
learner interactions, 69
procedure for developing, 67-
8
rationale for, 62
SEE cognitive maps
Directed graph, 53
Discovery method, 193
Distance matrix, analysis of, 42
Dynamic frames, 126
Elaboration theory
advantages of, 122
description of, 115-8
disadvantages of, 123
effectiveness of, 121-2
examples of, 118-9

procedure for developing,
120-1
rationale for, 117-8
Eliciting knowledge, 25-51
through card sorts, 45-51
through similarity ratings,
37-43
through word association
proximities, 25-35
Epitomes, 115, 120
Expert ratings, using similarity
ratings, 39
Expert-novice differences,
rationale for structural
knowledge, 10-1
using pathfinder networks,
76-9
Explicit methods for conveying
structural knowledge,
advance organizers, 189-99
causal interaction maps, 145-
53
concept maps, 155-63
cross classification tables,
173-78
graphic organizers, 165-71
semantic features analysis,
179-188
semantic maps, 135-43
Expository organizers, 190
Far transfer, 193
Formative evaluation, 33
Frame game,
advantages of, 228
classroom applications of,
225
content (task) interactions,
228
description of, 221-2
disadvantages of, 228-9
effectiveness of, 227
examples of, 223-5
for acquiring structural
knowledge, 226
for assessing structural
knowledge, 225-6

for conveying structural
knowledge, 226
learner interactions, 228
procedure for developing,
226-7
Frame theory, 173
Frames and slots,
advantages of, 132
as class exercises, 129
content (task) interactions,
132
description of, 125-6
disadvantages of, 133
effectiveness of, 131
examples of, 126-8
for acquiring structural
knowledge, 130
for conveying structural
knowledge, 130
learner interactions, 131-2
procedure for developing,
130-1
rationale for, 126
to evaluate textbooks, 129
Free word association, 25,26
Graph similarity, 76
Graph theory, 74
Graphic learning strategies,
frame games, 221-9
networks, 231-41
pattern notes, 205-11
spider maps, 213-9
Graphic organizers, 28
advantages of, 170
content (task) interactions,
170
description of, 165
disadvantages of, 171
effectiveness of, 169
examples of, 166-7
for acquiring structural
knowledge, 168
for assessing structural
knowledge, 166-7
for conveying structural
knowledge, 168

learner interactions, 169-70
procedure for developing,
   169
rationale for, 165-6
Ideational scaffolding, 168, 190
Implicit methods for conveying
   structural knowledge,
   content structures, 101-13
   elaboration theory, 115-23
   frames and slots, 125-33
Integrative reconciliation, 190
Integrative understanding, 5
Internal connectedness, 5
Knowledge, objectivist
   conceptions of, 12
Knowledge comparison, 22
Knowledge elicitation, 227-9
Knowledge maps, 234
Knowledge representation, 22
Knowledge structures, 155
Latent structures, in data, 73
Learner control, 117
Learner's mental set, using
   similarity ratings, 40
Learning, as a generative process,
   16
Link-weighted network
   representations,
   SEE pathfinder networks
Memory structures, rationale for
   structural knowledge,9
Multidimensional scaling, 27, 38,
   61, 68
NAIT, SEE Node acquisition and
   integration technique
Networks,
   advantages of, 239-40
   content (task) interactions,
      239
   description of, 231-2
   disadvantages of, 240
   effectiveness of, 237-8
   examples of, 232-3
   for acquiring structural
      knowledge, 235

for assessing structural
   knowledge, 234
for conveying structural
   knowledge, 234-5
learner interactions, 238-9
procedure for developing,
   235-7
rationale for, 232-3
Node acquisition integration
   technique,
   advantages of, 252
   as general learning strategy,
      251
   content (task) interactions,
      252
   describing the relationships,
      251
   description of, 243-4
   disadvantages of, 253
   effectiveness of, 251
   examples of, 244-9
   for acquiring structural
      knowledge, 249
   for assessing structural
      knowledge, 248
   for conveying structural
      knowledge, 248-9
   learner interactions, 252
   procedure for developing,
      249-51
   rationale for, 244
Organization, as defined by
   depth of tree, 87
Pathfinder nets,
   advantages of, 79
   compared with cognitive
      maps, 74
   compared with
      multidimensional scaling,
      78
   content (task) interactions 79
   description of, 73-5
   effectiveness of, 78-80
   examples of, 74-6
   for acquiring structural
      knowledge, 77

for assessing structural
knowledge, 76
for conveying structural
knowledge, 77
learner interactions,
procedure for developing, 77-
8
rationale for, 74-5
Pathfinder networks, 38
Pattern notes,
advantages of, 211
assumptions of, 208
description of 205
disadvantages of, 211
effectiveness of, 211
examples of 205-7
for acquiring structural
knowledge, 208
for assessing structural
knowledge, 206-7
for conveying structural
knowledge, 207-8
procedure for developing,
208-11
Pattern-indexed schemata, 10
Personal construct theory, 5
Predicting school performance,
using pathfinder
networks, 76
Prior knowledge, 101, 135, 155
Problem solving, rationale for
structural knowledge, 10
Problem/solution content
structures, 105
Procedural knowledge, 3-4, 10, 12
Procedural organizations, 115
Propositional knowledge, 16
Recall and comprehension,
rationale for structural
knowledge, 8-9
Relatedness coefficients, 25, 27
Relationship judgments,
applications of, 92
description and examples of,
91-2

procedure for developing, 92-
3
Relationships, types of, 90, 221-3,
243-4
Representing structural
knowledge, 53-95
through cognitive maps, 61-
72
through pathfinder networks,
73-82
through tree construction
task, 53-59
through tree representations,
83-87
through verbal tests, 89-95
Schema theory, as theoretical
base for structural
knowledge, 6-7
Schemas, 3, 6, 126, 173
Script theory, 173
Semantic distance, 15, 37
Semantic features analysis,
advantages of, 186
and text comprehension, 182
and vocabulary learning, 183
content (task) interactions,
185-6
description of, 179
disadvantages of, 186
effectiveness of, 185
examples of, 180-1
for acquiring structural
knowledge, 193
for assessing structural
knowledge, 182
for conveying structural
knowledge, 182-3
learner interactions, 185
procedure for developing,
183-5
rationale for, 179-80
Semantic maps,
advantages of, 142-3
and vocabulary learning, 140-
1
as pre-reading activity, 137

content (task) interactions, 142
description of, 135
disadvantages of, 143
effectiveness of, 141-2
examples of, 136-9
for acquiring structural knowledge, 140
for conveying structural knowledge, 138
learner interactions, 142
procedure for developing, 141
rationale for, 135-6
stimulus to writing, 140
Semantic network theory, 11
Semantic networks, as theoretical base for structural knowledge, 7
Semantic proximity, 53
Semantic relationship tests,
applications of, 90-1
description and examples of, 89-90
procedure for developing, 91
Similarity ratings,
advantages of, 41
content (task) interactions 41
description of, 37-8
disadvantages of, 41-2
effectiveness of, 41-2
examples of, 38
for acquiring structural knowledge, 39
for assessing structural knowledge, 38-9
learner interactions, 41
procedure for developing, 39-41
rationale for, 37-8
Spider maps,
advantages of, 219
content (task) interactions, 219
description of, 213
disadvantages of, 219

effectiveness of, 218
examples of, 214-5
for acquiring structural knowledge, 216
for assessing structural knowledge, 214-5
for conveying structural knowledge, 215
learner interactions, 218
procedure for developing, 216-8
rationale for, 213
Spreading activation theory, as theoretical base for structural knowledge, 7-8
Static frames, 125-6
Story schemas, 6, 9
Structural knowledge learning strategies,
frame games, 221-9
networks, 231-41
node acquisition and integration technique, 243-53
pattern notes, 205-11
spider maps, 213-9
Structural knowledge,
as cognitive structure, 4-5
as conceptual knowledge, 5
as knowledge structure, 5
assumptions of, 11-2
concept map of, 13
conveying, 15-6
definition of, 4
definitions of, 3-5
graphic organizer of, 11-2
limitations of, 11-2
of a group, 70
rationales for, 8-10
representing/assessing, 14-5, 21-95
Structure in knowledge, rationale for structural knowledge, 8
Structured overviews,
SEE garphic organizers
Student misconceptions, 33

Study strategies, support
strategies, 231
Subject content, relevance of, 117
Subject matter structure, 9
Subsumption theory, 118, 191-2
Symbolic processing model, of
cognition, 11
Tacit knowledge, 4
Theoretical organizations, 115
Top level structures, 101
Transcendental schema, 9
Tree construction task, 33
advantages of, 59-60
content (task) interactions, 59
description of, 53
disadvantages of, 60
effectiveness of, 58-60
examples of, 54-6
for acquiring structural
knowledge, 57
for assessing structural
knowledge, 56-7
for conveying structural
knowledge, 57
learner interactions, 59
optional method, 58
procedure for developing, 57-
8
Tree representations, 61
advantages of, 88
description of, 83-4
disadvantages of, 88
effectiveness of, 87-8
examples of, 84-6
for assessing structural
knowledge, 84
procedure for developing, 86-
7
rationale for, 84
SEE ALSO ordered tree
technique
Verbal learning strategies, node
acquisition and integration
technique, 243-53
Verbal tests
advantages of, 95

disadvantages of, 95
analogies, 93-4
rationale for, 89
relationship judgments, 91-3
semantic relationship tests,
89-91
Word association proximities,
advantages of, 34
content (task) interactions, 33
controlled association
procedure, 29-31
description of, 25-6
disadvantages of, 35
effectiveness of, 32-5
examples of, 26-7
examples of, 26-7
for acquiring structural
knowledge, 28
for assessing structural
knowledge, 28
for assessing structural
knowledge, 28
for conveying structural
knowledge, 28
free association procedure,
28-9
learner interactions, 33
procedure for developing, 28-
32
rationale for, 26
scoring for, 30-2